Cold War on the Campus

Cold War on the Campus

Academic Freedom at the
University of Washington, 1946–64

JANE SANDERS

UNIVERSITY OF WASHINGTON PRESS
Seattle and London

Copyright © 1979 by the University of Washington Press
Printed in the United States of America

All rights reserved. No part of this publication may be reproduced or trans-
mitted in any form or by any means, electronic or mechanical, including
photocopy, recording, or any information storage or retrieval system, without
permission in writing from the publisher.

This book was published with the assistance of a grant from
the Andrew W. Mellon Foundation.

Library of Congress Cataloging in Publication Data

Sanders, Jane, 1940–
   Cold war on the campus.

   Bibliography: p.
   Includes index.
   1. Washington (State). University. 2. Academic
freedom. 3. Loyalty-security program, 1947–
—Washington (State) I. Title.
LD5753.S26   378.797′39   78-21755
ISBN 0-295-95652-6

Preface

In the years following World War II, the United States and the U.S.S.R. plunged into a period of Cold War. The two superpowers struggled for control in the Far East and in Europe, and though the mutual suspicions of preceding decades provoked the Cold War, the factor central to its prolongation was the nuclear capability of both countries.

At home, concern for U.S. national security, combined with congressional determination to assert power over the executive branch, exacerbated long-standing internal animosities. Under the aegis of various congressional committees, Americans projected their hostility onto those whose past and current views seemed incompatible with undivided commitment to U.S. superiority.

The issue of Communist subversion at home and abroad thus emerged as a dominant strain in postwar politics. The activities of rightist pressure groups, given legitimacy by the sensational tactics of congressional leaders, preyed upon the predispositions of Presidents Truman and Eisenhower and the entire Congress to produce an era of security programs that exceeded wartime restrictions on civil liberties. In what Telford Taylor has named the "Cold Civil War," liberals vied with conservatives to prove their patriotism; all pretense of due process was abandoned when, in 1954, the Congress passed the Communist Control Act outlawing the Communist party. The near unanimity of the vote is symbolic of the lack of dissent at that time surrounding Communism as a political issue.

The consequences of World War II, the Cold War, and the Cold Civil War for higher education in the United States were, and are, immense. During the war, scholars provided an invaluable source of expertise in almost every phase of the effort to defeat the Fascist powers, from the Office of War Information to ·the Manhattan Project. Increased demands for trained personnel to maintain technological, scientific, and managerial superiority in the postwar years perpetuated the symbiotic relationship between higher education and the "military-industrial complex." Though the billions of dollars in federal grants and contracts brought back to American campuses after the war were an immeasurable boon to the growth of higher education, the accompanying pressures to conform to the political demands of national security became an increasing threat to the autonomy of scholarship in the United States. Academics, like most Americans, acceded to the prevailing view that the Communist party of the United States was an agency of international conspiracy directed from Moscow. As the pattern of legislative investigation and loyalty programs spread through the states, competency for teaching and research increasingly was determined on the basis of political criteria. The erosion of civil liberties in the United States was thus accompanied by increasing restraints on the political and academic freedom of teachers, researchers, and students.

The general picture of the impact of the Cold War on American higher educational institutions and attitudes has been told by others. But each institution responded to the exigencies of the era in different ways. This study examines the reactions of University of Washington administrators, faculty members, and students to external and internal pressures on the integrity of the educational process. Through consideration of the central factors that impinged on university decision-making, it is possible to glimpse what members of the university community worked for as well as what they worked against, and to gain a better understanding of the paths they chose. Two themes pervade this study: the debate concerning academic freedom in relation to the perceived threat of Communist subversion, and the effect of that debate on efforts by the University of Washington faculty to achieve greater professional autonomy and national recognition for the university in a state traditionally critical of that university.

As one of the values distinctive to a university and to the academic profession, academic freedom can be defined as the right of teachers, researchers, and students to an atmosphere in which they may freely investigate and discuss whatever it is they are interested in, an atmosphere conducive to disinterested scholarship and characterized by a lack of inhibiting pressures or restraints from colleagues, the administration, the state, or other outside agents. As the history of education in the United States shows, it is only since World War I that administrators generally have come to respect the right of faculty academic freedom, and its parameters have always been subject to dispute. Violations of the principle are most likely to occur during times of social crisis, when the activities of teachers are perceived as either sustaining or undermining majority morale and beliefs. Regents and administrators, in their eagerness to promote a sober image of their institution, may be inclined to sacrifice individuals whose teachings or writings threaten that image. Likewise, faculty members rely on academic freedom as a buffer against intolerant or intemperate majority opinion, as a tool to preserve their position, and as an instrument of status and power in academic battles. Academic freedom issues thus may cause strains between the university and society, between administrators and faculty, and within the faculty itself. In the Cold War era under consideration, Communist and left-wing activities by current and prospective faculty members posed such an issue.

The decision to concentrate on this period arose from personal interest (I was a student and teacher in the late 1950s and early 1960s) and from awareness of the availability of archival materials that had not previously been explored. Although I have tried to present a balanced view of why things happened the way they did, and to keep in mind the limits imposed on historical characters by their frames of reference, I believe much of the record must be judged deplorable. The choices confronting the university faculty and administration were problematic, but their failure to clearly enunciate the necessity of an untrammeled atmosphere for the pursuit of truth in the midst of a social crisis must stand as a violation of the ideal of academic freedom.

I have derived a good deal of my information from the Manuscripts Collection of the University of Washington Library. My chief source was the President's Office Records and the available papers of private individuals. Memories of those who participated in events and the usual public records were valuable as cross-references, but the ad hoc character of university affairs has precluded certainty concerning the dynamics of some situations. I have tried to make explicit my own speculations when documentation failed.

While I assume the burden for any mistakes that occur in this account, I wish to thank all who have helped me and encouraged this effort. For their criticisms and counsel I am indebted to the members of my graduate committee, Professors Donald T. Williams, Jr., Malcolm Griffith, David Madsen, and Robert Cope. Others who have read and corrected misapprehensions in early and late drafts include

Donald K. Anderson, Robert Burke, Garland O. Ethel, Ronald Geballe, J. Richard Huber, Solomon Katz, Arthur Kobler, Melvin Rader, and Edwin and Ruth Uehling. Richard Berner, Gary Lundell, and Robert Mittelstadt of the University of Washington Manuscripts Collection have been unfailingly gracious and helpful.

I am also grateful to those who shared their time and memories with me in interviews: Donald K. Anderson, Joseph Cohen, Giovanni Costigan, Harrill Dabney, Garland O. Ethel, Ronald and Marjorie Geballe, Alex Gottfried, Gordon Griffiths, Robert B. Heilman, W. Stull Holt, William S. Hopkins, J. Richard Huber, Mrs. Boris Jacobsohn, Solomon Katz, Abraham Keller, Laurel Lewis, Roger Loucks, Charles E. Martin, Howard L. Nostrand, Arval Morris, Charles E. Odegaard, Herbert Phillips, Melvin Rader, Rex Robinson, Leonard Saari, Max Savelle, Alfred Schweppe, George Taylor, Edwin and Ruth Uehling, and Lloyd Woodburne.

Contents

Illustrations

Cold War on the Campus

I

Prologue to Controversy:

The University of Washington to 1947

> If the University ever loses its dispassionate objectivity and as a University espouses causes and incites or leads parades, it will die. It will die because it will have lost its integrity as an institution and have abandoned the timeless, selfless quest of truth.
> —Raymond B. Allen, Inaugural Address as president of the University of Washington, May, 1947

The inauguration of Raymond Bernard Allen as president of the University of Washington was a scholarly celebration of the era of expansion that followed World War II. Among those participating in the three-day festivities were Nobel Prize-winner Robert A. Millikan of the California Institute of Technology, Edward U. Condon, director of the Bureau of Standards, and Robert G. Sproul, president of the University of California. Symposia on the Humanities, Science, and Labor reflected the theme of continuity and change, of unity in diversity in areas challenging the university's role in postwar society. Ebulliently emphasizing the dynamic growth of the Pacific Northwest, Allen pledged the continuation of the university's role as "a flexible instrument of development to serve the needs of the state." While Allen's vision of the mission of the state university was not unique in emphasizing service to society, it did reveal a great deal about his concern that American science and technology be used to relieve the tensions and troubles of a war-torn world community:

> What is this thunder o'er land and sea that troubles still our times? Can it be that Thor's anvils ring again? Or is it the throbbing voice of conscience, "thundering the laws of right and wrong," stirring the souls of men? Can it be? It *must* be that men at last are freed to make come true their age-old dream of peace and a better world to be.[1]

Allen's inaugural address reflected the ringing enthusiasm, idealism, and faith in rationality that he brought to the tasks of the presidency.

In contrast to his predecessor, Lee Paul Sieg, a reserved optical physicist, Allen was a gregarious man who dominated gatherings and exuded the confidence of past success. At age forty-three, he had extensive administrative experience in medical education. A 1928

3

graduate of the University of Minnesota Medical School, he had interned in Minneapolis and practiced in Minot, North Dakota. Following a fellowship at the Mayo Foundation, he received his Ph.D. in 1934. As associate dean in charge of graduate studies at the College of Physicians and Surgeons, Columbia (1934–36), and dean of Wayne University College of Medicine (1936–39), he prepared himself for his efforts as executive dean of the professional colleges of the University of Illinois in Chicago and dean of the College of Medicine of the University of Illinois.[2]

President Lee Paul Sieg's plans to retire had been postponed due to the war. During the planning for the university's new medical school, authorized by the 1945 legislature, Sieg and the regents had often consulted Allen, and eventually offered him the deanship; he refused. But Allen's energy impressed Washington officials, and he was added to their list of presidential candidates. When the regents met with the Executive Committee of the Faculty Senate in January, 1946, the list had narrowed to Allen and Henry Schmitz, dean of Forestry at the University of Minnesota, a Washington alumnus (1916). After more investigation among Allen's Illinois colleagues, Dean of Faculties Edwin A. Guthrie reported to Allen a "rather remarkable tendency to agreement on you among all parties." On February 18, Allen was invited to the regents' meeting and was asked to become Sieg's successor. After consultation with his advisors in Illinois and Minnesota, Allen telegraphed his acceptance of the presidency on February 22, 1946. Soon the campus at Washington was "buzzing with enthusiasm" over the choice.[3]

Local newspapers praised the regents' wisdom in choosing someone who was simultaneously committed to the university's venture into medical education and familiar with the Pacific Northwest. Allen's parents had lived in Seattle after leaving North Dakota in the 1930s; two brothers had attended the University of Washington, and another brother was a Seattle contractor. In an interview with the *Seattle Post-Intelligencer* a few days before officially assuming his duties, Allen stated that he expected to fulfill his ambition to move beyond medicine into a broad range of education-related areas. Noting that the University of Washington had the tenth largest enrollment in the United States, he vowed to reduce the thirty-to-one student-faculty ratio, raise salaries, and support the development of first-rate research and graduate study facilities. The advent of the atomic bomb, he declared, had made education more important than ever, compelling all men to move beyond their narrow lives to commit themselves to the future of humanity. He pledged to continue the work of the university by stimulating good relations with Pacific nations. Above all, Allen saw the university as the property of the people; he hoped to make it even more responsive to their needs.[4]

When Allen began his presidency on September 1, 1946, the University of Washington was straining its personnel and facilities to meet the demands of postwar enrollments. After a low of 6,770 in 1944, the student population surpassed its prewar high of 10,000 in 1945. The autumn of 1946 brought 15,594, of whom almost 10,000 were veterans. A hastily expanded faculty taught into the evening due to shortages of space, especially in engineering and chemistry laboratory courses. Construction had begun on classroom buildings and the health sciences complex, but shortages of materials and work stoppages caused delays. The housing shortage for faculty and students, many of whom were married veterans, was met with prefabricated units.[5]

In meeting the pressures of expansion, Allen had the support and confidence of the regents. Led by Teamsters International Vice-President Dave Beck, newly appointed by Democratic Governor Mon Wallgren, the regents convinced the legislature of the need for a generous biennial budget. They pointed out that enrollment would not peak until 1949–50, that no building or normal replacement of equipment had occurred during the war, and that inflation had increased the cost of everything, including the cost of living for faculty members. Beck, who had pledged to make the campus "the showplace of Seattle," helped get an extra $1,795,000 for buildings from the State Development Board to cover the costs of inflation. Despite the large budget request, the regents noted, "the University's average cost per student will continue to be low as compared to other institutions."[6]

While the regents exerted pressure for more buildings, Allen, as chief articulator of faculty concerns, was aided by the accumulated evidence of faculty leaders whose efforts to overcome the effects of geographical isolation and the regional economy were long-standing and well documented. Since the turn of the century, the University of Washington faculty had shared the increasing aspiration toward autonomy that characterized faculty development across the nation. Frederick M. Padelford, one of the formulators of the American Association of University Professors' 1915 Statement of Principles, was dean of the Graduate School from 1924 to 1940. With his colleagues he labored to upgrade salaries, working conditions, and the quality of the faculty and sought to gain professional recognition through membership in the Association of American Universities. But despite those efforts and the recognition brought by the achievements of J. Allen Smith, Vernon Louis Parrington, William Savery, Edwin Guthrie, Frederick Kirsten, Trevor Kincaid, and other faculty members, the university failed to be widely respected in the academic community. A report of the American Council on Education issued in 1933 showed that only seven of nineteen University of Washington departments rated had adequate staff and equipment to prepare candidates for the doctorate.[7]

Though in part due to the university's remoteness from the East, its low rating was a product of other more basic factors. The university was a regional institution; in 1934, 91 percent of the students were from west of the Cascade Mountains. Competition between the university and the State College at Pullman kept its share of the tax monies limited, a condition exacerbated by traditional political and social disparities among the constituents of both institutions. The results were inadequate library and laboratory facilities and poor working conditions for the faculty. Classes were large, and time for research and graduate instruction limited. Salaries were lower than at the seven institutions with which the university compared itself. These conditions led to an in-bred faculty, and dependence on faculty who were themselves candidates for the Ph.D. By 1945, 37 percent of the associate professors and 25 percent of the assistant professors with the advanced degree had received them from the University of Washington.[8] The dangers of such insularity perpetuating itself would be great in the press of postwar expansion.

Beyond salaries and working conditions, faculty efforts were directed toward expansion of administrative recognition of their professional prerogatives. With Sieg's encouragement and cooperation, the faculty had developed a Faculty Senate and an Administrative Code, which became effective in 1938. The code had the effect of clarifying the internal workings of the university, and gave the faculty a greater role than previously in the management of university affairs, especially at the departmental level. Though tenure and promotion regulations were added to the code, Sieg still had to contend with autocratic department chairmen who obstructed the code's intent by refusing to follow its provisions for faculty participation in departmental decisions, and who continued to use arbitrary standards for promotion. Sieg retained the chair of the senate, and rejected faculty wishes to exclude the deans from membership. Throughout the remainder of his administration, Sieg looked upon the code as a means for the faculty to conduct its own affairs. The regents were informed of its existence, but were never asked to endorse it. Thus it remained a kind of "gentlemen's agreement" between the faculty and administration, a reflection of Sieg's views about the nature of university government.[9]

While the Faculty Senate, through its committees, gradually replaced the old Instructors' Association (founded in 1919) as articulator of faculty concerns, its limitations led many of the faculty to join organizations with national affiliations such as the American Association of University Professors (AAUP), and the American Federation of Teachers (AFT). Membership in the University of Washington chapter of the AAUP grew from 87 in 1939 to 251 in 1947. The institution of the senate and code and the growth of the AAUP reflected the faculty's increasing professional consciousness and their need to band together amid the economic and political conditions of the 1930s.[10]

But these movements also constituted an alternative to Local 401 of the AFT, which had been formed on campus in 1935. While some of its sixty members belonged to the UWAAUP and the senate, other AFT members held appointments at the instructor level funded by the Works Progress Administration (WPA). Some of these lower echelon faculty members were reputed to be "young, cynical, ultraliberal, anti-establishment types." One of these, Hugh DeLacy of the English Department, was asked to resign by Sieg when he ran for a city council seat in 1937.[11]

Like their national counterparts, the members of Local 401 believed that solidarity with labor unions would strengthen their demands for federal aid to education and salary and tenure rights. Locally, they engaged in direct political action and lobbied the legislature for tenure laws and the repeal of the 1931 Washington State Loyalty Oath for teachers. Though the AFT was part of the AFL, some members of Local 401 such as Harold Eby, Hugh DeLacy, and Ralph Gundlach worked against what they considered to be "thug elements" in Dave Beck's Teamster's Union. They also favored affiliation with the allegedly more progressive CIO. Since Beck's was the most powerful union in Seattle, and was engaged in jurisdictional disputes with Harry Bridges' Longshoremen's Union (CIO), such actions were embarrassing to the university. As Local 401 moved further left, and increasingly followed the "Communist line" on such issues as the Nazi-Soviet Pact, some faculty members dropped out of the union. Its activities continued to trouble President Sieg and others on the faculty who were mindful that one consequence could be political interference in the internal affairs of the university.[12]

Sieg himself was no stranger to the constraints that could be brought to bear on university freedom. As dean of the College and

dean of the Graduate School at the University of Pittsburgh, Sieg had
participated in the dismissal of Frederick Woltman, a graduate assistant in philosophy, whose actions on behalf of striking Pennsylvania
coal miners were "offensive to powerful interests." In Pennsylvania
those interests lay with coal mine operators like the Mellons; in
Washington, though the pressures exerted by lumbering, transportation, and farming interests were more diffuse, they were equally real.
Sieg had hesitated to take the Washington presidency because it and
the regents positions had historically been political footballs. Regents
appointed by one governor were removed by his successor, and several presidents preceding Sieg had likewise been dismissed. The most
famous case was that of Henry Suzzallo, who, after serving as president from 1915 to 1926, was fired by regents newly appointed by
Governor Roland Hartley. During his eight-year tenure, Hartley had
kept the internal affairs of the university closely in hand. The elections of 1932 returned the Democrats to power; Governor Clarence
D. Martin appointed new regents and restored administrative autonomy to the university. Only after assurances from the regents that
he would have a free hand internally did Sieg leave Pittsburgh for
Washington.[13]

Though family and political ties continued to play a role in their
appointments, regents after 1932 were essentially free to fulfill their
role as managers of the public affairs of the university. That is not to
say that they were immune to political attack from groups holding
disparate views of their function. In 1937, for instance, Representative Ed Henry, an alumnus of the University of Washington Law
School, introduced a bill which would have changed the composition
of the board to include one woman, two representatives of the manual
trades, one faculty member, and one dirt farmer. The measure was
defeated. In 1943, however, the legislature instituted the Regents
Tenure Law, making removal of regents before expiration of their
six-year term a matter for judicial review. Governor Martin had vetoed a similar measure in 1934 because, as he later explained, "If
the president, regents, and other high officials are not jacked up
with the idea of being removed for unsound work, they might get
out of line."[14]

Such pressures could not be lightly dismissed, but the political confusions of the Roosevelt era, combined with U.S. neutrality abroad,
allowed Sieg and the regents to maintain a cautious aloofness toward
politically active faculty members. On the one hand, he considered
them noisy beyond their strength, and their political involvements
annoying. On the other hand, he warned faculty about making "ex-

tempore, random, and facetious remarks." He also watched for proof that they were wandering outside their areas of scholarship in the classroom. If that should happen, he confided to one of the regents, he could legally discharge them, "not because their opinions differ from mine, but because their day by day actions tend to destroy the much greater number of constructive and helpful activities in promoting the good relations of the University with the public." Meanwhile, he continued, he rarely questioned faculty members about their political affiliations because he was aware that arbitrary action on his part would lead to

> a very serious commotion, a serious doubt as to whether this University is conducted along the lines of a sound university and, in the long run, will not only tend to discredit the good name of the University, but will, through the promotion of the martyr complex, cement together the really subversive elements of our population.[15]

Sieg did resort to less apparent measures to demonstrate his displeasure. Shortly after coming to Washington, he demoted the dean of the College of Engineering, R. G. Tyler. The move, ostensibly occasioned by economy measures, was widely regarded as a rebuke to Tyler for his activities with the Technocrats and antiwar groups. The president's sub rosa pressure was also illustrated by his refusal to promote Ralph Gundlach and Melvin Rader. Gundlach's psychology courses, he was told, dwelt too heavily on political and economic theory, and infringed on the territory of other departments. When faculty salaries were restored to pre-Depression levels, Sieg told Rader he had not followed Philosophy Department recommendations that Rader's also be restored. Rader's political activities in connection with the Spanish Civil War and other issues were such, Sieg said, that the regents would not have accepted such a recommendation. Despite Rader's publication record, he was not promoted to associate professor until 1944. At the same time, however, Sieg told Garland Ethel, an English professor, that his politics were not important so long as he was a good teacher.[16]

Sieg's subtle measures and mixed signals served him fairly well, for he was able to maintain faculty unity. The president exhibited similar adroitness in responding to such potentially volatile episodes as the student strikes for peace and against compulsory R.O.T.C. which occurred in the 1930s. In cooperation with various faculty committees and the regents, he was able to sidestep another major student issue, the "Ban on Political Speakers." The problem first arose during the presidential campaigns of 1912, when the regents decided that "no political speakers outside of the student body be invited or permitted

to speak on the campus or at the University in advocacy of or in
opposition to any candidate for public office." Though this rule was
later amended to permit some speakers under "equal conditions," the
matter rankled students eager to take sides on the great questions of
their era. From 1933 through 1939 the regents reconsidered the restrictions on speakers five times at the behest of students and alumni,
but they never did see fit to relax the prohibition against partisan
meetings open to the general student body and the public.[17]

Sieg's steady management of university affairs also prevented
major meddling by outside groups such as resulted in the dismissal of
President Charles H. Fisher of Western Washington State College in
1939. Fisher allegedly allowed "subversives" to speak on campus. The
college was censured by the AAUP for "yielding to the pressure of
President's Fisher's critics," who included the Grand Dragon of the
Ku Klux Klan and Governor Martin. By maintaining an ostensibly
neutral posture toward right and left politics, Sieg avoided the provocation of an alliance between conservatives and the radical right,
which had been Fisher's undoing.[18]

When the faculty invited Marxist economist Harold Laski to a
Walker-Ames lectureship during the Winter Quarter of 1939, however, the vulnerability of the university became apparent. Groups
traditionally suspicious of the "radical" character of the university
such as the Daughters of the American Revolution, the American
Legion, and Pro America joined with newspapers such as the *Seattle
Times*, Hearst's *Seattle Post-Intelligencer*, and the *Catholic Northwest
Progress* to protest Laski's appearance. The British Labor party leader
was linked with the unionization of teachers and other public
employees, the United Front with the Communist party, and such
Washington State groups as the Washington Commonwealth Federation (WCF) and the Old Age Pension Union. Sieg remained firm in
supporting Laski's appointment, citing his faith in the intelligence of
college students and in the durability of democracy. Laski did not
make Sieg's task any easier when, on February 9, he addressed a mass
meeting at the Moore Theater in downtown Seattle. The meeting was
sponsored by a wide range of leftist groups; among them the American League for Peace and Democracy, the WCF, the Social Workers'
Committee to Aid Spanish Democracy, and the Friends of the Abraham Lincoln Brigade. The fears of rightist groups were confirmed.[19]

Laski's appointment coincided with legislative consideration of the
university's biennial budget, and it was from Olympia that the most
serious objections were raised. Thomas Balmer, president of the
Board of Regents, wrote Sieg of the "friends the University has lost

through having Laski here, and how much more difficult it has made our efforts to obtain an adequate legislative appropriation for the forthcoming biennium." Though Sieg admitted to a "fault of judgment" in the timing of the lectures, he denied that anyone at the university was deliberately trying to provoke the legislature, as was being charged. The president pointed to the world renown of the Marxist scholar and argued that since students would hear these views eventually, they might as well be heard from an expert in a forum conducive to open debate. The controversy died amid threats from State Senator Joseph Drumheller that the legislature would investigate the university, but it cast a long shadow in the memories of both supporters and detractors of the university.[20] Meanwhile, events beyond the university assumed a major role in its future.

World War II changed the University of Washington. As civilian enrollments dropped, faculty members were called upon to train increasing numbers of Army and Navy personnel. Cooperation with the federal government brought new prestige to the Engineering, Mathematics, Chemistry, Physics, and Far Eastern departments. University scientists contributed to the success of the Manhattan Project. Applied Physics Laboratory personnel were given a postwar Navy citation for their development of an effective torpedo exploder, and instruments used in the Bikini testing of the atomic bomb further enhanced its reputation. The university's aeronautical engineers and its wind tunnel were important to the development of the nation's air power during and after the war.

Following the war, these departments attracted grants and personnel for the continuation of basic research. More than any other event in the university's history, the war brought the faculty into contact with others in their fields; industrial and governmental ties were forged with the university which assured the future growth of all concerned. An example of this is the Far Eastern and Russian Institute which was organized within the Far Eastern Department following the war. With grants from the Rockefeller Foundation and in cooperation with the Chinese history project at Columbia, the university's departments of History, Political Science, Economics, and Anthropology developed an extensive language library and exchange program with the Far East nations. The major impetus in the development of this program was the area studies concept used during the war for the Army Specialized Training Program at the university.[21]

World War II also changed the social and economic character of the State of Washington. Urbanization and industrialization of the Puget

Sound region were accelerated as shipyards, aircraft plants, and other defense-related concerns attracted thousands of workers. Seattle became a boom town which constantly outstripped the efforts of government planners who allocated meat, oil, steel, and other rationed items. The cost of living skyrocketed along with wages; housing became scarce as military and industrial personnel competed for space. The population of Seattle swelled to 480,000 in 1943, a 20 percent increase over 1940. Moreover, the migration to the Pacific Northwest continued after the war; by 1949 the region had experienced a 48.7 percent increase in population over 1940.[22]

The importance of this overall growth to the University of Washington was appreciated by those responsible for planning its future. In the year preceding the end of the war, university officials presented a detailed plan to the legislature. Emphasis was placed on the needs of veterans, adult education programs, and continuation of university programs to assist community planning in the region. Expansion of the physical plant was anticipated as materials and manpower became available. In early 1945 the state legislature allocated funds for medical and dental schools to be established at the university.[23] A Commission on Public Education in Washington was set up to identify solutions to problems of overcrowding and lack of teachers in elementary and secondary schools, and to present a unified plan for the growth of the state's higher educational institutions. George D. Strayer of Columbia Teachers College coordinated the study, the results of which were published in September, 1946, as Allen took office.

The Strayer Survey pointed to the general growth of the state during the war and forecast the increased need for skilled labor which could only be met by increased training. The reporters found that a larger percentage of the state's population attended college than was true for the nation as a whole—1.54 percent versus 1.13 percent—yet the people of the state invested only two-thirds as much in higher education as the people of other states. The solution offered by the survey was a restructuring of the state's tax system.[24]

With respect to the university, the commission recommended a thorough-going reorganization of the president's office to include vice-presidents in charge of faculty and educational programs, student personnel and welfare, and business operations. The Board of Regents was urged to adopt a code to define the lines of authority, and procedures and practices among the regents, faculty, and administration. Though such a code had been formulated, the commission pointed out, "the status of the code is obscure," leaving "the faculty ignorant about the attitudes and desires of the administration and the board." The regents were chided for their "apparent preoccupation with other matters."[25]

But it was in the area of faculty development that the survey noted the most pressing need for change. Based on the fact of 20 percent inbreeding, money should be provided to bring a wide range of candidates to campus for evaluation; qualifications other than seniority should determine promotion; a more adequate retirement system should be adopted, and salaries raised. Due to its distance from the East and Midwest, the university should pay *higher* salaries than comparable institutions. The survey's wide-ranging recommendations also included sabbatical leaves, more travel funds, and support services such as an audio-visual system and a placement office.[26]

The most important effect of the Strayer Survey was that it lent credence to faculty suggestions aimed at making the university a first-rate institution. During the war years, the university chapter of the AAUP had continued gathering and transmitting faculty opinion to the administration by the use of polls and questionnaires. In 1944, AAUP questionnaires had been used to suggest standards and procedures for faculty promotions which would eliminate some of the "cronyism" pervasive among deans and department chairmen. The poll technique had also been used to win a 10 percent salary raise in 1945–46. In April, 1946, 255 of approximately 700 faculty members returned a questionnaire which showed overwhelming approval for a regent-approved code (177–45), a more equitable plan for promotions and salary increases (214–16), faculty consultation on appointments of deans and chairmen (199–43), and a more favorable retirement program (215–33). In response to the question "Should deans and chairmen be subject to a vote of confidence each four years?" 185 faculty members answered "Yes." These findings confirmed earlier AAUP studies which showed that a large minority of department chairmen failed to hold meetings as required by the Faculty Code, thus eliminating faculty input on appointments, promotions, and travel disbursements. The Strayer Survey, in turn, confirmed AAUP's polls by urging a more democratic system of governance and an end to what it termed "kitchen-cabinetry."[27]

Allen's response to the concerns of the faculty demonstrated his sympathy with their aspirations toward building a great university and his own loose, open style of administration. While he worked actively with the regents, alumni, and various faculty groups in securing broad increases in salary and retirement benefits from the legislature, he urged faculty members to contact legislators on an informal basis, a decided departure from past policy. Though the student-faculty ratio remained at the unacceptable level of twenty-seven-to-one, Allen cautioned against undue haste in hiring faculty who lacked competence. Travel funds were increased, and the level of research grants reached unprecedented heights. While meeting these immediate problems, Allen also endorsed faculty desires for more autonomy, as well as further revisions of the Faculty Code, which included strong tenure provisions. He acceded to faculty requests to exclude the powerful deans from the Senate, and relinquished his chairmanship of that body. Allen depended heavily on the advice of Dean of Faculties Guthrie, and as a result the faculty gained more policy-making power than they had ever before enjoyed. In an era of expansion, Allen gave top administrators virtual carte blanche, and released the pent-up ingenuity of the faculty.[28]

Speaking for the faculty at Allen's inauguration, Austin Eastman, chairman of the Electrical Engineering Department, paid tribute to Allen's innovative style: "In the few months you have been with us you have already inspired us to increased efforts by your constructive leadership, your encouragement of our various activities and your personal interest in the problems and needs of the various departments and colleges of the University."[29] But if many of the problems left over from the past appeared to be settling themselves through the industrious, rational energies of Allen and the faculty, another more stubborn cloud was growing on the horizon with each passing day. As war had brought a new era of growth to the university, so too its aftermath was to bring a period of uncertainty and fear which threatened the hallmark of the university, academic freedom.

The Genesis of the Canwell Committee

Like the problems associated with faculty development faced by Allen and the faculty, the emerging difficulties had their roots in the thirties, the developing Cold War, and Washington State politics. The elections of 1946 were an indication of the dissatisfaction of the American public with the state of the economy and the world. At home, Americans were confronted with sharp rises in the cost of living, labor strikes, and shortages of commodities; general prosperity coexisted with memories of the Great Depression. As Truman struggled to manage the economy, those who had been silenced by the popularity of Roosevelt and the war began to reassert their criticisms of his legacy of New Deal regulations. Added to economic uncertainty were indications from abroad that winning the war had not won the peace. The alliance with the U.S.S.R. had begun to disintegrate long before Churchill's Iron Curtain speech in mid-1946; old suspicions of Communism were revived and gained new credibility in the face of Russian intransigence in Eastern Europe. Earl Browder's Popular Front leadership of the Communist party of the United States (CPUSA) had ended in 1945, and his successor, William Z. Foster, no longer spoke of collective security. Liberals who had supported Roosevelt now found themselves divided on foreign policy and attitudes toward domestic Communists. For the first time since Herbert Hoover the electorate chose a Republican Congress, which included Richard Nixon and Joseph McCarthy. In the ensuing struggles between the Truman administration and a Congress reasserting itself over a strong executive branch, "Communism in government" became an important political issue. The Cold War abroad was thus complemented by the Cold Civil War at home.[30]

In the State of Washington, the 1946 elections featured a campaign by Republicans against "Communist-controlled Democrats." The focus of this effort was a clique of Democratic legislators who had espoused "United Front" politics during the 1930s, and were members of the Washington Commonwealth Federation. The WCF was an alliance of unemployed and/or disaffected liberals, laborers, and farmers which supported candidates favorable to an expansion of the New Deal locally and nationally. One of the more successful "Popular Front" groups, the WCF numbered among its affiliates the Washington Pension Union, the American Federation of Teachers, and other labor union locals. A special subject of Republican attack was Hugh DeLacy, a one-time University of Washington English instructor, AFT member, and leader of the WCF, who had won election to Congress in 1944. In his campaign for reelection, wide publicity was given to the fact that DeLacy had been cited twice by the House Un-American Activities Committee for membership in Communist "front" organizations. In his stead, Washingtonians elected a former state commander of the American Legion; they also chose a Republican senator and a Republican-controlled legislature.[31]

After the elections, conservative Democratic leaders resolved to rid themselves of the alleged Communists in their ranks. The 1947 legislature had not yet convened when a coalition of Democrats and Republicans held a caucus to discuss the possibility of a legislative investigation into Communist infiltration of the Democratic party and state institutions. With regard to one of those institutions, the University of Washington, the caucus report stated: "It is common knowledge in many quarters that the Communists have infiltrated the University of

Washington campus and that their supporters have found important places on the faculty . . . the Communists are trying everything in the book to reach American youth through the schools." [32]

In succeeding days, the *Post-Intelligencer* reported the demands of leading Democrats for a purge of their party. Among these were University of Washington regents State Senator Joseph Drumheller and Teamster Union leader Dave Beck. Drumheller, a member of a pioneer Washington family and grandson of University of Washington President Leonard J. Powell (1882–87), was the head of a Spokane chemical firm. Beck had been active in Seattle labor politics since 1918; in the course of his battles with more radical labor groups, such as Harry Bridges' cio-backed Longshoremen and Warehouse-men's Union, he brought his own type of peace to the city's unions and gained the respect of businessmen, politicians, and the Hearst-owned *Post-Intelligencer*. Beck had helped elect Democratic Governor Mon C. Wallgren in 1944; Wallgren, in turn, appointed Beck to the Board of Regents in 1946. [33]

Legislative concern with university affairs was further demon-strated when two regents appeared before the Senate Committee on Higher Education prior to confirmation. John L. King, educational director of the Washington State Grange, and John Fox, official of both the Seattle Local of the Masters, Mates and Pilots (AFL) and the Mariners Union (CIO), stated to the senators that they had no knowl-edge of "subversive activities" by University of Washington faculty. Senator Thomas Bienz, one of the coalition leading the move for legislative investigation of Communist activities, was moved to express bewilderment at such ignorance:

> For years and years we members of the Senate have heard it. There isn't a student who has attended this University who has not been taught subversive activities and when they come home it is very hard for parents to change their minds. I have reports that show definitely that five pro-fessors teach subversive activities at the school and other reports that the number is as high as thirty. If Mr. Fox and Mr. King haven't heard about these things, I don't think they should stay on the Board of Regents another two days. [34]

Though the Bienz allegations were denied by President Emeritus Sieg and President Allen, and though both King and Fox had been active in wcf politics, King was confirmed by the senate, but Fox was not. Some legislators reportedly feared that as a labor leader he would not be responsive to the problems of university management. Dave Beck, who did not appear before the senate committee, was confirmed. [35]

In and of themselves, Senator Bienz's remarks were illustrative of legislative attitudes toward the university which had often found expression in the past. In the circumstances of 1947, however, they also reflected a determination to take action to stem the tide of social unrest. Amid the turmoil over a "people's march" on the state capitol, which was sponsored by the Washington Pension Union to demand increased aid to schools, veterans, and the elderly, the legislature acted. A proviso to the 1947 Appropriations Act demanded, from all persons employed by the state, an oath disclaiming membership in organizations that advocated strikes or the forcible overthrow of the government. On March 3, the day before adjournment, a "Joint Legislative Fact-Finding Committee on Un-American Activities" was empowered to "investigate, ascertain, collate and appraise all facts concerning individuals, groups or organizations whose activities are such as to indicate a purpose to foment internal strife, discord and dissension; infiltrate and undermine the stability of our American institutions; confuse and mislead the people; and impede the normal progress of our state and nation. . . ." Included as subjects for investigation were the educational institutions of the state.[36]

Aside from conforming to the national pattern, and in some ways anticipating it, events in Washington State resembled a family feud. The political and economic fortunes of the state were historically tied to the basic industries of forestry, shipping, farming, and fishing. Within those industries there had always been pockets of right and left radicals who asserted themselves in times of stress. Attempts by workers to organize often involved violence, a result of frustrations engendered by poor conditions and the inability of government to meliorate them. Populism at the turn of the century, the activities of the Industrial Workers of the World, the Seattle General Strike of 1919, the Red Scare and union battles of the 1920s and 1930s, and the disorders of the Depression left scars on the memories of Washingtonians yearning for respectability. Despite the fact that state government was generally in the hands of conservatives, the state was considered progressive in labor and welfare legislation. Some thought matters had gone too far. "There are forty-seven states and the Soviet of Washington," a remark widely attributed to Postmaster General James Farley, both embarrassed and delighted the citizenry.[37]

In the eyes of some Washingtonians, the University of Washington had contributed to the state's reputation for radicalism. Over the years its faculty members were involved in controversial movements. J. Allen Smith's Progressive crusade for public ownership of utilities caused powerful men to call for his dismissal. When he died in 1924, he was still urging his students to disdain the excesses of the govern-

ment exemplified by Attorney General Palmer's campaign against
"Bolsheviks," and by the enforcement of prohibition. In the 1930s
faculty members continued to outrage citizens. They sought solutions
to the problems of the Depression and the dangers of Fascism
through organizations such as the Communist party, Bellamy Clubs,
the Technocrats, the Washington Commonwealth Federation, and
the American Federation of Teachers.[38]

Of course, political activism among professors was not unique to the
University of Washington, nor was the reservoir of suspicion of professors peculiar to Washingtonians. But as the university poised for an
era of unprecedented growth and national recognition, the threatening gestures of the 1947 legislature revived questions that had lain
dormant since the 1930s. Colleagues wondered again whether activist
faculty members were endangering the willingness of the public to
support university programs.

Beyond that immediate question was the issue of subversion. In the
chill of the postwar dawn, what were once mere academic differences
of opinion on Communist party membership and left politics began to
assume new significance. Events of the late 1930s—the revelations of
the Dewey Commission on the Moscow Trials and the Nazi-Soviet
Pact—had divided and confused liberal opinion on the merits of the
Communist movement in the U.S. The Committee for Cultural Freedom was formed in 1939 by intellectuals such as John Dewey, Sidney
Hook, and Reinhold Niebuhr to warn of the dangers presented to a
democratic society by the Communist party. Organizations such as the
ACLU and the AFT eliminated Communists from their leadership. On
the other hand, some academics refused to see Communism as a
monolithic conspiracy and urged adherence to traditions of civil liberties and academic freedom for individuals who were Communist
party members. As the mood of the American people became increasingly intolerant of Communists, however, faculty members who had
known one another for years questioned anew the legitimacy of some
types of activities in which their colleagues were engaged. What were
the bounds of academic freedom in an era of national insecurity?[39]

Such divisions marked the dilemma facing the faculty and administration of the University of Washington in March of 1947. Within
days after the legislature made it clear that the university would be
subject to investigation by the Un-American Activities Committee, the
Executive Committee of the AAUP chapter met with President Allen to
discuss the matter. On the committee were Charles E. Martin (Political
Science), president of the chapter, Stull Holt (History), J. B. Harrison
(English), R. G. Tyler (Engineering), P. E. Church (Meteorology), and

Vernon Mund (Economics). As veteran observers of Washington State politics, they were apprehensive about the implications of the legislative investigation, yet reassured by the overall favorable action of the legislature on the university's budget and faculty salary and retirement programs. Though a tenure bill supported by the AAUP chapter, Local 401 of the AFT, and the Faculty Senate had not passed the legislature, its provisions would soon be incorporated into the revised Administrative Code. As a working arrangement, it could protect faculty against unfounded allegations and provide a method for internal investigations of legislative findings. On the latter issue, Martin advocated negotiation with the legislative committee for university handling of the investigation, as President Gordon Sproul had done in California. The idea was rejected, however, since Allen had neither Sproul's connections in the state nor the backing of the regents for such a course of action.[40] Rather than risk the university's hard-won gains, which could result from resistance to the legislative committee, the group decided to proceed cautiously.

Given the backgrounds and future actions of the Executive Committee members, a wide spectrum of opinion was probably expressed on all the issues raised, but ultimately they agreed that the legislative committee "does not have in mind any interference with the intellectual freedom of the faculty or of the University." The committee also supported the position of the president who "has stated that he will give full cooperation should the committee request it, in setting up its investigations."[47] Allen wrote to the legislative committee expressing the cooperation of the whole university

> . . . in any studies you feel it desirable to make of the activities of the University of Washington which fall within the purview of your assignment from the Legislature. . . . Speaking for myself and the faculty, we would welcome an opportunity for a representative of the faculty, the Executive Officer of Academic Personnel, and myself to sit down with the committee to review any matters you wish to bring before us. We will be eager to cooperate with you in a fair and comprehensive study of the situation and discuss with you the areas of investigation about which you are most concerned.[41]

Dean Edwin Guthrie, the executive officer of Academic Personnel, later testified that he had warned Allen of his belief that there were three or four Communist party members on the faculty. Whether Allen believed that or not is perhaps immaterial. Since his strategy of co-operation with the legislative committee had the backing of faculty leaders, the initiative now lay with the committee, and the tactics could be worked out as conditions warranted. Allen's can-do approach to practical problems and his success with the regents, legislature, and faculty inspired further confidence that this matter could be met with reason and grace. Two months later, in his inaugural address, as he outlined his views on the role of the university in the postwar world, Allen warned that faculty members should guard their heritage of freedom through rational thought:

> And teachers in any field are also citizens and persons. They have likes and dislikes, and enthusiasms just as anyone else. Because of the rigors of truth in their intellectual discipline, however, we expect them to be more objective toward society and politics than some who have not had their peculiar advantages. It is for this reason that the teacher has a special obligation to deal in a scholarly way with controversial questions. Unless he can make his report so objective that it will withstand the fire of criticism from his colleagues, he should not offer a professional opinion. If he goes forth to battle the world armed only with half-formed judgments and prejudices, either those colleagues will expose him, or someone in the tough, hard-headed world of affairs will surely do so. Fortunately, few faculty men make this mistake. If they do make it, the institution from which they come will lose its academic standing, as they will lose their security.[42]

In coming months, the president would often use those passages to show that he had warned faculty members of the dangers of political entanglements. As the Cold War deepened abroad and at home, the road to truth narrowed, and those who strayed found themselves outside the university.

II

The Politics of Loyalty:

The Canwell Committee Hearings and the University of Washington

On the last day of the 1947 legislative session, the day after the AAUP chapter Executive Committee met with President Raymond Allen, the members of the Interim Committee on Un-American Activities were appointed. Composed of five Republicans and two Democrats, the committee soon became known as the Canwell Committee for its chairman, Albert F. Canwell, who had introduced the subversive activities measure in the legislature. A freshman Republican, Canwell traced his concerns about Communism to the Seattle waterfront strike of 1934. His credentials as an investigator were derived from his experience as deputy sheriff in charge of the Spokane County Identification Bureau. Canwell expanded his qualifications by conferring with members of the U.S. House Un-American Activities Committee (HUAC) and obtaining access to the extensive files on persons and groups accrued by the committee since 1935.[1]

Canwell's colleagues on the committee were motivated by similar apprehensions. Sydney Stevens, a freshman Republican from Seattle, expressed concern about Communists undermining parental authority through the school system, which he had learned about as a member of the American Legion. Of the three other Republicans on the committee, two were senators, but only one was an experienced legislator. All had favored creation of the committee and expressed confidence in Chairman Canwell's leadership. Senator Thomas Bienz, Democratic legislator since 1939, was a vigorous supporter of the investigation into Communist activities in the state, having introduced the Canwell-Stevens measure in the senate. His opinions on the subversive nature of Communism were developed during a 1927 trip to Europe, while he was a delegate to an American Legion convention.

21

Representative George F. Yantis was the only non-coalition Democrat
on the committee, and was its only lawyer. He confided to President
Allen that he had been appointed by the speaker of the house to
moderate Canwell's witch-hunting fervor. Yantis conveyed his own
misgivings about what he termed Canwell's "amateur detective" self
image. Yantis died in December 1947 before the committee began its
hearings.[2]

Following the legislature's adjournment, little was heard of the Canwell Committee, as it set about hiring investigators and gathering
information on subversive activities among the citizens of Washington
State. In the meantime, national and world events helped shape the
response to the Canwell Committee. In February, 1947, President
Truman announced his plan of military and economic aid to Greece
and Turkey aimed at preventing the southward surge of Russian
forces. He also ordered investigations into the loyalty of federal
employees. Seattle citizens formed a local branch of the Progressive
Citizens of America (PCA) and denounced Truman's provocative
stance. The PCA warned that in bypassing the United Nations, Truman signaled the "end of American policy based on one world and
presents a policy in which he divides the world into two camps." A
forerunner of Henry Wallace's Progressive party, the PCA also denounced the State Un-American Activities Committee and defended
the political and civil rights of Communists. Among the University of
Washington faculty members who joined the PCA were Albert Franzke
(Speech), Melvin Rader (Philosophy), Ralph Gundlach (Psychology),
and R. G. Tyler (Engineering). All eventually received Canwell Committee subpoenas.[3]

But for the most part, university students were more outspoken
than the faculty in the early days following formation of the Canwell
Committee. A "Committee for Academic Freedom" was organized by
the American Youth for Democracy around such issues as opposition
to the Un-American Activities Committee, the restrictions on Henry
Wallace's freedom to speak on campus, and university policy prohibit-
ing recognition of political groups like the AYD as legitimate student
organizations. The AYD attracted wide attention in October when the
head of the National Federation of Young Republicans stated that
Seattle was a center for Communist-dominated groups like the AYD.
President Allen responded to that report with a reiteration of his
stand that the university was no place for students who "incite riots
and lead parades"; however, he also pledged not to "raise an iron
curtain against the objective study of the world's problems."[4]

Communism and the University of Washington were again linked in headlines when a graduate student told of being forced to leap from a second story window to escape the threats of a faculty member and another graduate student. The student said that he had been accused by the pair of being an agent for the F.B.I. and the Canwell Committee, and in his attempts to avert a beating, broke his leg. Though investigations by the university and the King County prosecutor concluded that the student had been the victim of a practical joke, the follow-up stories were buried by both Seattle papers, leaving the reading public to its own conclusions.[5]

In the midst of that comic opera, *Times* columnist Ross Cunningham predicted a probe of university "Red Activity." According to Cunningham, there existed a "clique of faculty members which stresses the 'advantages' of the communist theory of government over our own." Also, he alleged, "a number of prominent Communist and pro-Communist thinkers are found among former students of the University." As proof, Cunningham cited the case of the Seattle girl who "rose to stardom and then found oblivion" in Hollywood. According to her own mother, he noted, this woman had become Communist while attending the university's drama school in the thirties.[6]

On December 8, the *Tacoma News Tribune* editorialized about University Regent George Stuntz's remark that "teachers of communist doctrines would be run off campus." The editorial pointed out that a "witch-hunt" on the university would undermine the faith of the young in the democratic tradition of the competition of ideas, drive the cpusa underground, and promote a martyr-complex which would make its activities attractive. Since only 60,000 out of 140 million citizens were estimated to be Communists or fellow-travelers, the editorial concluded, democracy was secure. Though the *Tribune* was paraphrasing the arguments of J. Edgar Hoover against outlawing the Communist party, Stuntz, who had replaced John Fox as regent, was expressing the determination of the regents to clean house once and for all.

The Canwell Committee held its first hearings from January 27 to February 5, 1948, in the Seattle Field Artillery Armory. Canwell's seven investigators had concentrated their efforts on the Washington Pension Union. Under the supervision of officers of the State Patrol the committee quickly set about using the testimony of national and local witnesses to show the subversive nature of the cpusa, and the domination of the Pension Union by Communists. "Expert witness" Louis Budenz, then professor of Economics at Fordham University, testified that in his former capacities as editor of the *Daily Worker* and member of the Communist party's National Committee, he had come to know Hugh DeLacy as a member of the Communist party. The former University of Washington English instructor was characterized as an effective agent in charge of the Washington Commonwealth Federation. Budenz also testified that the Seattle Labor School was a Communist party organization and that Professor Ralph Gundlach was "following the Party Line." Mostly hearsay, Budenz's testimony did not point to illegal activities, only certain associations. Canwell allowed no cross examination by defense attorneys because of the "fact-finding" nature of the hearings.[7]

After several more expert witnesses from across the nation had testified, local persons who had been members of the Communist party working within the Pension Union were called. All attested to Communist party leadership of the Pension Union. Kathryn Fogg, a member of the 1939 legislature, testified to the presence of Professor Harold Eby at Communist unit meetings. Instructor Joseph Butterworth had introduced her to Earl Browder at his home. H. C. (Army) Armstrong said that he belonged to a "professional unit" of the party which included Professors DeLacy, Butterworth and Gundlach. Mrs. Isabel Costigan's testimony included the information that after joining the party in 1938, she was assigned to a "secret University unit" with Eby and Butterworth; she also testified that she had once interrupted a Communist party meeting at Gundlach's home one evening by her unexpected arrival.[8]

There seemed to be little disposition on the part of the University of Washington faculty to defend their fellows named during the first Canwell hearing. The problem was posed to the Faculty Senate by its Public Relations Committee in February of 1948. Membership of the committee, which was concerned with good public relations, included legislative lobbyists R. B. Harris, the executive secretary of the Alumni Association, and Nelson Wahlstrom, comptroller. H. P. Everest, director of the School of Journalism and public relations assistant to former Governor Langlie, was experienced with the legislature and newspaper editors around the state. Donald Anderson, Allen's newly appointed director of University News Service, was a member of the committee, as were faculty members R. G. Tyler, Charles E. Martin, and Vernon Mund. Harold Eby, who had been named a Communist during the first hearing, was also part of the group. In its preliminary deliberations, the committee decided only that it should prevent publicity by "campus groups that might be tempted to rush into print," and suggested this policy to the senate.[9]

No debate on the matter is recorded; the senate endorsed the "no publicity" resolution, and concurred in the stance of the Public Relations Committee that the senate should provide the administration any assistance it might request. Since the first hearings had uncovered only vague charges against three faculty members, the senate was perhaps warranted in preparing no further strategy. Its members could hope no further actions against university faculty were forthcoming. By late March, however, it was evident that the university could not evade further scrutiny. Senator Thomas Bienz charged that, though President Allen had denied the figure of thirty, Bienz had evidence of "not less than 150 Communists or Communist sympathizers on the faculty." Bienz's statement brought immediate comment from Canwell, who said that the committee was not ready to say how many faculty were Communists. Regent Drumheller observed that such unsubstantiated attacks would "destroy the public confidence until now enjoyed by the Canwell Committee, and particularly its chairman." The former senator went on to say that the regents were well aware of subversive activities on the university campus, but that it was probably no worse than on any other campus in the state.[10]

Though Bienz protested that he was not trying to "smear the University," the state press picked up on the issue. When President Allen told the Spokane Alumni Association of the importance of academic freedom which permitted "fearless men to look into the future," and asserted that there were no Communists on the faculty, only some whose statements appeared subversive, he was challenged. "There is such a thing as being too zealous in this matter of academic freedom," warned the *Pasco Herald*; the editor of the *Aberdeen World* took the view that "indoctrination is not a right."[11]

In the face of such vitriolic commentary, Allen may have realized that he could do nothing to stave off an investigation, and he turned his attention toward the insurance of internal due process according to rules of tenure that the faculty expected him to follow. The president had been unable to convince the regents that they should endorse the tenure bill which had been placed before the last legislature by the faculty, and he had been equally unsuccessful in securing their approval of the tenure provisions in the Faculty Code. The regents saw these efforts as a threat to their power to veto faculty decisions. Beck wrote to Allen that he was in favor of faculty organizing for their own welfare; however, he disfavored a faculty organization that would interfere with Allen's position as chief executive. In addition, the regents had resolved to handle the public side of the investigation themselves. The university was undergoing a period of extensive growth which required the full attention of the president. As Beck wrote, "it is for this reason that I was unalterably opposed to your being placed out in front where opposition on the question of Communism and such would keep your office in constant turmoil." It was better that the board divert propaganda attacks to itself, he concluded, leaving Allen to do the job for which he had been hired. When they considered the Faculty Code in November, 1947, the regents did not look upon it as a constraint on their powers. At the suggestion of Regent Balmer, they prefaced the code with the state statutes describing the prerogatives of the Board of Regents. Tenure provisions notwithstanding, the president and the faculty served at the pleasure of the regents.[12]

Thus, while the regents clearly expected dissent in the matter of the Canwell investigation, they expected Allen to concur in its necessity. In order to fulfill his role as spokesman for the faculty, and to retain their confidence as well as that of the regents, Allen set about convincing the regents of the need for due process as prescribed by the Faculty Code. Given the nature of the regents, this was a problem. The public statements of Regents Beck, Drumheller, and Stuntz showed their determination to purge the faculty. Thomas Balmer had worried about radical faculty since the days of Sieg. A lawyer, Balmer was vice-president and counsel for Great Northern Railway, director of several Seattle business concerns, and a director of both the National Bank of Commerce and the Washington Mutual Savings Bank. Others on the Board of Regents included Clarence J. Coleman, an Everett lawyer, university alumnus, and Democratic National Committeeman, and Winlock Miller, a Seattle investment broker, who had been a member of the board since the days of Henry Suzzallo and the Seattle General Strike. John King, a moderate who had been attacked by Bienz at his senate confirmation hearing, was probably of greatest assistance to Allen, since he had many associates on the faculty.[13]

Allen at first met with only partial success. At their April 22 meeting, the regents assured Canwell of full administrative cooperation and of their intent to dismiss any faculty member proved to be engaged in subversive activities. Canwell, in turn, agreed to provide Allen with the names of suspected faculty and briefs of evidence in advance of the public hearings so that a committee of the faculty could interview the accused. To avoid disruption of the spring quarter classes, Canwell also consented to postpone the public hearings on the university until after the June commencement. At that same meeting, Joseph Drumheller was elected president of the board and Dave Beck vice-president. Afterward, the regents issued a statement expressing amity with Canwell and the activities of the committee.[14]

Twelve days later, Canwell announced that the hearings on the university would be conducted in public, as were those on the Washington Pension Union. Canwell said that his press release was designed to quell rumors that evidence concerning faculty subversion would be turned over to the regents for "a quiet investigation of their own." He made it clear that he would help the regents and Allen in "any remedial action they take on the Committee's evidence."[15]

The regents' actions regarding Canwell did not receive uniform public approbation. Attorney Herbert Little, who later served as a regent (1960–65), wrote Drumheller that mishandling of this situation could damage the reputation of the university just as it entered its greatest era. Deploring the manner in which Canwell's activities were being played up in the *Post-Intelligencer*, he urged the regents to emphasize publicly the necessity of fair hearings to guarantee the freedom of the university. Little also hoped they would emphasize their confidence in the loyalty of the faculty. Without such positive actions by the regents, he asserted, the effects of this episode could undermine Allen's leadership and destroy public confidence in teachers.[16]

Meanwhile, Allen's directives to the faculty that they cooperate with the Canwell investigation were being questioned. Though some faculty members were politely interrogated about their past activities and associations, others found the methods of the investigators contemptible. Giovanni Costigan (History), who responded to Canwell's subpoena on the evening before a long-planned trip to Europe, was able to convince the chairman that there was nothing sinister about his support of Spanish Loyalists in the 1930s. His encounter was not marked by the threats and innuendos that Brents Stirling (English), who was also an attorney, reported to Allen. Ernest Stith, a Canwell investigator, told Stirling that he had evidence Stirling was a member of the Communist party, but that things would go better for him if he turned state's evidence. The committee was out to "'get' Communists and those who have played ball with them," said Stith, who continually used the phrase, "'We are not out to smear anyone.'" Wrote Stirling: "I merely wish to point out that standard police methods of intimidation are being used on this campus—this in return for the University's willingness to cooperate with the Canwell Committee."[17]

In an attempt to keep Canwell somewhat in check, Allen reached out to one of Canwell's political allies, Harry P. Cain. As a Republican campaigning on the "Communism in the Democratic party issue," Cain had been swept into the U.S. Senate in 1946. He assured Allen that in his talks with Canwell he found no evidence that the committee was out to "besmirch the University's reputation." Though suspicious of some of the faculty, the chairman would not treat anyone unfairly; "Al feels that some of your advisors are working as best they can to whitewash any serious investigation . . . [though] the relationship between you is somewhat strained . . . I respect you both and I think you have much in common." Cain encouraged Allen to talk things over with Canwell often and to feel free to tell the chairman which of his investigators were being "indiscreet."[18]

Several days later, Allen called the faculty to a general meeting in which he outlined the predicament of the university and the thinking of himself and of the regents on the way out of it. The president assured the faculty that the regents would support the administration and the faculty in their wishes for due process according to the Faculty Code. To those faculty who thought their civil rights were being trampled, Allen stressed the importance of maintaining "our unity and our dignity . . . we cannot afford to engage in a public fight with the Canwell Committee." The previously developed strategy of silence would be maintained. His "reconnaissance of the situation" showed that "the climate of Public Opinion is strongly running against radicalism and is being currently conditioned against allowing proved Communists to hold public employment." The university was dependent on public support and its corollary, public good will. Allen referred to the unpredictable "motives, procedures, and policies" of the Canwell Committee, which threatened to turn the public against the university and further the frequent accusations of faculty activity in fostering communistic and atheistic teachings. "The secrecy of the methods and tactics of Communists makes it difficult for liberals to defend their academic privileges and immunities because we don't know what we are defending."

Allen then spoke of the strengths of the university in meeting the challenge of the situation, and in the process revealed the defensive steps he had taken. Pointing to the pride of the state's citizens in their university, "a national institution moving dynamically forward," Allen asserted that alumni, friends, and regents would defend it. Further, the managing editors of the Seattle papers, members of the Washington State congressional delegation, and the F.B.I. were fully advised of the seriousness of the situation. Allen claimed to have evidence "that Mr. Canwell at least now realizes that he must proceed cautiously and with due respect for *his* University" (Allen's emphasis).

The president's final comments served as a warning. Though he would fight to uphold the principles of due process and tenure, as well as safeguard the civil liberties of the faculty, Allen intimated that the Board of Regents would not defend individuals found to be engaged in secret activities of a dubious character.[19]

Though no transcript of Allen's address to the faculty exists, Allen later asserted that the intent of his final remarks was to induce individuals to come forward and tell him of "any affiliations which might embarrass the University," or they would lose its protection. It is questionable, however, whether Allen himself had made up his mind about Communist faculty persons as abstractions, much less what he would have done had a faculty member confided Communist party membership to him. His comments in May, 1948, indicate his feeling of being trapped between the legislative committee, public opinion, and the regents on one hand, and the faculty and the AAUP on the other. While publicly "welcoming" the coming investigation, Allen was searching for ways to alleviate or eliminate this menace to the university's future and his own ambitions. Allen's vacillations were matched by those of the faculty, who were themselves divided by the pressures of the Cold War.[20]

Because of the general proscription on public opposition to the Canwell Committee, faculty attitudes toward the idea of Communist teachers and the impending hearings were somewhat difficult to measure. However, in the spring of 1948, the Executive Board of the UWAAUP solicited the opinion of its members on its "Statement of Principles." Of approximately seven hundred Washington faculty, half belonged to the association. In a vote of 142–93, support was given to the statement, which condemned those who advocated acts designed to overthrow the government by force, and defended the rights of teachers as citizens to be members of any legally constituted political party. In support of these ideas, the statement threatened the administration with censure if the guidelines for due process as outlined in the Faculty Code were not followed, should the university take action against any faculty member as a result of the Canwell investigation. The UWAAUP also asked that certain procedures be adopted by the Canwell Committee to protect the rights of those faculty subpoenaed to appear before it, including the right to counsel, to cross-examine, and to present defense witnesses. The statement also urged the committee to admit only testimony that constituted clear evidence of advocacy of forcible overthrow of the government.[21]

The vote of 142–93 indicates that even before the Canwell hearings, a sizable group of AAUP members questioned the right of their colleagues to belong to the Communist party. In the face of the swiftly deteriorating international situation, the civil liberties of citizens who seemed less than zealous in opposition to Communists were threatened. Among liberals, the campaign of 1948 deepened old divisions. The Americans for Democratic Action, a group founded by assorted politicians and intellectuals such as Reinhold Niebuhr, Eleanor Roosevelt, Sidney Hook, Hubert Humphrey, and Arthur Schlesinger, Jr., were militantly anti-Communist and endorsed the Truman loyalty program and the Truman Doctrine of freedom and globalism. Liberals who took a more conciliatory approach toward Russia, and a more relaxed approach to Communism, as well as to international disarmament, tended to join the Wallace branch of the Democratic party, the Progressives. While these political divisions were a function of the Cold War, they allowed only limited action against the political conservatives who increasingly captured the "Communism in government" issue.[22] In many cases, liberals found themselves with the choice of either out-conserving the conservatives or risking the label "fellow-traveler." The problems of liberals in the Cold War era were a rough approximation of the difficulties faced by Allen and the faculty. Though some faculty were able to separate the issues of the Cold War abroad and at home, their attitudes toward the notion of "communists as teachers" precluded a unified response to the Canwell Committee.

Part of the problem, of course, was that the political differences of the 1930s had resulted in a hardening of attitudes of faculty toward each other. An example of this is a June, 1948, faculty statement on "Civil Liberties at the University of Washington." Essentially a manifesto of the left liberal viewpoint, it argued for the rights of Communist party members as citizens and faculty members, and asserted the illegality of the Canwell hearings. Perhaps because the legality of the legislative committee was being challenged by the Washington Pension Union, the subject of its first hearings, only fifty faculty signed the statement. One who refused to do so was George Lundberg, a nationally recognized sociologist, and chairman of the Sociology Department. In an open letter to Allen, he stated that his refusal was based on the "mass movement" character of the action and his misgivings about the movement's leadership. He also defended the legality of the committee. In addition, he objected to the implication of the statement that Communist party membership was a special case, since "anyone who acknowledges or *in practice observes* a higher allegiance to any political doctrine than to the established methods of science is *ipso facto* occupationally disqualified for scientific work. I think it is a false and indefensible idea of academic freedom to assume that it confers immunity from the consequences of participation in pressure group activities."[23]

Allen mimeographed Lundberg's letter for the whole faculty and invited comment; though few faculty wrote to express themselves on the subject, several did. J. B. Harrison (English) warned against giving the current hysteria its head; Communists have civil rights like anyone else, he stated, and while the Canwell Committee was probably not extralegal, it had violated the spirit of the Bill of Rights by allowing gossip and innuendo to pass for testimony. A. I. Melden (Philosophy) objected to Lundberg's implication that defense of Communists was a defense of Communism. Brents Stirling of English noted that faculty have a right to belong to pressure groups such as the AAUP. The right of teachers to speak freely "has not always existed and will exist only so long as university teachers are willing to constitute themselves in appropriate . . . 'pressure groups,'" he wrote. H. K. Benson, professor emeritus of Chemical Engineering, evoked past battles when he told Allen that he had signed the petition "in the interest of unity and cooperation" among the faculty. "Going back to the days of J. Allen Smith, faculty members defended their colleagues against charges of disloyalty."[24]

That the Canwell Committee's activities were having a chilling effect on faculty members' willingness to speak out can be inferred from Lundberg's private reply to Harrison in which he indicated general agreement with the signers of the statement. Lundberg not only condemned the committee for its "unwisdom," he labeled it "an unqualified nuisance, unwise, ineffective, and obscene." On the principle that the university should consider all viewpoints that have a following, Lundberg said he would publicly advocate having Communists and Fascists on the faculty, if doing so would not add fuel to the fire. The half-dozen faculty the committee would find objectionable made the situation "laughable," though Lundberg doubted the "public will see the humor."[25]

Student reaction to the impending Canwell hearings on the university was associated with the movement to have the Speaker's Ban lifted in the spring of 1948. The election of 1946 had occasioned some action in this regard, but the preoccupation of returning veterans who made up two-thirds of the student body, had been mainly with school, housing, and inflation. The policy of having the president approve off-campus speakers remained in effect, and partisan political speakers were not allowed to use university facilities. In February of 1948, just after the conclusion of the first Canwell hearing, presidential candidate Harold Stassen was denied permission to speak on campus because he refused to abide by the nonpartisan rule. Though he spoke at the YMCA near campus, the room was too small, and many students were unable to hear his address. As a result, Brock Adams, vice-president of the Associated Students (ASUW), led a movement to have the ban lifted, citing the fact that many presidential hopefuls were scheduled to visit the Northwest. As might be expected, Students for Wallace supported this move. The faculty, however, found it inadvisable to back the students because of the Canwell Committee: "It would only work hardship on faculty members who have been named by the Committee," said R. G. Tyler (Engineering).[26]

Though the students were divided on the wisdom of opening the campus to various soapboxes, the major issue soon became Communist speakers. In one telling debate, a student who favored lifting the ban on all political speakers except Communists said: "The University has had a lot of adverse criticism as a communistic hotbed. I am in favor of cleaning up that reputation. What I propose is a public relations measure, hitting out and out Communists." The president of the ASUW responded: "So long as the Communist Party is not illegal, we can't cut them out. . . . As we are looking at the issue now, we are thinking: how much money will we get from the State Legislature?" Said another, "I came all the way from Philadelphia to attend the University. Nobody ever told me it was a communistic university. . . . We don't have to be afraid of being called Communists if we invite Communists." A second Pennsylvanian chimed in, "I heard that the University was a hotbed of Communists and that Washington was the Soviet of the United States. . . . If this amendment is passed, we may be doing our public relations a favor, but denying our intellectual integrity. Freedom of educational opportunity is involved; we're supposed to be intelligent citizens, able to sift and choose between ideologies." The amendment barring Communist party speakers was defeated.[27]

Though the ASUW Board of Control voted to lift the ban, the regents reaffirmed it at their April 22, 1948, meeting. Undaunted, the student government voted to petition the regents and the governor to rescind the ban so that Wallace, Dewey, and Truman could appear on campus. The *Seattle Times'* associate editor, Carl Brazier, attacked this student effort in his column: "Of course, they'll deny it; but those who are this week clamoring for opening the campus to politics are commie sympathizers—they may not actually be Communists, but they very definitely cannot be pegged as anti-Communists." By May 21, six thousand of the sixteen thousand students had signed the petition;

some nonsigners stated they were "afraid of being checked by the Canwell Committee," others disagreed with or were suspicious of the objective of the action. Most probably did not care. The petition effort fizzled, and the regents upheld the ban at their May 21 meeting. They also announced that President Harry Truman would speak on campus in a nonpolitical capacity.[28]

On that same day, Henry Wallace, addressing 2,500 students from atop a sound truck positioned across the street from campus, expressed his amazement that Washington, "one of the most progressive states," would have a Canwell Committee, and that the university should be accused of harboring 150 Communists.[29] Though the appearance by Wallace and the activities of the vocal minority of students provoked a few letters to regents, university officials had little cause for concern. The general tenor of the *Daily* in 1947–48 supported what was probably the majority opinion among students: Communism was a danger to the U.S.A., but the issue was overshadowed by quotidian problems.

Indeed, their attitudes were close to those of their parents. An April, 1948, survey of public opinion showed that "communism" was an issue spontaneously mentioned by only 3 percent of Washingtonians when they were asked about their chief concerns. Inflation, war, elections, employment, and transportation were considered most important. This finding is consistent with other opinion research done during the 1950s which showed that Americans generally were not paralyzed with fear of Communism. Though Westerners were found to be better educated and more tolerant toward nonconformity than the nation generally, they had, like most Americans, consistently registered opposition to Communists, and were willing to deny Communists the same rights as other citizens. Teaching had been barred to Communists by general public opinion since the 1930s.[30]

In many ways, intolerance of Communism, which had been building since World War I, reached a high plateau in 1948. Throughout the world, in Czechoslovakia, Italy, Finland, in the Near and Far East, agents backed by the U.S.S.R. seemed to be gaining power. The Berlin Blockade and the Alger Hiss trials were final blows for some liberals who had been wavering in their support of Truman's foreign policy and loyalty programs. Thomas Dewey and his running mate Earl Warren accused Truman of "coddling Communists" while mainstream Democrats and ADA liberals continued their red-baiting of the "wild-eyed Wallasians" who would not renounce their belief that American aggression stimulated Russian aggression. In this atmosphere, Raymond Allen and his faculty tried to meet the issues of academic freedom for Communists and ex-Communists. With majority sentiment and most of the state press against Communist teachers, and liberal opinion divided, the University of Washington's position was guarded as it prepared for a long summer.

Early in June, Canwell provided President Allen with a list of seven persons on the faculty who would be cited as past or current members of the Communist party. Canwell also gave Allen the names of thirty-three faculty who would be subpoenaed as witnesses during the hearings, which were to begin July 19. Informing the regents of this development, Allen indicated that a special faculty committee had been set up by the Faculty Senate to be of aid to the faculty and the president. This committee would review the transcripts of the Canwell hearings to decide if charges should be brought against any subpoenaed members, and if so, refer the cases to the standing Faculty Committee on Tenure and Academic Freedom for hearing. Allen also received the regents' permission to hire lawyers to attend the hearings in the name of the university.[31]

Canwell's statements to the press on the subpoenas were even-handed. He declined to name those faculty members who had been called to testify, since not all were regarded as Communists or even fellow travelers; from some he hoped to get "information which may be helpful in shaping new legislation at the 1949 session. . . . The University of Washington is a great and fine institution. This committee hopes to contribute toward keeping it so by exposing the Communists who have been active on the faculty and on the campus." Canwell warned that contempt charges would be levied against those who refused to testify. The *Times* reported that Canwell stated: "We have a fine University here, but the faculty members who are Communists are not representative of this state or of the principles of academic freedom."[32]

Shortly after Canwell's press conference, Allen met with the president of the University of Washington chapter of the AAUP, R. G. Tyler, and Executive Committee members J. B. Harrison (English), and Max Savelle (History). All three were under suspicion by the Canwell Committee because of their affiliations with front groups in the thirties, and Tyler had been subpoenaed. Joining the president and these faculty leaders in discussion of the situation was E. R. Guthrie, the influential dean of faculties. The group agreed that faculty members under subpoena should state the truth of their position in the Canwell hearings, but that they should not feel obliged to comment on the activities of their colleagues, even if it meant a contempt citation. Allen called Chairman Canwell immediately to find out what he thought of that position; Canwell replied that "he was not out to persecute anyone on campus." As a result of this meeting, Tyler talked with each subpoenaed person to inform them that if they had anything to report to the administration about past membership, they should do it before the hearings, rather than keep Allen ignorant of their position. Assuring them of administration support if they admitted past membership, Tyler made sure to point out that Committee A of the AAUP would not support those who falsified the facts of their situation.[33]

The situation of faculty members who might be current members of the Communist party does not seem to have been discussed. It is reasonable to assume, however, that the faculty members present felt that truthful admission of such status would also gain administration support: Allen was ensuring that the administration followed AAUP guidelines for hearings; the Communist party was not illegal, and the code did not refer to such activities as cause for dismissal.

Meanwhile, the faculty who had been subpoenaed by Canwell began to break the agreed-upon silence. In a letter to the University of Washington *Daily*, Professor Herbert J. Phillips (Philosophy) elaborated some of the difficulties met in dealing with Canwell's investigators. Not only did they use intimidation and spread rumors about various members of the faculty, they also defined Communism as the advocacy of the violent overthrow of the government as an agent of a foreign power. Wrote Phillips: "I wish my colleagues and students to know that I believe the theory of force and violence as a means of social change is fascist doctrine, that its advocacy constitutes treason and deserves the severest punishment."[34] Since Phillips' commitment to Marxism was well known on campus and he would later admit membership in the Communist party, this letter could be regarded as both a protective measure and as an index of his beliefs about the nature of his involvement.

Ralph Gundlach (Psychology) expressed his hopes for support from his professional colleagues. As president of the Western Psychological Association, he told colleagues in the Society for the Psychological Study of Social Issues (SPSSI) of his concerns, and revealed what he considered to be the divisive tactics of the administration: "The university has virtually forbidden faculty members or groups to make any statements criticizing the methods, or pointing out the objectives of the committee; and the faculty has been fairly well paralized [sic]. Now school is out and everyone runs to the four winds. . . ." Gundlach predicted that the administration would feel compelled to protect its legislative appropriation by dismissing some faculty, despite an adverse reaction from the AAUP.[35]

Gundlach also attempted to initiate unified action on the part of the subpoenaed faculty members, but rejected the notion of some of them that they should refuse the subpoenas. In a letter to his lawyer and some of his colleagues, he suggested that a battery of prestigious attorneys protest the actions of the Canwell Committee. Referring to the impotence and disintegration of faculty support which the tactics of both the administration and Canwell had perpetrated, Gundlach lamented the fact that "personal safety" seemed the uppermost consideration in everyone's minds, even among subpoenaed faculty. Some, he said, will be fired "to the great relief of those challenged but missed; but who can then thankfully fight a losing battle for those discharged. And those remaining, thinking that this skirmish is the whole war, ended with this blast; not aware that they are the next targets." After all, Gundlach added, the Canwell Committee needed a few live victims to justify its demands for more money to continue operations in 1949.[36]

These attempts at unity went awry. On June 30, nine of the subpoenaed persons announced that they would not respond to their subpoenas because of the "unconstitutional and basically un-American" character of the Canwell Committee. Among these nine were Professors Phillips, Butterworth, and Gundlach. Reaction to the move was immediate and adverse. Seattle papers termed the action "defiance," and University of Washington Regent Dave Beck stated that these faculty should "stand up and be counted. . . . I have no time for any group attempting to hide behind technicalities and injunctions in order to protect themselves from an open opportunity to study their conduct. . . . Those professors should come out on the public rostrum and denounce Communism and put themselves 100 percent against Russia and the ideologies she stands for."[37]

Ralph Gundlach was the first to reverse his stand, deciding that he could "contribute more to the maintenance of our centers of education and culture" by joining his colleagues in appearing. To a still-defiant colleague, Herbert Phillips, who was teaching at Columbia University's summer session, Gundlach described the effects of the action on the campus. Other faculty, he said, looked upon it as an admission of guilt, a flaunting of the university, bravado, or animosity. Though Gundlach had not wanted to go along with the action, he said he had been talked into it, unaware that the other subpoenaed faculty had not been consulted. Now he felt ostracized: "My own position I found untenable. Whatever support and good will I might have from my department, university, college, and through them, profession, appeared to vanish." Gundlach stated that his intention was to keep beliefs and associations out of the picture, and to keep his testimony before the committee confined to criminal matters.[38]

Organized public sentiment against the proceedings of the Canwell Committee was sparse. Most vocal were the Students for Wallace, the Washington Young Progressives, and Local 401 of the AFT. A "nonpolitical, nonpartisan" group of about one hundred citizens calling itself the Washington Committee for Academic Freedom was formed "to take counter-action against the Canwell Committee." A coalition of teachers, professors, members of the ACLU, and unaligned citizens, the WCAF attracted some of the most prominent liberals of Washington State. The executive board included Stimson Bullitt, an ADA member from an established Seattle family, Seattle attorney Kenneth MacDonald, and Max Savelle (History). Its founder and chairman was Benjamin H. Kizer, Spokane attorney and expert on Asian affairs. Kizer had been honored with a Walker-Ames Lectureship at the university in 1947. The major activity of the WCAF was lobbying the regents, Allen, and the legislature.[39]

Given the chance, however, most citizens would probably have agreed with the *Daily* editorial: "We feel that the period has long passed whereby certain faculty members can continue to dabble unhampered in an ideology that has for its ultimate aim the destruction of the American way of life." Citizens had a right to know, the *Daily* asserted, how the university was spending its $29 million appropriation. Given the chance for deeper thought, many might have agreed with the *Longview Daily News*, which urged caution in evaluating the "verbal blasts" which absurdly attacked the university as a "hot bed of Radicalism." The editorial doubted whether the eleven thousand veterans on campus had the time or the inclination to "chase Red banners," and urged that the "crux of the investigation should be whether professors have passed on Red doctrine." A few days later, the Longview paper dared Canwell to set a national precedent by allowing defense witnesses the right to answer charges, and to cross-examination by counsel.[40]

The tide, however, was against such reasonable notions. Canwell had learned well the lessons of Martin Dies and J. Parnell Thomas. On the eve of the hearings he asserted, "We have not prejudged anyone. We will develop the facts as we have found them, based on a four-month investigation in which hundreds of faculty members were interviewed." Those subpoenaed would have the right to the advice of

counsel, but not the right of defense or cross-examination, since this
was merely a fact-finding hearing. "The Communist element has engaged attorneys in the past as a device to use public hearings as a
sounding board for the dissemination of agitational doctrine. They
will not be permitted to get away with any such ruse at the University
hearings. I am serving warning now to any who may be thinking of
trying it. They will be ejected." [41]

The week-long hearings concerning the University of Washington
faculty were stormy. The Field Artillery Armory was picketed by various groups protesting the proceedings; their chants were loud
enough to stop the hearings, and several protesters were arrested by
the State Patrol. The pattern of this second hearing followed that of
the first. Witnesses were called to testify concerning the activities of
the Communist party nationally and locally, and various faculty
members were alleged to be members of the Communist party or
operatives in front groups. A star witness was Dr. J. B. Matthews, a
former Communist party member, who testified about the aim of the
Communist party to undermine education in the United States by
recruiting teachers, especially university professors. Matthews mentioned Albert Einstein and Arthur M. Schlesinger, Jr., as examples of
academics with a wide reputation who were proven "friends" of the
Soviet Union, and whose support was invaluable to the goals of the
Communist party. But most of the testimony concerned the activities
and associations of faculty members in and with organizations such as
the Abraham Lincoln Brigade, the League Against War and Fascism,
the Washington Commonwealth Federation, the Consumer's Union,
and the Harry Bridges' Defense Committee. Local 401 of the AFT
(AFL) was singled out as being the most important of these front
groups, since most of its membership was university faculty. The Seattle Labor School, the Progressive Citizens of America, and the Independent Citizens Committee of the Arts, Sciences and Professions
were also alleged to be Communist-dominated through use of Attorney General Tom Clark's list of subversive organizations. Because
these organizations "followed the Communist line" those who belonged to them were de facto suspect: little attempt was made to
evaluate the motives of individuals who joined them. Subpoenaed
faculty members responded to questions about their political activities
in various ways. Herbert Phillips, who had answered his subpoena
only after suspension from the faculty by Allen (he had been on the
summer faculty at Columbia), refused to answer questions concerning
his political affiliations. Joseph Butterworth and Ralph Gundlach fol-

lowed Phillips' example. Garland Ethel, Harold Eby, Maude Beal, and Angelo Pellegrini (all of English), and Melville Jacobs (Anthropology) admitted past membership in the Communist party but refused to testify about others. Sophus Winther (English) admitted past membership and named colleagues he believed were members of the party. Joseph Cohen (Sociology) denied past or current membership. Surprise witness George Hewitt, a former Communist from New York, had testified that Ralph Gundlach and Melvin Rader were Communists. Rader denied any such affiliation.[42]

The Canwell Committee hearings on the university provoked a good deal of comment in newspapers across the state. The *Seattle Post-Intelligencer*, through reporter Fred Niendorff, provided readers with detailed looks at the background and testimony of the committee's star witnesses. In one case, Niendorff got witness Isabel Costigan (ex-wife of former WCF leader Howard Costigan) to go beyond her testimony to state: "It was the actual work of the University English Department to get young people into the Communist Party."[43]

The *Seattle Times* also provided extensive coverage of the hearings, but its reports included criticisms of the committee proceedings by J. B. Harrison of the English Department and Arthur Smullyan of Philosophy. *Times* columns followed those articles with a reply by the former head of the university Alumni Association, A. R. Hilen, who pointed to his defense of President Henry Suzzallo against Governor Hartley in 1926 as evidence of his commitment to academic freedom. Hilen stated that if a professor were under attack because of membership in the Socialist party, he could be defended because that was "a truly American Party, led by a great and patriotic American citizen, Norman Thomas." But the Communist party, a foreign party and agent of a foreign conspiracy, "is today the greatest menace to free people throughout the world. Membership in it, when thousands of American boys are daily risking their lives by flying food into Berlin, to maintain American honor by keeping faith with a defeated foe, is akin to treason. There is no such thing as academic freedom to commit treason."[44]

Following the conclusion of the hearings, President Allen issued a statement in which he pointed out that most of the professors implicated in Communist party or front group activities were tenured faculty, and therefore would be given "full opportunity to be heard by a committee of their colleagues under the provisions of the Administrative Code of the University. Because of the seriousness of the charges growing out of this investigation, it is especially important that the University observe to the letter the due processes that are precious not only to our academic traditions, but, more importantly, to our American way of life." [45]

Within a week after the conclusion of the Canwell hearings, Allen wrote to the regents recapitulating the performance of the sub-poenaed faculty, and outlining the administration's projected course of action. A brief, in preparation by university counsel, would be passed on to the special Faculty Senate committee set up to advise the president. If this committee found charges against any faculty warranted, the cases would be referred to the Senate Committee on Tenure and Academic Freedom. Allen then indicated that counsel was giving first priority to the records of the three faculty who had refused to tell the committee about their activities: Professors Gundlach, Phillips, and Butterworth. In the second group of faculty, those who admitted past membership but refused to implicate others, Allen emphasized the cases of Professors Eby, Ethel, Jacobs, and Beal, though he did not think their positions at the university would be jeopardized. In setting out the cases as he did, Allen seems to have been subtly preparing the regents for the acceptance of his own position, which had the merits of following the general guidelines of due process, yet left the door open for the judicious elimination of true subversives, which he termed a "healthy outcome" of the proceedings ahead. [46]

Allen's summary to the regents is interesting also because of the faculty he chose *not* to mention. Rader and Cohen had been named by various Canwell witnesses as being Communists; though they denied it, they were still under suspicion. Pellegrini, like Beal, had been a member of the party for a year (1936). Sophus Winther, who admitted being a member of the party for about a year, had cooperated with Canwell to the extent that he named others on the faculty as former associates in the party, including Cohen, Jacobs, Ethel, Beal, Pellegrini, and Butterworth. Perhaps at this stage of the investigation, Allen preferred to err on the side of caution. But why then did he name Beal? He later admitted that he did not know her. [47]

As the momentum shifted from Canwell to Allen, the president enlisted the aid of the special committee appointed by the Faculty Senate to ascertain whether charges should be brought against any of the faculty members implicated in the Canwell hearings. Shortly after this committee was authorized to assist the president and the faculty, its chairman, Charles E. Martin, had written Allen of the need to take action based on "educational and academic reasons," and to avoid the implication that Canwell was forcing the university to take action.

Martin pointed out the differences between "hardened Communists" who still clung to the party after 1945, and those who had joined it in the thirties and dropped out after 1939. No "right thinking person," he felt, could defend the deplorable tactics of Russia in Czechoslovakia, Berlin, and Yugoslavia. It was surely not a good example for students to have Communists teaching, since they were no respecters of civil rights and the Constitution. Party members should either disavow allegiance to the party or get off the faculty. While Martin realized that many faculty and the AAUP upheld the rights of faculty to be members of the Communist party, he felt the faculty, president, and board should investigate the matter further.[48]

The task facing the Martin Committee was two-fold: interpreting the Tenure Code and justifying its own function in light of its mandate from the senate. The tenure provisions of the code, which had been adopted in May of 1947 and as yet were untried, listed as grounds for dismissal incompetency, neglect of duty, physical or moral incapacity, dishonesty or immorality, and conviction of a felony involving moral turpitude. The evidence, as prepared by Allen and counsel for the administration, was based on their assessment of the character of the Communist party, a foreign party acting within the United States as an agent of a foreign power; membership of certain faculty in "front" groups; and Allen's assertions that in private conferences in June some of the men had lied to him about their activities. Those under consideration had all appeared before the Canwell Committee, and some had refused to cooperate. Did the evidence meet the prescribed reasons for dismissal? In answering this question, two Law School members of the committee, Dean Judson Faulkner and Alfred Harsch, pointed up the legal ramifications of the situation: the legality of the CPUSA, the implications of the 1947 loyalty oath which all faculty had been required to sign, the Truman loyalty program, the position of the AAUP. Bryan McMinn (Mechanical Engineering) was concerned less with legality than the basic moral principles involved in the activities of the faculty in question. H. K. Benson, who had spoken out against the tactics of the Canwell Committee, was at the same time solicitous of the loyalty and security issues involved.[49]

The issue of whether the special committee was acting within its mandate "to assist the president and the faculty" was raised by Thomas Thompson (Oceanography) and Donald Cornu (English). Thompson was eventually convinced by Martin and the others that the faculty members in question deserved a fuller hearing, and that it was the duty of the committee to insure due process by considering the evidence. Cornu, who was also a lawyer, argued that the committee's proper role was the defense of the faculty, not their prosecution. Cornu remained unconvinced by the majority position. By mid-September, the committee's deliberations had produced recommendations to Allen warranting the preparation and filing of charges against Butterworth, Phillips, Gundlach, Eby, Ethel, and Jacobs. However, the recommendations were not unanimous concerning the basis for the charges. Two members held that membership in the Communist party was grounds for dismissal, two felt there was lack of honesty with the president, and two felt that there was sufficient doubt about the activities of the six to require investigation by the Committee on Tenure and Academic Freedom. Though the committee considered charges against Beal, Pellegrini, Rader, and Cohen, no further action was advised.[50]

The deliberations of the Martin Committee suggest the depth of doubts aroused among University of Washington faculty by the Canwell investigation. As Martin wrote to Benson, "The fact is that the Canwell Committee proved the existence of conditions here which we hoped they would not be able to prove. Having to deal with this situation, or to put it as Dean Guthrie described it, something washed up on our beach, we have had to proceed in the best manner possible."[51]

But the actions of the Martin Committee should also be considered against the background of the summer's world events. Beginning with the Berlin Airlift in June, the nation entered upon a war scare which lasted until the following May. The Alger Hiss case, which broke in August of 1948, would preoccupy intellectuals for years to come. The ongoing presidential campaigns featured Republican red-baiting of both Henry Wallace's Progressive party and of the Truman administration. In counterattack, Truman's Justice Department indicted Communist party leaders for violations of the Smith Act. Implications of domestic subversion were coupled with the deteriorating situation in China and in Europe.

Despite Cornu's objections, the Martin Committee felt that if it did not act, the accused faculty would be thrown to the wolves by the regents. Indeed, the committee did prevent further university action against Beal, Pellegrini, Cohen, and Rader. It also assured the other six the right to counsel and defense witnesses at hearings in a less charged atmosphere, where they and the university might be cleared of long-standing suspicion. Allen's consultations with the Martin Committee also met the AAUP's standards for protection of academic freedom, and assured most faculty that the president was acting judiciously. When Allen was attacked in the *New Republic* for watching "in silence as his faculty members have been smeared and shamed," William S. Hopkins (Economics), UWAAUP chapter president, defended Allen.[52]

As soon as Allen received the Martin Committee's recommendations that charges be filed with the Tenure Committee against six of the faculty, he informed the regents and assured them of speedy due process. The president received permission to hire two attorneys to prepare the university's briefs. His choices were A. R. Hilen and Tracy Griffin, both University of Washington Law School alumni. The regents also issued a press release in which they expressed gratitude to the legislative committee for "securing essential facts that have long been alleged but have never before been available from a responsible source," and promised that charges would be filed against some of the faculty members involved in the Canwell investigation.[53]

As Cornu pointed out, and as the August regents' meeting made clear, the events of the summer had moved Allen from a mediating role to that of an advocate of the position that some of the faculty would have to go. The resistance of the accused faculty to his efforts to counsel them in June, and then the defiance of the Canwell Committee by Phillips, Gundlach, and Butterworth, led Allen to conclude that they were unfit to be members of the faculty. Given the adamancy of the state press, public opinion, and some of the regents, Allen set about laying the groundwork for a rationale that would save those faculty whom he felt had acted honorably. As he became aware of the precedent-setting nature of the unfolding events, he moved to put his position squarely before those who would eventually judge his conduct of the cases: the AAUP and his fellow academic administrators.

In July, Allen went East, where he visited Dwight Eisenhower at Columbia, and the general secretary of the AAUP, Ralph Himstead. Since Allen was a member of the Hoover Commission studying national security organizations and a member of the Armed Forces Medical Advisory Committee, his visit with the new president of Columbia was designed to elicit his advice on a number of topics. Allen later wrote him to extend a formal invitation to be the main speaker at the 1949 commencement. Continuing what was evidently a prior topic, Allen declared concerning the Canwell hearings, "I am still of the mind that, conducted as they are in an atmosphere of some dignity and consideration of individual rights, it is going to be extremely healthy for the University and the State as well as for the individuals concerned." Allen's point was that civil and academic rights were often confused, and he expressed the hope that through events at the University of Washington "we can sharpen the edge of thinking among our fine liberal-minded friends." He advised Eisenhower to talk with Ralph Himstead, "a straight thinker . . . who does not believe in falsifying political affiliations by lying and subterfuge. He knows that the final arbiter of the destiny of education generally is the American people."[54]

Allen wrote in a similar vein to other influential university administrators who, like Eisenhower, were meeting pressure from the public about Communist professors, urging them to read between the lines of the AAUP's report of Committee A to find the reasonableness of the association's position. Himstead's cooperation was evident in his actions; Allen noted that he had refused to send observers to the University of Washington campus as the local chapter had requested. "He advised our chapter in no uncertain language that each accused person should be advised to take the stand and tell the truth." The AAUP was interested in protecting principles, not individuals; the local group, he went on, presented a problem because they seemed bent on protecting only individuals and did not abide by the principles of "fair and honest communication between employees and administration."[55]

He used a variation of this argument in his defense against potential critics. When an old Chicago colleague, who had helped Allen to his present eminence, wrote to Allen that he was sure the president would not "buckle down to this temporary hysteria in your state," Allen replied that the Canwell Committee had a reputation for being fairer than most of those about the country, and that he was convinced that it could be useful. Its investigations might help resolve

> difficulties which the University has experienced over a long period of years in its relationships with the Legislature due to unconfirmed allegations of communistic and atheistic teachings on the campus. . . . Perhaps partly due to the efforts of the University, no members of the faculty who are not members or past members of the Communist Party have been publicly embarrassed by the proceedings other than the embarrassment that attaches to the University itself in the circumstances. In other words, men who are not, in this instance, being branded Communist.[56]

Allen also pointed out that despite his efforts to help them, only two of these faculty were completely frank with him, and that most tried to defy and discredit the committee. In giving his side of the picture, Allen failed to mention that at least two faculty members, Rader and Cohen, who had not been and never were Communists, were at that moment engaged in the agonizing process of clearing their names, and that at least a dozen more had been smeared because of their participation in organizations called "fronts." Such rationalizations clearly pointed up Allen's solution to the dilemma of Communist professors.

Early in October, President Allen publicized his position on the issues raised by critics of the administration's course of action in "Communism and Education, An Open Letter to Friends of the University of Washington." To those who called for the immediate dismissal of all past and present members of the Communist party, Allen asserted the right of the university "to its own opinion of the validity of those facts and of whatever actions are called for by reason of those facts." The Canwell Committee was merely a fact-finding agency of the state, with no power to dismiss university personnel. No action would be taken by the university "except through the procedures laid down in existing University regulations."[57]

The bulk of Allen's remarks, however, was directed to the left. The Canwell Committee was not a "witch hunt" since there was no attempt "to smear liberals with a red brush." To those who thought the university should have conducted the inquiry, Allen emphasized that "definitive finding of facts on this subject by the University itself is impossible," but once the facts were uncovered, the university was required to act to consider their validity. Allen termed "patently ridiculous" the charge that there was some mysterious collusion between himself and the board with the Canwell Committee. There had been no prejudgment of the issues, the president was not the "prisoner" of any "understanding" between Canwell and the board; there was merely a recognition of the legitimacy of the committee's investigation. "Academic freedom has not been abridged," he wrote; the issue was not whether citizens have the right to be members of the Communist party, but whether the exercise of that right alters the faculty member's qualifications as a teacher. "For example, are the competency, honesty and attention to duty stipulated in the Administrative Code compatible with the secrecy of the Party's methods and objectives, with the refusal of the Communists to hold their party membership openly, and with commitment to dogmas that are held to be superior to scientific examination?" Allen warned that though there were no obvious answers to the questions, it was incumbent on the university to find some that were "wise and satisfactory . . . lest its functions of setting the qualifications of its faculty be taken over by some other agency to the serious and lasting curtailment of academic freedom."[58]

The "Open Letter" concluded with Allen's thoughts on "Communism and Education," in which he cautioned readers of the danger of "subversion by ideas that are hidden and falsely painted in colors not their own." Academic freedom's maintenance depended not only on lack of institutional restraints placed upon the individual teacher, but also on "an absence of restraints placed upon him by his political affiliations, by dogmas that may stand in the way of a free search for truth, or by rigid adherence to a 'party line' that sacrifices dignity, honor and integrity to the accomplishment of political ends. . . . Men must be free, of course, but they must also be free, and willing, to stand up and profess what they believe so that all may hear."[59]

Allen reiterated his beliefs about academic freedom to anyone who would listen. As the academic year opened, he addressed students at a university convocation; while in the East he lunched with Henry Luce of *Time* and *Life* magazines, an important figure in the China lobby. Allen later wrote Luce of his conviction that the "publishers of this country are the greatest potential force for adult educational programs that exists. Naturally, I am most pleased that the policy of your publications is so strongly and wisely oriented toward public education." On this trip East, Allen also consulted with Whittaker Chambers, then famous for his testimony against Alger Hiss, and secured his consent to testify for the administration at the upcoming tenure hearings.[60]

The president continued his efforts to have Eisenhower speak at the university's commencement in 1949. After Eisenhower tentatively turned him down, Allen held out the prospect of an honorary degree, which if conferred would have been only the second in University of Washington history, the first having been given Marshall Foch in 1919. Since Columbia and its president were under attack by the Hearst newspapers at the time for harboring Communists, Allen continued to advise Eisenhower of the course of events at the University of Washington: "We are at some pains that the issue of the Communist in education is met squarely and the record of the hearings I think will be of some value when the history of these times is finally written."[61]

III

Hearings before the Faculty Committee

on Tenure and Academic Freedom

This faculty Committee is not a prosecuting agency; it is not a defense agency; it is not charged with a missionary duty for the cause of academic freedom; it is a trial committee and nothing more. Its functions are limited to hearing evidence in the cases filed with it, and, at the conclusion thereof, to the making of findings of fact and recommendations to the President of the University.

    —Introductory statement to the Report of the Faculty Committee on Tenure and Academic Freedom, January 7, 1949

On September 8, 1948, Dean Edward Lauer of the College of Arts and Sciences filed complaints against six tenured faculty members with the University of Washington Faculty Committee on Tenure and Academic Freedom. Charged with membership in the Communist party were: Joseph Butterworth, teaching associate in the English Department since 1929; Ralph Gundlach, member of the faculty since 1927 and associate professor of Psychology since 1937; and Herbert J. Phillips, faculty member since 1920 and assistant professor of Philosophy since 1934. From that charge flowed the other five alleged violations of the Faculty Code: neglect of duty, for failing to inform President Raymond Allen of said membership after his request to do so at the May, 1948, faculty meeting; dishonesty, for failure to tell the president of said membership when asked during individual conferences with Allen; dishonesty and incompetence consequent of following the Communist party line; neglect of duty due to time spent in political activities; and dishonesty and immorality arising from failure to cooperate with the Canwell Committee. The remaining three against whom charges were brought were also long-time faculty members. Harold Eby had been a member of the faculty since 1927 and a full professor of English since 1947. Garland O. Ethel had been an instructor in the English Department from 1927 until he was promoted to assistant professor in 1947. Melville Jacobs had joined the faculty in 1927; he was promoted to associate professor of Anthropology in 1945. These three were not charged with current party membership, but their past membership made them liable to the other five charges, stated Lauer. As their immediate superior, Lauer's preferment of the charges was *pro forma*, the complaints themselves having been formulated by Allen and counsel for the university.[1]

In compliance with the Faculty Code, the Senate Committee on Committees set about appointing the eleven faculty members of the Committee on Tenure and Academic Freedom who would hear the charges. The chairman of this standing committee had been Sophus Winther, who was slated to be a witness. He was replaced by J. Gordon Gose, professor of Law at the university since 1946. J. B. Harrison of English, who had often protested against the Canwell Committee, resigned due to the code stipulation that members of departments could not hear complaints against colleagues. Besides Gose, the committee finally consisted of Merritt Benson, professor of Journalism since 1933 and assistant director of the School of Journalism; H. B. Densmore, chairman of the Classics Department and professor since 1907; Melville Hatch, professor of Zoology and Entymology since 1927; Rex Robinson, professor of Chemistry since 1929; Jennie Rowntree, director of the School of Home Economics and professor since 1925; J. Richard Huber, chairman of the Economics Department and member of the faculty since 1939; John Sholley, professor of Law since 1932; Curtis Williams of Education, professor since 1920; George Goodspeed, chairman of the Geology Department, on the faculty since 1919; and Thomas G. Thompson, professor of Chemistry and director of the Oceanography Laboratory, a university faculty member since 1919. Thompson had also served on the Martin Committee, which had advised Allen to press the charges.[2]

At one of its first meetings, the Committee on Tenure decided that the hearings would be closed, and that witnesses would not be sworn. Though these regulations were in accord with the committee's view that the proceedings were a hearing and not a public trial, the decision for closure provoked Professor Phillips to ask the King County Superior Court to enjoin the committee to open the hearings. When the court decided that the committee had power to set rules for the hearing and turned aside Phillips' complaint, some students expressed fear that this was part of the administration's plan to deprive the accused faculty of their academic freedom. A graduate student in English contrasted the atmosphere of fear and restraint on campus with the vital spirit before the war when Laski appeared, and charged that the faculty was afraid to speak up. William S. Hopkins, head of the local AAUP chapter, however, expressed confidence in the Tenure Committee's rules. Throughout the hearings, students petitioned to try to curb the tenure proceedings.[3]

When the hearings began on October 27, Professors Butterworth and Phillips stipulated that they were current members of the Communist party. Their attorney, John Caughlan, stated his concern that the charges were not precise enough, that "wrongful conduct" was a vague term which did not allow the respondents to know what they were being charged with. The hearings could be shortened, he said, if the actions of his clients, not their beliefs, were the subject of testimony. Also, he noted it would be easier to prepare a defense if he knew who was going to testify against his clients. Ethel's attorney, Benjamin Asia, protested the blanket nature of the charges and asked for a pre-trial conference to make the delineation more specific; was his client to be charged with responsibility for all that the Communist party did while he was a member? Gundlach's attorney, Clifford O'Brien, reasserted the motion to dismiss the charges against his client, which he had filed with Gose on September 27. Because Gundlach had never been a member of the Communist party, the charges were not germane to him, he asserted.[4]

Counsel for the administration, A. R. Hilen, announced that all charges against Professors Phillips and Butterworth would be dropped except that of Communist party membership, to make the issue before the committee definitive. He also stated that there was to be no examination of students to see if courses were taught in a biased manner, because such testimony could be easily balanced by other students who detected no bias. "So we make the direct issue that he becomes incompetent by the very fact of remaining a member of the Communist Party and participating in its activities for any length or period of time."[5]

In order to establish the nature of the Communist party, the administration brought in four former members of the Communist party. Joseph Kornfeder, who had also testified before the Canwell Committee, described his activities with the party in New York from 1919 until he left it in 1934, and stated that the aim of the Communist party was, and had always been, the violent overthrow of the U.S. government. As an "expert" on Communist Front groups, he affirmed the subversive nature of various organizations in which the respondents had been active: the Citizens Committee for Harry Bridges, the Consumers Union, Seattle Labor School, the Teachers Union, and American Youth for Democracy. When Kornfeder was questioned by several members of the committee who were themselves active in the Consumers Union, he said only that any organization concerned about the rights of the "public" against business was Communist because the Communists hate capitalism.[6]

Benjamin Gitlow, who had been active in the New York Communist party from 1919 until 1936, testified that the CPUSA still advocated the overthrow of the government and that Moscow still controlled it. But the administration's attempts to get other "star" witnesses who could bring the committee up to date on recent party activities failed. Both Louis Budenz and Whittaker Chambers begged off at the last moment, and the committee had to content itself with local witnesses.[7]

Professor Sophus Winther of the English Department repeated the testimony he had given during the second Canwell hearing concerning his one-year stay in the Communist party (1935–36). Winther's testimony implicated several of his colleagues who were also respondents, but otherwise did not do a great deal to help the administration's case. Under cross-examination by Caughlan, Winther admitted that he was the author of the article in *Harpers* magazine entitled "A Professor Quits the Communist Party." In the article he described how he was drawn to the party: the Depression, the university pay cuts, the lack of support by the president when professors were attacked in the newspapers, his fear of Fascism's assault on intellectual liberties, and his belief that the Communist party offered an alternative, a closeness with the workers. The article also described his rather easy exit from the party when he decided it was all talk and no action. Winther admitted that his article was rather loosely based on reality, but though an exaggeration, it portrayed his disgust with the party. He testified that he never felt obliged to support the Communist party line, or inhibited from expressing his own opinions. In answer to Caughlan's question about whether Communist party membership interfered with his university duties, he responded:

> I think professors are often interfered with in their time—sometimes by committee meetings and sometimes by golf, and I do not know whether this is proper, but the worst time I ever spent in this University was from March 27 of this year to the end of summer school. I came back with a book two-thirds done, and I did not write one word from March 27 until the summer session was over. My classes were interfered with; my home was continually called up; I had investigators standing at my door. . . . I was driven to a state of nervous insecurity by the Canwell Committee. . . .

Administration counsel hastily dismissed him from further testimony.[8]

The administration's final witness was Howard Smith, a minor Communist party figure in Seattle from 1941 to 1946. His testimony had been taken at both Canwell hearings and served to point out the important positions held with the party by Phillips and Butterworth, but otherwise it was considered ineffective by both the committee chairman and administration counsel.

On November 17, Attorney Caughlan objected to the nature of the hearing thus far. In the name of all six respondents, he reiterated their belief that the Communist party was not on trial, and should not be the focus of the hearing. However, in rebuttal to the administration's picture of the party, Clayton van Lydegraf, secretary of the Washington State Communist party was called by Caughlan. He testified that the CPUSA had withdrawn from the Comintern in 1941 or 1942, and since then had not received communications or directives of any kind from the Soviet government. He stated that the Communist party advocated evolution of capitalism to socialism by constitutional means, not violence. Though there were no restrictions on teachers per se, it was understood that once a question had been decided by the national convention, party members would support the position taken by the CPUSA. Members could not favor the Marshall Plan as it was currently conceived, for example, and expect to remain in the party.[9]

The remaining rebuttal was given by Paul M. Sweezy and Edward W. Strong. Sweezy, who had taught economics at Harvard, considered himself a socialist and had never been a party member. On the basis of his studies, Sweezy emphasized the evolutionary nature of Marxism-Leninism; though belief in revolution was central, its nature was capitalization on existing circumstances rather than instigation. When revolution happened, the Communist party would be ready to use it. Strong, a member of the University of California Philosophy Department, also testified as an academic expert who had never been a member of the Communist party. Strong testified that Communists believed a majority, not a minority, was to seize power—the majority would be workers, and the revolution would be nonviolent.[10]

So ended the testimony on the nature of the Communist party. Though over one-third of the total testimony concerned this question, it makes for very unsatisfying reading even today. As Attorney Caughlan pointed out, the Communist party as portrayed by the administration's witnesses differed considerably from that witnessed to by the defense. Thus the task Caughlan set for himself was to prove Butterworth and Phillips objective, fair, and competent in fulfilling their duties as University of Washington professors.[11]

To do that, Caughlan brought in five students who testified that Phillips was a dynamic teacher careful to reveal his biases toward theories that favored the working class, specifically Marxism. Six of Phillips' university colleagues, four from Philosophy and two from English, all agreed that he was an avowed Marxist and that his membership in the party came as no surprise. Support for his objectivity was derived from their testimony that he was sympathetic to the philosophy of A. N. Whitehead, to the validity of religious experience, and to belief in the existence of God. The strongest affidavit came from Phillips' department chairman, Everett Nelson, who said he was not only aware of Phillips' Marxism, but considered it desirable to have a Marxist in the department. Like his chairman before him, Nelson had not made Phillips' political activities a matter of concern since he did his job well, and was considered one of the department's best teachers.[12]

When Phillips took the stand in his own behalf, he revealed that he had come from a Populist family background, and that when he joined the Philosophy Department in 1920, he already had socialist leanings. He became a member of the Communist party during the Depression because he believed that a capitalist society must eventually become socialist, and that the Communist party was the most effective means to that end. His membership in the party did not mean that he believed in the violent overthrow of the government, nor had he been pressured to adopt the Soviet way of thinking. In response to President Allen's question, "You have never felt any restraint on yourself as a teacher and a scholar?" Phillips said, "Not relatively. Every person feels restraint in their conduct . . . the Communist Party is [not] peculiar in that way. . . . People don't go in there unless they have a general view. . . ." The philosopher maintained his independence of thought throughout the cross-examination, though he admitted it was difficult to convince others of his integrity when his ideas about politics happened to coincide with the "so-called Party line."[13]

Joseph Butterworth testified that he had been a specialist in Old and Middle English language at the university since 1929. His decision to join the party in 1935 was founded on his belief that the party was the most organized vehicle for opposition to Fascism, which was on the rise in Europe and in the United States at the time. Like Phillips he had never felt Communist party membership was a damper on his intellectual freedom, though he had followed the main line of its thinking. He also espoused the peaceful substitution of communism for capitalism, and denied any connection between the CPUSA and other Communist parties of the world, except philosophical, due to differing circumstances in each nation. Five graduate students from the English Department testified to his competence as a teacher, and denied any attempts to indoctrinate through his work in the English language.[14]

At the close of the hearings, when the Committee on Tenure came to evaluate the administration's position and the charge against Butterworth and Phillips, eight of the eleven committee members decided that Communist party membership, alone, was insufficient grounds for dismissal. Examination of the Tenure Code led the committee to conclude that the Removal for Cause section was definitive, as the respondents had argued, and not illustrative, as the administration contended. In other words, membership in the Communist party was not listed as a cause for dismissal in the code.[15]

In making Communist party membership the only charge against Butterworth and Phillips, the administration had hoped for a clearcut decision from the committee. Professors Densmore, Gose, Hatch, Rowntree and Thompson attempted to respond to that hope; despite their conclusion that the tenure of the two should not be disturbed, they made a list of seven adverse findings about the nature of the party and recommended that "some competent authority, whether it be the faculty as a whole, the President, the Regents, or the legislature," put the question to rest by making exclusion of Communists part of the code. They did not, however, suggest that dismissal be retroactive, nor did they charge that Butterworth and Phillips subscribed to all the pernicious aspects of Communist party membership they listed. They also expressly stated their dissent from the position of the AAUP which protected party members.[16]

Committee members Benson and Goodspeed disagreed with the majority's strict construction of the code, and recommended the dismissal of Butterworth and Phillips:

> It is our opinion that active present membership in the Communist Party, U.S.A., is an overt act of such reckless, uncritical, and intemperate partisanship as to be inimical to, and incompatible with, the highest traditions of academic freedom and scholarship, and that such active present membership should be declared sufficient grounds for dismissal of any faculty member so committed.

Professor Williams joined this recommendation for dismissal, but on different grounds. As a member of the College of Education, he considered institutions of public education instruments of the will of the people. He wrote, "I have no doubt that it is the expectation of the parents of students at the University of Washington that their children shall not be instructed by members of the Communist Party, U.S.A."[17]

Only three members of the committee, Robinson, Sholley, and Huber, were unequivocal in upholding the tenure of Butterworth and Phillips. In their view, the code did not address the question of faculty membership in the Communist party. Therefore, the tenure of Butterworth and Phillips was inviolable on those grounds. They criticized the majority's general findings about the party as irrelevant to the matter of tenure. Nor did this group approve of the suggestion that the Tenure Code be amended to forbid future faculty membership in the party. The dissenting three wrote, "With that implied recommendation we do not concur, and furthermore, we do not conceive it to be the function of the committee to make recommendations as to legislative policy."[18]

When Allen submitted the committee's finding to the regents, he reminded them of a fact unknown to the committee during their deliberation: "The Board of Regents never at any time specifically approved or ordered into effect the existing provisions of the Administrative Code." Though Allen had approved the code with the consent of the regents, the board "clearly retains within its power the right to determine the conditions of employment of the faculty and staff generally." Based on this interpretation, Allen recommended to the regents that they hold with the minority of the committee for the dismissal of Butterworth and Phillips because their membership in the Communist party, kept secret until the proceedings, rendered them unfit for faculty membership.[19]

The president applauded the seven-point finding of fact, the committee's severe indictment of the nature and characteristics of the CPUSA as the first of its kind rendered by a faculty body, and proof that a majority of the committee (eight of eleven) would support the regents' exclusion of Communists from the faculty. Allen discounted the claim of Robinson, Sholley, and Huber that findings of fact about the party were not germane to the decision: "It seems to me that theirs is an unrealistic point of view. If a policy cannot be determined from these cases, the University is powerless to act. This of course is not the case. The Regents have full power to settle the issue."[20]

Allen further bolstered his case for the dismissal of Butterworth and Phillips by taking issue with the majority definition of incompetency. Eight members of the committee construed incompetency to mean unfitness in a faculty member's field of scholarship and teaching. Allen defined it in broader terms as "any action, condition, or attitude which interferes with the proper and adequate performance of his duties." In other words, a teacher could not be a sincere Communist and at the same time a "sincere seeker after truth, which is the first obligation and duty of the teacher." Faculty members, he went on, have a "higher duty" than ordinary men to pursue truth objectively; and infidelity to that concept, implied by membership in the party, rendered Butterworth and Phillips "incompetent, intellectually dishonest, and derelict in their duty to find and teach the truth."[21]

Perhaps in an attempt to square his recommendations with the position of the AAUP, Allen assailed the secrecy of membership in the Communist party. Though such political activity was not illegal, Allen construed his inaugural address and his speeches to the Faculty Senate as constituting university proscription of party membership. By keeping their activities secret, Butterworth and Phillips acknowledged the serious nature of their activities, violated their duty to protect the integrity of the university, and through their disingenuousness proved themselves unfit for the academic profession. Despite testimony which showed no consistent university policy on faculty membership in the party, and despite the fact that a majority of the committee could find no evidence of such policy, Allen insisted there was, and urged the regents to accept his view.[22]

In thus recommending dismissal of avowed Communists Butterworth and Phillips on two grounds, Communist party membership and its secret nature, Allen implicitly posed the dilemma of a person who denied membership yet engaged in "activities sanctioned by the party." Such were the issues in the Ralph Gundlach case. Since Gundlach had refused to answer the questions of the Canwell Committee as to his political affiliation, the administration's efforts to prove that he was a member of the Communist party were more elaborate. Four former members of the Communist party testified that since he was involved in meetings at which they were present, and since he was "accepted" as a Communist, they assumed he was. His active involvement in "front" organizations over a period of years, and the allegation that he had gone along "with every twist and turn of the Communist Party line" were further evidence in the minds of the witnesses.[23]

Questioned by his attorney, Clifford O'Brien, Gundlach told the committee that he had joined the Psychology Department in 1927, had been active in research and writing, and introduced evidence to that effect. His involvement with the Seattle Labor School had come about through his work on the university's Committee on Adult Education. In a statement submitted to the committee, Gundlach charged that the case against him was founded on differences of professional perception between himself and Dean Guthrie, who was also a member of the Psychology Department. This rivalry had kept him at minimum pay for his rank since 1937, despite majority departmental recommendations for raises and promotions. His fundamental position on psychology he stated, had led him to become a psychotechnologist—looking to man's fundamental drives and motives to determine the conditions for complete human development. This had led him to study race relations, propaganda, and labor management, all of which he said he had been advised to abandon in favor of more scholarly subjects. When he became an admirer of Kurt Lewin and joined in founding the Society for the Psychological Study of Social Issues (1936), he claimed to have been derided as a "quack, or nut." But, he said, those activities and involvement with the Consumers Union were a reflection of his "fundamental position in psychology."[24]

Though Gundlach denied to the committee that he had ever been a member of the Communist party, university counsel demonstrated through questioning that the psychologist supported the Washington State Communist party's position on several issues: opposition to the Mundt Bill, prosecution of the leaders of the New York Communist party, advocacy of federal anti-lynch laws, price controls, and fair employment practices laws, and repeal of the Selective Service Act. With Gundlach's permission, members of the committee then asked Ethel, Eby, and Jacobs if they had any knowledge of Gundlach's membership in the Communist party; all said no. Gundlach later withdrew his permission to have Phillips and Butterworth answer that question because he said he realized he was putting them in a position of potential harm to themselves: they could either testify against the administration's case on him, or they could refuse to answer.[25]

The committee next heard testimony from Albert Franzke of the Speech Department on the involvement of Gundlach in the Seattle Labor School. He discussed the genesis of the school as an expression of the need for adult education by union officials. Contributing unions selected a board of directors for the school, among whom were himself, Gundlach, and John L. King of the Grange, currently a regent. Franzke and Gundlach had dropped out in early 1947 when they learned that Communists had become deeply involved in it. Franzke testified that he had never been a member of the Communist party.[26]

In addition to the extensive evidence Gundlach introduced to show his scholarly ability, two former students and three graduate students testified to Gundlach's objectivity as a teacher. A statement to the same effect was signed by forty graduate and senior students. Testimony by three of Gundlach's colleagues in the Psychology Department, including Chairman Roger Loucks, revealed the wide support Gundlach commanded from others in his field. Loucks told the committee that a Psychology Department poll showed Gundlach's political bias in teaching to be about average; he also told of his colleague's weakness as an undergraduate teacher and of his skill with older students. Loucks stated that Gundlach was a truthful man and that he believed his denial of Communist party membership. Department members, however, had decided after the first Canwell hearing in February that Gundlach should not teach the Social Psychology course during spring quarter because of its content. Loucks also introduced letters from about forty psychologists from other institutions who had written in Gundlach's behalf.[27]

Guthrie's testimony against Gundlach revealed that the dean had discussed the probable presence of Communists on the faculty even before the Canwell investigation. The president had assumed that the oath required of faculty members by the 1947 legislature was a guarantee that there were none, but Guthrie told Allen that he believed there were three or four, and that Gundlach was one. Guthrie attributed his suspicion to Gundlach's interest in the Labor School, though he himself had been interested in the school's possibilities for adult education through the University of Washington. Guthrie also testified that he was present at a meeting between Gundlach and Allen on June 2, 1948. The first issue discussed at that meeting pertained to a questionnaire which Gundlach had sent to the Washington press corps, asking them to evaluate the performance of each member of the House of Representatives. The results had been favorable to Hugh DeLacy, and when the poll's findings turned up in a paid newspaper advertisement in 1946, they were attributed to the University of Washington Psychology Department. Guthrie charged that, as a personal friend of DeLacy's, Gundlach had allowed the university's name to appear in a purely political connection, i.e., support for DeLacy's 1946 reelection effort. When in May, 1948, Gundlach attempted to mail a similar questionnaire, Guthrie intercepted it in the university mail room. At the June meeting, Gundlach explained that he needed to validate the results of the earlier questionnaire in order to write a publishable article, and that he had the permission of Loucks to send it. When Allen requested him to withdraw it, Gundlach did.[28]

The second topic discussed at the meeting was Canwell's allegation that Gundlach was a member of the Communist party. When Allen asked him directly about his current or former membership, Guthrie told the committee, Gundlach replied that the Canwell Committee could not prove he was, and he (Gundlach) could not prove that he was not. Though Allen did not pursue the question further, Guthrie said, he did warn Gundlach that the Canwell Committee was empowered by the legislature to ask such questions.[29]

Guthrie further testified to the "forensic" nature of Gundlach's use of two questionnaires. One had to do with prejudice against Jews, the other was slanted toward noncraft unions. Both had provoked reaction in the community, and both had come to the attention of current and former regents. Though Guthrie admitted under cross-examination that all three questionnaires were considered "legitimate" research by many psychologists, and that the poll of Washington correspondents was also legitimate, he objected to them because they were not primarily intended to "establish general knowledge, but specific knowledge relating to a specific political proposition."[30]

In rebuttal to Guthrie's testimony, Gundlach told the committee that the questionnaire on anti-Semitism was one developed by Nevitt Sanford; however, he admitted that he had hurriedly passed it out at the end of a class period without adequate explanation to the class. The questionnaire relating to unions was used at the request of Theodore Newcomb at Columbia, who was studying the attitudes of union members toward their union. Under cross-examination, Gundlach acknowledged that he had favored DeLacy in the 1946 campaign, and realized that the results of his poll might be used by DeLacy's staff, but he denied knowing how they had gotten hold of the results. Later, under questioning by Chairman Gose, he contradicted that statement by admitting that he had given the results to DeLacy's staff.[31]

In response to a question from committee member Hatch, Gundlach denied that he was an "Intellectual Marxist." He also said that he had been equivocal with Allen about Communist party membership because he believed that the attorney general had wrongly attached the "subversive" label to organizations he was involved in, and that the word "communist" was used in an infinite number of ways; "Many words have no denotation at all, but are only tone words . . . in the charges against me, one of the definitions of a Communist is a person who denies he is a Communist." Also, Allen told Gundlach at the June meeting that "anyone who refused to answer directly that question before the Canwell Committee would receive no support from the University." Gundlach saw little point in being clear with Allen, who, he felt, did not understand the subtleties of his argument. President Allen had refused to accept the letter he had brought to the meeting; in it he asserted his anti-authoritarianism and defended his outside activities as an integral part of his work. Allen then corroborated Gundlach's account of the June conference, stating to Chairman Gose that he had not directly asked Gundlach if he was ever a member of the Communist party. When asked what support he would have given Gundlach if he had answered the question directly, Allen replied, "My support would be trying to advise with them to a greater extent than I would if I found they weren't willing to cooperate with me."[32]

Earlier, the president had testified in support of the charge against Eby, Ethel, Jacobs, and Gundlach that they had not communicated with him concerning their Communist party membership as he had directed in his May, 1948, address to the faculty. Allen pointed out that on two occasions prior to the May meeting these faculty members had been warned about the perils they faced. His inaugural address had carried one such caution, and the second was delivered at a December, 1947, faculty meeting. At that time, Allen testified he said that "if there were any Communists, and I was not assuming that there were any on our faculty, but if there were, I thought that they ought to get off the faculty . . . before they were smoked out." At the May, 1948, meeting, Allen stated, his intent was to convey his belief "that no Communist should or could look to the University Administration, the Board of Regents, and I am quite sure I added the faculty in general, to defend a secret activity of an organized character."

When cross-examined by Caughlan, Allen said that meant that if a faculty member would disengage himself from secret political activity, "there was some hope for the University to come to the defense of any person so involved." Allen then admitted his position really had nothing to do with whether a faculty member was a "secret" or open member of the Communist party, but rather it was based on public opinion:

> Well, I think that if the gentlemen who have admitted that they are past or present members of the Communist Party had admitted that, not necessarily when they first came in, but at some time prior to the present period, and had professed or had stated clearly why they were working towards those objectives, and at the same time they were people who were qualified in their respective fields of teaching and scholarship, I think, along with Mr. Conant, who I am glad to associate myself with, and it is an honor, I would defend their profession, because I feel that it was an honest profession. But I hasten to say that I do not think I would have a prayer of a chance of getting away with it in a public institution now. At one time I think that might have been accomplished.

> Q: And you feel therefore . . . that the general good of the institution is best effected by driving from the faculty persons who now acknowledge their membership in the Communist Party. Is that correct?

> A: I would not put it that strong, though it would appear that I did in
> the first faculty meeting. . . . I would phrase it thus, that if a faculty
> committee and the faculty generally, in the traditions of the University,
> felt that it was inimical to the total behavior of the University—a public
> institution—I would be compelled by my personal convictions to agree
> with them.

Caughlan then warned the committee that they were bucking the current of public opinion and "what is wanted by the Administration." Allen interjected with a statement that universities are great "because of disloyalty to Administration opinions." [33]

When Caughlan questioned Allen concerning his views on the 1947 Report of Committee A of the AAUP, which stated that Communists should not be denied faculty positions per se, the president referred to a footnote in the report which, he stated, was "the most important statement in the whole article." Allen's reference is to page 126 of the 1948 *AAUP Bulletin*, which reads: "Here and elsewhere in this report it is assumed that the teacher has not falsified his political affiliation. Lying and subterfuge with reference to political affiliation are in themselves evidence of unfitness for the academic profession." Further, in response to one of Caughlan's questions, Allen agreed that there was nothing in the nature of the teaching profession which would automatically exclude Communist party members, and that an attempt to exclude them would endanger the educational system. [34]

Allen's equivocations about his real position on the question of Communists in faculty positions, as can be seen, continued throughout the hearings. An ambitious man, eager to retain majority confidences, Allen eventually decided that the balance of opinion was running against Communists, as was seen in his decisions on Butterworth and Gundlach. Perhaps none of the defendants in the tenure hearings saw this as clearly as did Gundlach. An incident during the hearings illustrates this point. On November 12, Allen received a letter from A. W. Martin, the chairman of the Zoology Department, who had recently returned from an AAUP Council meeting. Martin told Allen with pride of the university's "increasing stature in the eyes of our colleagues about the country" and of the many queries he had received about the Faculty Senate, the code, and the methods of promotion developed by Guthrie, the dean of faculties. He also told Allen of the "high regard" for Allen held by Ralph Himstead arising from their July conference, which ". . . made a lasting impression upon him. Little as we may like the present circumstances here, it must be granted that in this fairly liberal state we are a school which had in formal operation a most completely defined set of regulations for the safeguard of the faculty. The test of these safeguards under such ideal conditions is hence an object of great interest. . . ." Martin also discussed the thinking of the "average Council Member" concerning the issues at hand: individuals who followed the party line and refused to answer the questions of a duly constituted investigative committee should be discharged; individuals who resigned from the party long ago should not be dismissed, even if they refused to name colleagues. Given "intelligent and courageous decisions" by the Tenure Committee, and a "moderate" course by the board, "the reputation of the University of Washington will emerge unblemished and establish a notable standard for the rest of the country." [35]

Though Martin stressed that his account was only his own estimate of AAUP Council thinking, it did reflect the dissension that must have existed within the association over the 1947 Report of Committee A. Accordingly, Allen had the letter copied for university administrators, the regents, deans, and the lawyers involved in the tenure hearings. Reaction was immediate. Himstead telegraphed his fury to Allen, stressing that the council had no authority over the matter, had made no decisions, and had endorsed Committee A's position. Himstead relayed the same message to the UWAAUP chapter. Allen's action also earned the displeasure of attorney John Caughlan. Allen apologized during the hearings for his "act of poor judgment," but denied that circulation of Martin's letter was an attempt to prejudice the "jury." But, as Gundlach noted in a letter to his wife, "one may think that the reason the President prints and mails this out at this time is to encourage the Senate Committee to fire two or three persons with the understanding that the AAUP will back them up. Instructions, almost." [36]

While Gundlach appreciated the political subtleties and behind-the-scenes maneuvering surrounding the tenure hearings, there seemed to be little he could do to prevent himself from obscuring his own case. In his efforts to show how he had been misunderstood by the administration, he offended the committee. In his attempts to show that Dean of Faculties Guthrie had failed to understand his work, he came across to the committee as an uncooperative, sarcastic, deceptive person. Though witty and brilliant, he had equivocated to the committee about his role in the DeLacy campaign. As his success with graduate students and professional psychologists showed, he could get his points across in a one-on-one situation better than he could in large group situations, such as an undergraduate class or a tenure hearing. His didactical nature often won out over his tactical sense. During the course of the hearing, for instance, he helped to sponsor Dean Hewlett Johnson, "the Red Dean of Canterbury," who appeared in Seattle on a speaking tour. Administration Counsel Tracy Griffin called the incident to the attention of the committee as an example of Gundlach's "non-helpfulness" to the university, and espousal of the party line. Though Attorney Caughlan retorted that Allen had suggested the committee listen to testimony by Johnson while he was in the city, the incident certainly did little to convince the committee that Gundlach was apt to refrain from "embarrassing" the university in the future.[37]

At the close of the hearings, Chairman Gose asked Andrew Hilen, chief administration counsel, if it would be possible for the committee to use the evidence concerning Gundlach to support something other than the Communist party membership charge. Of course, Hilen agreed, saying that the evidence could be used as circumstantial indication of party membership, and that the committee's power as a rule-making body allowed it to apply the testimony to other facets of the code not specifically covered by the original charges. Since Gundlach and his counsel were not present during this exchange, there was no argument recorded, and the majority of the committee eventually adopted the view set forth by Gose: "Evidence tending to show lack of ability to engage in objective scholarship met no issue raised in the original pleadings, but the Committee deems it reasonable to consider the pleadings amended to conform with the proof."[38]

With regard to the charge that Gundlach was a member of the Communist party, committee members Gose, Rowntree, Thompson, and Williams found no evidence to show that he was, and none to show that he was not. Pronouncing themselves unsatisfied with Gundlach's "evasive" and "self-serving" testimony, they concluded that he was surely a "sympathizer" with the party, and that his non-membership could be a consequence of his desire to avoid adverse results connected with membership. Despite their opinion that Gundlach could have adduced more positive proof of his nonmembership in the party, they decided that he could not be dismissed from the faculty as a mere sympathizer. Committee members Hatch, Huber, Robinson, and Sholley concurred, but took sharp issue with the "findings" of their colleagues. Not only did the evidence not show that Gundlach completely supported the Communist line, they wrote, but the inference as to Gundlach's motives in not joining the party was irrelevant and unjustified. Despite the fact that Gundlach said he was not a Communist, Benson and Goodspeed found for dismissal on Charge I. Though they too found the evidence "contradictory and confused," they concluded that since he had never opposed the principles of the Communist party and had been active in front groups,

Gundlach was "a more effective agent for Communism" than Butterworth and Phillips.[39]

On Charge II the committee found unanimously that Gundlach had no affirmative duty to tell President Allen of possible Communist activities following the May, 1948, faculty meeting, since there was no evidence that he desired the assistance of the university in his defense against the Canwell Committee.[40]

Seven committee members found for Gundlach's dismissal on Charge III. The substance of this charge was that he had failed to answer Allen's questions directly concerning Communist party membership. Gose, Rowntree, Thompson, Williams, and Densmore found the incident a "serious and substantial neglect of duty to the university" for two reasons. First, it was typical of Gundlach's history of unsatisfactory relations with the university administration. Testimony by Dean Guthrie and Allen showed improper use of his position with the university in the DeLacy campaign. Second, this incident gave weight to the committee's perception of Gundlach as being more concerned about his own position than considerate of the university, an impression confirmed by his lack of frankness with the committee. These five placed Gundlach in the "crypto-Communist" category enunciated by the AAUP: those who used "covert, deceitful methods." Benson and Goodspeed concurred with this finding and went further to say that the evidence presented by Gundlach to show productivity in psychology raised some doubt about his "ability to perform objective scholarly work." [41]

The dissenting four—Hatch, Huber, Robinson, and Sholley—pointed out that Allen had not insisted upon an unequivocal answer from Gundlach, and certainly did not warn him that his answer would be grounds for dismissal. Likewise, they stated, Gundlach probably realized he was antagonizing Allen, but had not understood he was jeopardizing his tenure; had he been cautioned of the possibilities involved, he might have been more cooperative. These members also placed the conference with Allen in the context of Gundlach's relations with the administration, but in a different manner than the majority. Giving him the benefit of emotional response, they reasoned that he was seeing the conference as just one more indication of "persecution" by the administration, and thus reacted less than rationally. Gundlach's elaborate presentation of evidence concerning his use of the questionnaires could be seen as his capitalizing on a chance to explain his research in a more favorable light than had the administration. Though granting that his testimony left much to be desired, it could not be used to add weight to the conference with

Allen. These members expressed puzzlement that Gundlach should be charged with "crypto-Communism" since his "sympathy with the underdog" was sanctioned by the AAUP, and was forthright and undisguised.[42]

The fourth allegation against Gundlach was that as a member of the Communist party he had followed instructions from Moscow, which prevented his exercise of honesty and academic freedom in his role as teacher and researcher. Gose, Rowntree, Williams, and Thompson found it "inconceivable" that Gundlach "can efficiently and fairly deal with the subject of his special interest, social psychology. His views on social problems are strongly biased in favor of those advocated by the Communist Party, which he so closely follows." Though they found his research biased, they deferred to the wide-ranging support and judgment of his colleagues, and decided not to recommend dismissal on this charge. Densmore concurred in finding Gundlach biased, but refused to trust the judgment of psychologists unfamiliar with "circumstances prevailing in this University," who seemed most concerned about safeguarding "academic freedom in general, a matter in no way germane to this hearing." Densmore also refused to consider the views of students who had testified in Gundlach's behalf, since there were "other students who might have given contrary testimony if called." He recommended dismissal, as did Benson and Goodspeed, who found Gundlach's research "forensic rather than scientific." Hatch, Robinson, Huber, and Sholley concurred with the majority in exonerating Gundlach on Charge IV, but assailed the unnecessary publication of "their personal and relatively uninformed opinions" on his competency.[43]

Except as discussed in connection with Charge IV, the committee found no violation of the code under Charge V, which alleged that Gundlach had neglected his duty to the university by spending too much time on party activities. The committee refused to find fact on Charge VI, which alleged that Gundlach refused to answer questions at the Canwell hearings, despite Allen's recommendations that he do so to protect the general good of the university. The committee felt that to comment would prejudge contempt proceedings initiated against Gundlach by the King County prosecutor. Further, they took the position that professors should not be dismissed for refusal to testify at a public tribunal.[44]

When Allen relayed his analysis of the Gundlach case to the regents, he emphasized the opinion of Benson and Goodspeed, remarking on Gundlach's Communist party activities, lack of objective scholarship, and evasive and uncooperative stances toward the committee and the administration. Pointing to the testimony which showed that important party members were not required to carry membership cards, Allen came to the conclusion that "Gundlach has done more for the Party than any other respondent." Allen also upheld Densmore's questionable shift of the burden of proof and found Gundlach biased in his research regardless of the testimony of his students and colleagues. Perhaps to show impartiality, Allen refused to pass judgment on the finding that Gundlach had neglected his duty by refusing to give Allen a straight answer to questions about his party membership. However, the president cited Gundlach's "No one can prove that I am, and I cannot prove that I am not," statement to show the professor's implicit membership in the party.[45]

The administration's case against Garland Ethel, Melville Jacobs, and Harold Eby was essentially the same as that against Gundlach. Though these three had admitted past membership in the Communist party and denied current involvement with it, the contention was that they, like Gundlach, should be dismissed because they had followed the Communist line during those years. Besides the shadow this cast upon their honesty and competence, the three were accused of failure to tell the Canwell Committee the whole truth; i.e., they had refused to reveal the names of their colleagues involved in party activities, and had equivocated in their conferences with the president in June.[46]

Garland Ethel told the Tenure Committee that he began reading Marxist and Socialist literature early in his life. As the son of a poor Missouri couple, he witnessed the perils of early attempts to unionize the railway system. Furthermore, the writings of muckrakers convinced him that the law was made for two types of persons, the haves and the have-nots. The Armistice ended his career in the Army, and Ethel grasped the opportunity to become the first in his family to go to college. As he worked his way through the University of Washington, the Seattle General Strike and the activities of the Industrial Workers of the World further convinced him of the merits of Marxism. In 1927, the year before he received his Ph.D., he joined the university's English Department. A six-month tour of Europe in 1932, much of it in Russia and Germany, allowed him to grasp the dangers of Fascism; but on his return to the United States, he found the Hearst papers carrying articles written by Mussolini, and labor silent on the issues of the day. The Communist party won his allegiance in 1934, since it was the only organized group opposing Fascism. When he recognized that

England was going to fight, he dropped out of the party and enlisted in the Army Air Force. He served until after the defeat of Japan, and rejoined the faculty in the fall of 1946.[47]

Ethel testified that Dean Lauer had praised his work on several occasions, and introduced commendatory letters Lauer had written to him over the years. Five members of the English Department and two graduate students vouched for his competence and objective teaching. Asserting that he had kept Allen informed of his views before and after talking with the Canwell investigators, Ethel refuted the charge that he had not cooperated with the president. Though he had originally told Allen he would not affirm or deny past membership in the party, he acquiesced to Allen's request that he do so, stating only that he would not inform on others. Since Allen and Guthrie did not directly ask him about his party membership, Ethel did not tell them; on the advice of R. G. Tyler, Ethel later sought out Allen and gave him the specific dates of his membership. Allen's testimony confirmed Ethel's accounts of their meetings. On cross-examination, Ethel said that he was still a "philosophical, convinced Marxist," but that he had not engaged in political activity since the war.[48]

In its deliberations, the Tenure Committee found no reason to disturb the employment of Ethel. In praising the straightforwardness of his testimony, the committee stated that intellectual Marxism as professed by Ethel was not grounds for removal, nor was past membership in the party. The committee could find no evidence that such past membership had interfered with the proper discharge of Ethel's duties as a faculty member. The charge that Ethel had not answered all the questions of the Canwell Committee was left to the jurisdiction of "other tribunals duly constituted for that purpose."[49]

Melville Jacobs' account of his drift into the Communist party revealed a childhood spent reading in the Carnegie branch of the New York Public Library and listening to socialist soapbox speakers. When he attended the College of the City of New York he came into a world populated by ghetto Jewish students, a new experience for a person from a "stuffy, apolitical" family. There and at Columbia graduate school, many of his socialist preconceptions took root. As he put it, a mild socialism was in the intellectual environment of the teens and twenties, a kind of apolitical gradualism. Jacobs came to teach at the university in 1927 while completing his Ph.D. in Anthropology from Columbia. Jacobs and his wife often drove across the country to New York and were able to see the effects of the Depression first hand; his father lost everything in the Crash of 1929. Part of 1933 was spent in Germany where he saw Hitler assume power. Like most of his colleagues who joined the party, Jacobs was recruited by an ubiquitous and persuasive Communist party recruiter named Roberts, a "fascinating young man" who added a good deal of interest to the parties and open houses attended by faculty members. Roberts gave Jacobs the works of John Strachey and Earl Browder, which assured readers that the Communist party was an effective tool for fighting Fascism through nonviolent, constitutional means. Jacobs and his wife joined the party in 1935, paid dues and attended as few meetings as possible, since they found Communism ideologically "archaic," and their membership was merely an expression of horror concerning the anti-Semitic aspects of Fascism. As soon as the war ended, the Jacobses withdrew completely from the party.[50]

Like other members of his professional group of Communist party members, Jacobs realized the dangers inherent in membership; attacks by Fascists and informers could threaten his job. For this reason secrecy was attempted, though it was always clear to Jacobs that his membership was known to many outside the party. In 1943, for example, he and Eby were attacked on the radio program of a Teamster columnist named Lester Hunt. Also, the inept recruitment of a military intelligence man to his Communist party unit during the war further convinced Jacobs that his activities were no secret to the government. Thus, when the Canwell Committee subpoena came through, it was a shock, since he had been inactive and indifferent for so long. Jacobs, who had built a good reputation as an American Indian languages specialist, feared that he would lose his job, and actually began looking for employment in other countries. A curious sidelight was that during the hearings and on into 1949, Jacobs was the science news broadcaster for the university's weekly radio shows.[51]

Jacobs told the Tenure Committee that his chief concern at the moment was his scientific research, and that "in my present frame of mind, something would have to happen to some of the cells in my cerebrum before anybody could persuade me ever to touch politics with a ten-foot pole after what I have been through." Like other people, scientists change their minds, he said; followers of Boasian anthropology were not excluded from anthropological societies despite the discrediting of some of the theories of Franz Boas.[52]

Jacobs admitted that he had at first told Allen he had never been a member of the party, but that he had done so on the advice of counsel, and later told the president of his past activities. Allen's testimony corroborated Jacobs's account, as did that of the attorney who had given the earlier advice: "I told him that I didn't think it was any business of the President of the University as to what lodge or what political party he belonged to, and that he could either deny or refuse to answer the question," especially since the Canwell Committee was using "ultra-legal" methods. The chairman of the Anthropology Department, five of his colleagues, and two graduate students testified concerning his excellent reputation and ability as an anthropologist; through letters, many of his colleagues from other institutions did likewise.[53]

The committee found no reason to dismiss Jacobs, though they did express disapproval of both his untruthfulness and his purely emotional commitment to the Communist party. It was clear, however, that his indifferent participation in party affairs could not have seriously interfered with his university duties. As in the case of Ethel, the committee noted that though the Canwell hearings resulted in a contempt citation against Jacobs, the appropriate tribunal had refused to bring charges.[54]

Edwin Harold Eby's early life experiences also conditioned him toward a socialist perspective on the troubles of the thirties. The son of an eccentric Spokane mining engineer, Eby became interested in government ownership of railroads (a current Populist notion) while in high school. After studying at the University of Chicago, he returned to the university to become a student under Vernon Parrington; Eby edited the final volume of Parrington's Pulitzer Prize-winning *Main Currents of American Thought* after the death of the author. The plight of the unemployed during the Depression made him want to do something to help alleviate their problems, since it appeared that the legislature would not. All over the Northwest various groups were organizing the unemployed, from Fascist-type organizations like the Minutemen and Silver Shirts, to education-minded Bellamy Clubs. Not really a Marxist, but a believer in government intervention, Eby joined the Unemployed Citizens League, which later became part of the Washington Commonwealth Federation (wcf). Disturbed by worker hostility to university faculty members, Eby and his friends joined the AFT to work with labor leaders (some of whom were former iww's) in seeking solutions to common problems. At this point, Robert Roberts entered the scene as one who represented an "active organization," the Communist party. After receiving assurances that violence was not part of the plan to achieve justice for the workers, Eby joined the party in 1935, and became a respected theoretician of the wcf. At first able to accept the Communist party notion of a dictatorship, Eby eventually could no longer justify its confusion of means with ends. The mechanical thinking and rationalization that accompanied the Nazi-Soviet Pact caused him to begin withdrawing from the party, but not the wcf, in 1939. Eby ended his membership in the party in 1946, after the demise of the wcf.[55]

Eby also realized the dangers involved with Communist party membership. Like Jacobs, he had been attacked in the media for his activities. While maintaining that these attacks were motivated by anti-trade union, anti-liberal forces which also were hostile to the university, Eby asserted that politics did not interfere with his teaching and research. Eby related an encounter with President Sieg in 1939 when he received a promotion to associate professor. Sieg said to Eby, "I have heard rumors that you are a Communist or a 'Red.' I do not care one way or the other about that. That is not germane. The question is, are you going to produce?" When Eby was promoted to full professor in 1947, there was no question from President Allen. Eby also testified that his membership in so-called Communist fronts such as Local 401 of the aft, the Seattle Labor School, and the Independent Citizens League of the Arts, Sciences and Professions was consistent with his beliefs. The Labor School was, after all, supported by the churches, libraries, and the university. Three of Eby's colleagues and five students testified to his competence; his former chairman did likewise, but stated under cross-examination that he had warned members of the English Department about becoming involved with the wcf. J. B. Harrison, one of his colleagues, stated he would have recommended Eby for promotion even if he had known of his Communist party membership: "A man's political beliefs make no difference at a University unless he misuses them."[56]

After he had been named as a Communist in the first Canwell hearings of February, 1948, Eby told the committee, he went to Allen and denied that he was a Communist. As a member of the Teachers Union, he had obeyed Allen's requests to refrain from public statements concerning Canwell's activities, and convinced others to do likewise. He also worked with the aaup leadership to relieve pressures on the university. At the June 3 meeting with Allen and Guthrie, Eby had repeated his denial of membership, but when he later learned that Allen had gotten the impression that Eby had never been a member of the party, he returned to Allen's office and told him that he had been a member in the past. Eby also testified that he told Allen that, like Ethel and Jacobs, he had no intention of naming colleagues in the upcoming Canwell hearings. Allen told him that though he was risking contempt charges, it was a position that the university could defend, and that it was "certainly within the mores of the American people. The American people do not like informers."[57]

R. G. Tyler, former president of the UWAAUP, corroborated Eby's understanding that the university would not bring charges if subpoenaed members refused to testify about the activities of their colleagues. He said that he also relayed to them Himstead's warning that the AAUP would not support them if they falsified the facts of their Communist party activities. Committee member Benson then asked what the AAUP's Committee A meant by "crypto-Communists." Attorney Caughlan asserted that it was a reference to the teachers who appeared before the Rapp-Coudert Committee (in New York, 1940–42), falsified their affiliation with the Communist party, and were denied AAUP intervention.[58]

President Allen said that he had gained the impression from Eby at both the February and the June conferences that he had never been a party member, and that Eby came in to correct that impression in July. Allen also said that he put the matter of naming colleagues in an ethical context—one to be decided by each person. Attorney Henry reminded Allen of a conversation that he had had with him on the same question, in which he had gotten the impression he could advise his clients "that the Administration would not discipline them for refusing to name their colleagues. . . ." Allen replied, "You have a correct impression . . . I accept that fully."[59]

Despite Eby's recent and active involvement in party affairs, no grounds for his removal were discovered by the committee. Nor could they find that his past activities had impaired his usefulness to the university. Though the committee found itself uncertain as to what had actually transpired in the meetings with Allen, they were convinced that no grave violations of the code had occurred.[60]

When Allen submitted his analysis and recommendations to the Board of Regents, he refused to pass judgment on Jacobs' case because of his denial of membership prior to the Canwell hearing. Allen said he felt the incident was serious and a violation of the AAUP's admonition against "lying and subterfuge." Allen also indicated his disapproval of Jacobs' reasons for joining the party: "It is incredible to me that a scholar, of whom the University has rights to expect rational rather than emotional conduct, could and would accept, without investigation, obligations such as those inherent in Communist Party membership"—especially when he knew that such action "would bring discredit and disrepute upon the University." Allen also noted that Jacobs remained in the party after the "rapprochement of Nazism and Communism in 1939." Against these evidences of dishonesty and incompetency, Allen set Jacobs' record of productive research and devotion to teaching, apparently lapsing for the moment from his view that no Communist could be competent.[61]

The president upheld the recommendations of the committee concerning Ethel and Eby despite their dereliction of duty during their period of Communist party membership. Allen also expressed support for the "intellectual Marxist" views entertained by Ethel, and Eby's "left of center" ideas: "I think it is necessary that we maintain a place in the University for the holding of such philosophies, regardless of how strongly we may disagree with them. . . . To close the University's doors to honest nonconformist thought would do violence to the principles of academic freedom that we must maintain at all costs."[62]

Thus, after six weeks of testimony, Allen's definition of academic freedom was drawn to exclude those whom he believed had renounced their freedom by joining the Communist party or by following its political "line." In recommending the dismissal of Butterworth and Phillips to the board, he pointed out that eight of the committee agreed: three explicitly, and five implicitly. The regents had the power to remove any doubts about the meaning of the code, and Allen recommended that exclusion of Communists be given the status of policy. In siding with the seven committee members who recommended the dismissal of Gundlach, Allen cited the findings of three committee members who decried the psychologist's "ambiguous relationship" with the party, and his "biased research." Allen cited, but refused to comment on, the recommendation for dismissal which came from five committee members who felt that Gundlach had neglected his duty by failure to cooperate with the president. Allen further demonstrated his commitment to intellectual freedom by urging that Eby and Ethel should not be dismissed because they had demonstrated their capacity for objectivity by leaving the party. He made no recommendation to the regents on the Jacobs case, due to the June "incident of falsification," but noted that the committee had unanimously upheld Jacobs' tenure rights.[63]

Allen's analysis for the Board of Regents reflected his own beliefs about the nature of the internal Communist threat to the future of democratic institutions, but it was also tempered by his personal feelings toward the men involved and his perception of what the regents would allow. An additional factor was his concern about the position of the AAUP. On January 19, a few days before the regents met to consider the cases, President Allen supplemented his major recommendations with further suggestions to the board. To illustrate the

university's lack of "punitive" intent, he urged that the university pay
the lawyers' fees for the defendants and continue their regular
salaries up to April 1, 1949. "Much as we might think they had earned
such [financial] embarrassment by past behavior . . . it would look
good in the record that we will have done this." The gesture, he
noted, would exempt the university from giving the dismissed faculty
a year's notice, as the AAUP recommended, because "more than a year
ago all members of the faculty were warned in an official faculty
meeting that members of the Communist Party should resign or be
forced out." Despite the fact that the attorney general of the state later
ruled that the University of Washington could not legally pay persons
beyond the date of severance, or their attorneys' fees,[64] Allen's memo
illustrates his determination to consider the faculty forewarned—even
though the Tenure Committee majority felt the university had no
"policy" toward Communists. Obviously, Allen knew that the regents
would dismiss some faculty even before the final hearing.

IV

The Regents' Decision and Aftermath

There is no question at all that the University of Washington Board of
Regents is about to set a precedent that will command nationwide atten-
tion in the educational field.
—Regent George R. Stuntz, January 20, 1949

On January 22, 1949, five weeks after the Tenure Committee hearings and five months after the Canwell Committee hearings, the University of Washington Board of Regents met to hear the final arguments of administration and defense counsel regarding the six faculty
members. Prior to that Saturday afternoon the regents had been lobbied from both sides. Arguments for retaining the six were quietly
made from within the academic community by alumni such as Neal E.
Miller, professor of psychology at Yale. Miller urged the board to
remember the mistakes of past regents: "I feel that the Suzzallo and
Fisher cases have already detracted from the educational honor of my
native state." He asked the regents to uphold the tolerance and freedom of the university. The rationale for dismissal of the six professors
appeared in the pages of the local press. Fred Niendorff reported that
the members of the thirty-first legislature were awaiting the regents'
decision before considering the university's budget requests for the
next biennium. He also stated that three of the seven regents would
move for immediate dismissal of all six faculty members.[1]

In contrast to the quiet deliberation of the tenure hearings, the
regents' hearing was open to the flashbulbs and notepads of the press.
Attorney John Caughlan urged the board to put off a decision until
they had had time to read fully the 3,900 pages of testimony and
examine the 125 exhibits. Pointing out that only three of the Tenure
Committee had unequivocally recommended the dismissal of Phillips
and Butterworth, he asked the board to consider the dangerous implications of Allen's support for the minority view. Already, he said,
Professor Henry Aiken of Harvard had declined an invitation to teach
at the University of Washington because of the charges against his

fellow philosopher, Phillips. In failing to advise the regents of the
dangers in following his recommendations, Allen was exacerbating
the divisions within society that imperiled freedom and American
traditions of liberty, said Caughlan.[2]

Phillips' statement to the board on behalf of Butterworth and himself was apparently meant as a defense of their membership in the
Communist party. The philosopher attacked Canwell, J. Parnell
Thomas, and the Hearst newspapers as anti-labor, anti-democratic
purveyors of "incipient fascism." Citing their acquittal by the Tenure
Committee, Phillips termed Allen's recommendation "simply a capitu-
lation to the Canwell forces . . . the local manifestation of decaying
capitalism." One can imagine Phillips looking board member Dave
Beck in the eye as he outlined the socialist goals of the Communist
party which he said were aimed at developing the working class despite the "consistent employment of deliberate misleaders of labor
. . . half demagogic, half terroristic." While reminding the regents
that the voters had defeated Canwell in the November (1948) elections, Phillips urged them to face their obligation to protect the public
interest by repudiating those in the legislature calling for continuation
of the Un-American Activities Committee.[3]

Administration counsel Tracy Griffin's rebuttal accused Caughlan
and Phillips of using Communist party tactics by propagandizing and
by insulting President Allen through suggesting "that he knows how
you seven gentlemen are going to vote." Allen had showed courage
and independence in his recommendations, Griffin said, because he
went beyond what the faculty committee recommended, and not as
far as he, Griffin, would recommend. Griffin urged immediate dismissal of all six respondents. He maintained that since only the last
few volumes of the transcript had been unavailable until recently,
board members had had enough time to consider their decisions.
Caughlan then apologized for implying that the board had not read
the testimony and that Allen was prejudiced. He urged the regents to
uphold the Tenure Code, which did not specify Communist party
membership as grounds for dismissal, and to judge only the competence of his clients.[4]

In Gundlach's defense, C. T. Hatten maintained that the only
charge against his client was Communist party membership. Since the
committee could not prove he was a Communist, it had shifted
ground; Hatten charged that "the findings of incompetency in teaching and research were clearly an afterthought." Echoing Caughlan, he
asked the board to postpone its decision so that it could give more
attention to this matter. Hatten also read a letter from Stanford

psychologist Lewis Terman, which urged that Gundlach's dismissal be based only on treasonable acts, not mere left-wing beliefs and activities. In rebuttal, Griffin told the regents that Terman had been cited by the House Committee on Un-American Activities (HUAC) for his alliance with subversive organizations: "that letter was not written by an amateur." Griffin also reminded the board that the Nazis had been able to undermine German universities because "old line professors" had upheld academic freedom indiscriminately. The only way to decide if a person was a Communist was to look to circumstantial evidence, he argued, and Dean Guthrie's testimony supported that assumption in Gundlach's case.[5]

Concerning Ethel, Griffin said that anyone who remained a Communist party member from 1934 to 1941 was not fit to be on the university faculty. That was even more true of Eby and Jacobs who "don't know when they quit, if they quit." Ed Henry, their attorney, told the regents that the three no longer concerned themselves with the Communist party: "Their sole desire is to continue in their field and devote all of their time to their academic field. . . . I am sure that they have had as severe a lesson as any man could possibly have, and I am sure that the Board may rest assured that these men have no desire to engage in any political affray from now on."[6]

The regents' deliberations resulted in the dismissal of Gundlach, Butterworth and Phillips, and two-year probations for Eby, Ethel, and Jacobs. Board President Drumheller told *Post-Intelligencer* reporter Fred Niendorff that the action "serves notice everywhere throughout the country that the University of Washington is notifying Communists to stay away from the University campus." Niendorff went on to state that Drumheller, Stuntz, and Beck argued for the dismissal of all six, and that only one vote saved the jobs of Eby, Ethel, and Jacobs. Probation for those professors was a warning that "participation in any Communist or Communist front activities henceforth will terminate their services." Most significantly: "The regents' action marks the first success in a struggle of more than a decade to penetrate the University of Washington pro-Communist teaching bloc, and break its influence in the classrooms," wrote Niendorff. The regents credited Canwell with finding the evidence necessary to oust the three professors. Several regents, he wrote, hoped that a renewed legislative committee would assist in "making all tax-supported state institutions of learning clean as a hound's tooth."[7]

While Butterworth and Phillips were denouncing "control of ideas" at the university, former representative Canwell called the action "partial" and reminded officials that "other members of the faculty

have been named in the legislative hearings, and no doubt President
Allen will see that proper action is taken. . . ." The state's Elks organization urged the legislature to expand and strengthen, not
merely continue, the Un-American Activities Committee. When President Allen announced that he would confer with the executive
officers of the AAUP in Washington, D.C., Regent Drumheller challenged: "Naturally we hope that the AAUP will not raise an issue over
these dismissals. But if it does, the issue will resolve into whether a
nation-wide organization of professors, or the taxpayers of this state,
are to be the judges of whether Communists shall teach their children." [8]

Most newspapers across the nation supported the decisions. The
Peoria Journal described the regents' action as "heroic," one which
"should blaze the way for every school and university that has Communists or fellow-travelers on its faculty. True to traditional Communist reaction, the three ousted professors have appealed to the
American Association of University Professors." The *New York Times*
and the *New York Post* took opposite views, with the *Post* upholding the
primacy of competence, not politics, in educational matters. [9]

Syndicated columnists Raymond Moley and Dorothy Thompson
praised the regents, while from the floor of the House of Representatives Democrat F. Edward Hèbert of Louisiana lauded Allen for "accepting the challenge of Communism." His comments were seconded
by John Rankin of Mississippi, who added that a "house-cleaning" was
long overdue at other leading universities besides the University of
Washington. Stands taken by organized labor followed predictable
lines. The Seattle Central Labor Council, affiliated with the AFL, sent
President Allen a resolution praising his good work, and urged him to
continue "until you have gotten rid of all that undesirable element
who are upholding foreign philosophies, so that red-blooded Americans in this country can point to the University of Washington with
pride as one that is upholding American principles. . . ." CIO-affil-
iated workers in the fishing and furrier industries protested the action.
The National Americanism Commission of the American Legion expressed the support of Legion posts around the country to Allen, as
did various chapters of the Daughters of the American Revolution
and Lions clubs. [10]

Benjamin Fine, education editor of the *New York Times*, declared
that Allen's actions were controversial but were supported by most
college presidents. Fine cited the statement released by Dr. Albert C.
Jacobs, provost of Columbia, which purportedly expressed the views
of President Eisenhower and the deans of the university: "To allow

the infiltration of such persons [who would destroy academic freedom] into the faculties of universities would tend to defeat the ends which academic freedom is designed to attain." Allen's correspondence bore out Fine's assessment. Chancellors von Kleinsmid of Southern California and Wilbur of Stanford, as well as numerous presidents and officers of higher educational institutions and organizations, wrote Allen with expressions of gratitude for his great service to education. Joel Hildebrand of Berkeley shared with Allen a letter he had written Committee A of the AAUP expressing his concern over the committee's 1948 report. In his view, the right of a faculty member to join the Communist party was abrogated by his higher obligation to reject membership in any organization that destroyed his independence and integrity.[11]

Meanwhile, reaction within the University of Washington campus was diffused. The student newspaper carried the protests of several faculty: J. B. Harrison of English wrote of the "Tragic Error" that had been made; Edwin Uehling of Physics forecast a "dark future" for the university. Protests by W. Stull Holt and Max Savelle of History were amplified by Melvin Rader of Philosophy and eight physics professors who wrote: "A university is above all a place where ideas are freely received and exchanged, developed or discarded without fear of administrative reprisals. These recent actions have impaired the ability of the University to fulfill this basic function." A Student Organization for Academic Rights (SOAR) garnered three thousand signatures on a petition of protest and drew one thousand students and faculty to an outdoor rally which Allen refused to address. Regent Stuntz discounted SOAR, calling it suspect because most of its leaders were followers of Henry Wallace. After a *Daily* poll showed that most students approved the decisions, a law student organized "Students Organization that Allen's Right," which he said was affiliated with a "Student Organization for Removal of Eccentrics." The only dues necessary was "100% disapproval of Communism."[12]

The resignation of Political Science professor Thomas I. Cook provoked brief reaction in the press. On leave of absence while teaching at the University of Chicago, Cook called a press conference to protest the abrogation of due process "vital to constitutional and democratic government, and to the performance of the role of teacher and scholar within these institutions." Allen told New York reporters that Cook's action was "half-cocked" and that his resignation would not be accepted until Cook examined the record and retracted his accusations against the university. Because Cook had sold his Seattle home before leaving for Chicago, his action was generally discounted as an empty protest. However, Cook later wrote that he had not been offered a permanent job at Chicago and that he made his decision only after consultation with friends Kermit Ely and Rexford Tugwell, who urged him to resign publicly to gain faculty support. The Chicago press conference, therefore, had put him in precarious position: "local inference that my resignation involved no sacrifice, and by inference was cheap publicity, seems to me unwarranted," he wrote.[13]

But actions such as Cook's were easily turned aside by Allen, who was now confirmed in his role as defender of academic freedom. When asked about charges of "thought control" at the university, the president told a reporter that it was "further away than ever" since Communist party members were removed from the faculty. Should a faculty member fear that he might be dismissed for matters other than politics, like religion? Allen replied, "Such a thing would be inconceivable, incredible, impossible and ridiculous. Spiritual matters, while they relate to academic life, are questions of individual privacy and are not matters of concern to the University." To Lawrence Davies of the *New York Times*, Allen said faculty fears that "adventurousness in teaching" would be discouraged were "perfectly absurd. If there are some young faculty members here on campus who have not thought this through and think they face thought control, they are just as immature as the Communists are." Indicating that he would not care if such men resigned, Allen said, "I think they are responding a little to the hysteria of the times. We have emphasized the importance of men of integrity. I should think men of that kind would be encouraged to come here and be men."[14]

The issues involved, however, went beyond individual integrity. Faculty could and did assume several stances toward the actions of Allen and the regents. Those who agreed with Allen did so for many reasons. They were offended by the unabashed truculence of the defendants—all of whom had "embarrassed" the university in the past—and felt a "house-cleaning" was indeed long overdue on either political or esthetic grounds. These men, after all, had lied to the president, and not even the AAUP condoned that. George Lundberg of Sociology, who claimed agreement with the stand of the AAUP against dismissing Communists per se, felt that the regents' action would sit well with Committee A. Since the best the defendants could get was a "hung jury" in the tenure proceedings, not even a "biased" group such as the AAUP could disagree. Traditional professional jealousies also played a role: those who agreed with the regents tended to be from "professional" schools such as Forestry, Business Administration, Engineering, Law, and Education. They upheld the authority of the president and the regents to hire and fire, dissented from the position of Committee A, and were generally suspicious of less precise disciplines such as the humanities and social sciences.[15]

Allen's "broadening" of the "professional" meaning of academic freedom appealed to this group: though the Communist party was legal, teachers had a higher duty in the current struggle among ideologies. But that notion also found favor with another larger group of faculty who feared the sinister qualities of international Communism which were enabling it to undermine governments in countries such as China, Italy, and other nations in Western Europe. Members of this group, however, disagreed with the dismissals because they went against the recommendations of the Tenure Committee and notions of faculty autonomy. In a debate on the issues, George Taylor of the new Far East Institute told of his experience with the leaders of the Chinese Communists: "These are serious people. This is no pinochle game. I am asking for a divorce between political thought and action only in reference to one political party . . . these men challenge the basis of our society. We cannot tolerate intolerance."[16]

Another smaller group concerned itself with protection of the civil and academic liberties of those dismissed or put on probation. For them, the right of faculty members to participate in legal political activities was inviolable. These included men like J. B. Harrison, Melvin Rader, and the minority group on the Tenure Committee: Huber, Robinson, and Sholley. Labeled "ritualistic liberals" by Sidney Hook, they preferred to think of themselves as conservators of constitutional rights. In the debate with George Taylor, Harrison warned: "If we ask teachers to divorce thought from political action, we are asking them to become political eunuchs." As one who knew Butterworth and Phillips well, he refused to believe that they constituted Justice Holmes's "clear and present danger." He went on, "I should be far happier if the University of Washington had made the headlines by issuing a ringing declaration of academic independence than by initiating this sinister chain reaction."[17]

Within these three major streams of faculty opinion existed many subtle variations occasioned by differences among individuals, and by the complexity of the situation both within the university and outside it. As a result, no "ringing declarations" were forthcoming from the Faculty Senate. In March, Stull Holt of History presented a resolution to the senate which recognized the right of the regents to make decisions on faculty membership, but termed its action in these cases "detrimental to the best interests of the University . . . just as the

Board of Regents accepts the decisions of the faculty in exercising its legal right of appointing members of the faculty, so also should it accept the faculty decisions in dismissing members of the faculty. Academic freedom can only be maintained if the competence and qualifications of a member of the faculty are determined by a jury of his peers." Even though it was offered by a veteran of two world wars and a recognized anti-Communist, the senate voted to table the resolution.[18] This ended faculty attempts to protest the decision through official university channels.

Following the senate action, Allen received memoranda of support from the deans and faculties of Engineering (E. O. Eastwood and H. Wessman), Business Administration (H. Burd), and Forestry (G. Marckworth). The final expression of opposition came in the form of an open letter signed by 103 faculty which asserted opposition to the Communist party, yet upheld the right of faculty to dissent through legal political action. Further, the dismissals and probations violated the principle of personal guilt by inferring dishonesty and incompetency from associations. The letter went on:

> We believe, finally, that the action taken has already done serious damage to the University and to the cause of education. The reputation of the University as a center of free inquiry and untrammeled teaching has declined; the *esprit de corps* that gives confidence and character to any institution has deteriorated; and the University of Washington has invited education in general to join it in a retreat from freedom, which, if it continues will weaken the morale which is democracy's best defense against totalitarian Communism.[19]

The signers were predominantly from the College of Arts and Sciences. Although sixty-four of them had received University of Washington appointments since World War II, signators such as C. L. Hitchcock, Everett Nelson, Walter Issacs, W. M. Read, and Linden Mander were chairmen or directors of departments and schools. The salient point about the letter, however, is that it received so little support among the university's over seven hundred faculty. This illustrated the confusions and divisions caused by the complexities of a situation that involved the Communist party, faculty authority, and the personal views of those asked to sign the letter. While some objected to actions against Eby, Ethel, and Jacobs, they approved the actions against Gundlach, Butterworth, and Phillips. Some would not sign the letter because it indicated disapproval of the Tenure Committee's findings about Ralph Gundlach; others were afraid to register an opinion, or pleaded ignorance of the issues.[20]

Meanwhile, the decision against allowing Communists to teach was the subject of extensive commentary in the national media, since it was the first such stand taken by an academic administration. In March, Allen and T. V. Smith of Syracuse University debated Harold Taylor, president of Sarah Lawrence College, and Roger Baldwin, director of the American Civil Liberties Union, on the question of allowing Communists to teach. Listeners to ABC's "Town Hall Meeting of the Air" heard Taylor point out that students were not readily susceptible to ideas from any source, that "students and teachers in America have already rejected the Communist Party," and that since there was no evidence that Butterworth and Phillips had corrupted students, they should not have been dismissed. Allen's notion of truth would close off a basic freedom, he said, "To refuse to encounter because of public fear is to betray the search and to yield to a failure of nerve." Allen countered with the familiar notion that Communists are not free and are therefore incompetent and intellectually dishonest; "education," he argued, "cannot tolerate organized intolerance." As a representative of an organization that denied all anti-democrats positions on its council, Baldwin argued for the exclusion of teachers only when they held beliefs inimical to their discipline; for example, a member of the Ku Klux Klan should not teach anthropology, a Communist should not teach government. Smith, who had reported on the University of Washington hearings for the *New York Herald Tribune*, tended to see the decisions as a "democratic Compromise," and the regents as "moral middlemen." He stated that Communists have no right to teach, since they disavowed the ends of education; the duty of society to itself is to exclude those who disrupt it. In response to a query from Taylor, Allen said that the investigation of the individual dishonesty of Butterworth and Phillips would have taken too long; they made their mistake when they joined the Communist party.[21]

The *American Scholar* Forum presented a resumé of the cases along with statements by Allen and the three dismissed professors and four commentary essays. Arthur O. Lovejoy, one of the founders of the AAUP, expressed his concern about hiring Communist party members in the future; current tenured faculty members, he said, should not be dismissed if they disavowed the aims of the Communist party to suppress political and academic liberties. Since the published record did not reveal such questioning of Phillips and Butterworth, he refused comment on their cases. Lovejoy did state that the probationary action against Eby, Ethel, and Jacobs was an unwise, unfair, unnecessary stigma for them to bear. Max Lerner of the *New York Post* castigated Allen for praising the search for truth on the one hand, and then throwing aside the truth sought out by the Tenure Committee. Citing the experience of the Chinese university system, Lerner warned that by paying too much attention to left-wing propaganda universities forget the dangers from the mainstream and the right. Soon, he wrote, professors would be like mandarins teaching only what Big Money wanted them to teach. T. V. Smith's "Academic Expediency as Democratic Justice *in re* Communists," was an expansion of his earlier arguments about the wisdom of the regents' midroad brand of decision-making: "It points to the use of intelligence rather than a surrender to hysteria." Helen Lynd, obviously the only one of the four to have read the committee hearing transcript and visited the University of Washington campus, concluded that the actions taken resulted from political pressures and budgetary concerns, not from any quest for truth. She also reported that more University of Washington faculty would have protested had they not feared for their jobs.[22]

Other academic luminaries who entered the fray in the pages of national journals included Sidney Hook, I. L. Kandel, H. S. Commager, Alexander Meiklejohn, A. M. Schlesinger, Jr., and R. M. Hutchins. Hook, himself a former doyen of radical politics, became one of Allen's most prolific defenders. His major line of argument was that Communist party members were prima facie not free, and that faculty who would not disavow membership should be dismissed. His views, and the decisions of Allen and the regents, were attacked by Meiklejohn who wrote that university officials were "misled by the hatreds and fears of the cold war." He continued, "the entire faculty is now on probation," due to the doctrine of guilt by association as preached by Hook. At Hook's urging, Allen countered Meiklejohn with the assertion that fully free faculty members had nothing to fear. The probationary action against Eby, Ethel, and Jacobs was a form of "social discipline," he said, an accepted way for society to deal with repentant criminals. Moreover, Allen continued, Ethel remained on the faculty despite his philosophical Marxism.[23]

I. L. Kandel also rejected Hook's notion of incompetence by association: "It is somewhat ironical that the flames started by superpatriotic organizations dedicated to crushing un-American activities should be fanned by intellectuals." Henry Steele Commager accused Allen of subscribing to deductive a priori methods which were both dogmatic and un-American. Schlesinger posited the lack of "clear and present danger" from those dismissed, and pronounced the decisions a devastating commentary on the other seven hundred University of Washington faculty and on the strength of democracy. In a reply to the historian, Merritt Benson denied that freedom was in danger on the University of Washington campus: Ethel's "right to loathsome ideas" was not questioned; Phillips had been given the largest auditorium on campus to express his defense after the dismissals; like Butterworth, he had been dismissed for his abandonment of scholarship. Gundlach, he wrote, was dismissed not for political beliefs, but for his actions and deceit. Francis D. Wormuth's reflections on the issues produced a concern that was never assuaged by the supporters of the University of Washington actions. If "guilt by association" was to be the norm for determining competency, he wrote, "intellectual plasticity" would be the result; there would be nothing to prevent Communist party members from resigning to retain their positions, and institutions of education would become the havens of intellectually servile men.[24]

As other states began investigations of institutions of higher education, the University of Washington cases were used as touchstones for action. Before the Illinois Broyles Committee, R. M. Hutchins was asked by J. B. Matthews if he approved of the dismissal of Gundlach for his affiliation with "a score of communist front organizations." The chancellor's reply was "No," and when he later addressed the Inland Empire Educational Association in Spokane, he assailed "thought control" at the University of Washington and warned of the critical pressures being exerted on higher education by special groups. Hutchins' comments provoked a storm of response in the state's press; Allen took public exception by saying that thought control directed from Moscow was the real danger.[25]

With such declarations, Allen succeeded in turning aside the criticisms of "naive academics" such as Hutchins, who were, after all, disunited. The combined complexities of the deepening Cold War and the University of Washington cases convinced many liberals to remain silent. Into this vacuum rushed small, well-organized groups and individuals eager to topple intellectuals from their positions of influence. Allen himself did not escape suspicion. H. L. Moody, an investigator in the state auditor's office, voiced the notion that Allen was trying to cover his own dubious actions by his public pronouncements. Citing the 1947 statutes against giving salaries to subversives, Moody pointed to the efforts of the University of Washington to exchange scholars with the U.S.S.R., and to two thousand dollars spent on "communistic literature" for the Far East and Russian Institute. The same institute, he wrote, published "Soviet Press Translations" and sent them to hundreds of universities, members of the government, and the Soviet embassy. The web of subversion widened

as Moody noted the guest list for Allen's inauguration: Edward U.
Condon, according to HUAC, "the weakest link in our security chain";
six atomic bomb physicists; and the Soviet consul-general. Moody
implied that by inviting these individuals to mix in a social setting,
Allen had jeopardized national security. Allen also served as a national vice-president for the Institute of Pacific Relations, cited by the
California Un-American Activities Committee, and retained Marxists
on the faculty despite the costly tenure hearings. Not enough attention was given to front and underground activities, said Moody; despite the Canwell Committee, Communist activities were still evident
at the University of Washington.[26]

Instead of treating the memo as the product of an overactive im-
agination, Allen enlisted the help of George Taylor of the Far East
Institute to put together a reply, which dealt with two of the major
issues that would shortly confront the United States: the "loss" of
China and the Russian atomic bomb. The attempt to recruit a professor of Russian Literature, said Allen, was meant to demonstrate the
"good faith" of the University of Washington in "opening cultural
relations with the U.S.S.R." after the war. Though the institute had
not expected cooperation from the Kremlin, and none was forthcoming, literature was chosen as the "least dangerous" subject for exchange. The Soviet Press Translations were widely used by newspapers: "Those organs of public education and opinion apparently believe as Universities do in the intelligence and critical capacities of the
American public." In defense of his inaugural guests, Allen noted that
the Soviet consul was the accredited representative of a recognized
nation, and that Condon had not been charged with anything before
May of 1947. While acknowledging that many faculty belonged to the
Institute of Pacific Relations, Allen defended the organization's "fundamental Americanism," pointing out that it did not appear on the
attorney general's list. Concerning the aspersions on his own patriotism, Allen pointed to his cooperation with the Canwell Committee,
"and for this I have been commended by numerous patriotic organizations and individuals. Of the more than 2,000 letters received . . .
10 to 1 [are] in favor of my activities and position." Allen also cited his
clearance to work in "sensitive departments" of the federal government. "I am surprised," he declared, "and not a little shocked. . . ."
Though Allen's resignation was averted by the Board of Regents, one
wonders whether he recognized the degree to which he had encouraged such preoccupation with conspiracy.[27]

Shortly after this, Allen announced that he had been offered the
first directorship of medical services for the military establishment by

Defense Secretary Louis Johnson, and that he intended to seek a year's leave of absence from the University of Washington to accomplish the task of unifying the medical branches of the Army, Navy, and Air Force. Probably due to pressure from the regents, he served in that capacity only from July to October of 1949. The regents had good reasons for wanting Allen at his desk.[28]

The university was undergoing a transition from the period of furious-paced expansion following World War II to one of consolidation of its gains. Enrollment dropped slightly and legislative appropriations were below the previous biennium because of inflation and a recession in the state's major industries. Consequently, wages and salaries were cut, and the student-faculty ratio hovered at eighteen-to-one—all this at the moment the new teaching hospital was trying to get on its feet. Bright spots were unprecedented levels of research support from the federal government ($798,514) and business and industry ($462,100), and increasing national faculty recognition in areas such as health sciences, fisheries, Far East studies, and the physical sciences.[29]

In addition to the material exigencies of university management, increasing pressure for conformity on institutions of higher education required Allen's hand at the helm. In March, two nontenured Oregon State College professors had been dismissed for their Progressive party activities, and the University of Washington faculty was still upset about the January decisions. In June HUAC Chairman John Wood, responding to pressure from the Sons of the American Revolution for an investigation of college textbooks, sent questionnaires to a sample of institutions. Since the state legislature had refused Canwell's recommendations for a similar investigation, Dean Guthrie replied, "In this university, our policy is to exercise the choice of instructors and to leave to these specialists the matter of choice of textbooks and reading." After appropriate apologies, Wood withdrew the investigation, and Republicans blamed Democrats for the national furor.[30]

The war scare, which had begun in April, 1948, with the Berlin Blockade, had resulted in the formation of NATO and the institution of the peacetime draft. In August, 1949, the State Department issued its White Paper on American policy in China, and in September the Soviets exploded their first nuclear device. Red-baiting of the Truman administration worsened after eleven CPUSA members were convicted of conspiracy to overthrow the government. Therefore, the president's attorney general, J. Howard McGrath, escalated the climate of fear by traversing the nation with warnings of the subtle subversion of students' minds. Emphasizing the need to promote anti-Communist books and speakers on campuses, he spoke of Communists "everywhere—in factories, offices, butcher shops, on street corners, in private businesses—and each carries in himself the germs of death for society."[31]

In such an atmosphere, citizens upon whom rested the merest suspicion, even though they had never been Communists, were hard put to defend their right to speak and freely to earn a livelihood. Melvin Rader is a good example of this. After the Philosophy professor was accused by a Canwell witness of attending a secret New York Communist school in 1938, Rader began the painstaking fifteen-month task of reconstructing long-past events to prove his innocence. In his book, *False Witness*, he recounts the difficulties involved in getting anyone to help him: state authorities, a judge in New York, and much of the local press presumed him guilty. Even President Allen, so proud that "honest liberals" had not been smeared at the university, revealed his bias. To A. C. Jacobs, Columbia's provost, Allen expressed approval of the decision to deny a teaching exchange agreement between Rader and Herbert Schneider: "Our friend here is going to be in trouble before long, trouble of his own making." The tone of Allen's letter was somewhat less encouraging than his statements to Rader had been.[32]

By May, 1949, when it became clear that neither the Canwell Committee nor the courts would exonerate Rader, the *Seattle Times* assigned reporter Ed Guthman to investigate the case. Using the information Rader supplied him, Guthman proved that Canwell investigators had tampered with a key piece of evidence—a hotel register—which disproved the testimony of the only witness who had accused Rader of being a Communist. After examining this evidence in October, 1949, Allen issued a statement declaring himself convinced that the charges against Rader were false. Though, as Rader later wrote, "misrepresentation and blind prejudice had been defeated by fair play and a free press," his vindication was not accepted by everyone. In ensuing years he would often be confronted with the same old charges and suspicion. As the Cold War grew more bitter, more and more citizens were called to account for their actions in a previous decade.[33]

The Controversy over Malcolm Cowley

Meanwhile, events had been put in motion that would further test the compromise the university had struck with its critics. In November of 1948 Robert Heilman, chairman of the English Department, wrote to Malcolm Cowley, a literary critic and expert on twentieth-century American literature, asking him to consider a Walker-Ames Lectureship at the university. In his reply Cowley expressed interest for winter quarter, 1950, but warned Heilman that his political past might pose difficulties in light of current events nationally and at the University of Washington: "If the legislative committee is still at work on your faculty next year, they might call me up as one who belonged to various left-front organizations before 1939 including one (League of American Writers) which Attorney General Clark has put on his famous list of subversive organizations." The former editor of the *New Republic* went on to say that he had resigned from the organization and political activity in 1940, after the Nazi-Soviet Pact: "I thought I'd tell you all this, because legislative committees have been digging far into the past and taking over a field that properly belongs to Egyptologists." Heilman, who had only recently come to the University of Washington, thanked Cowley for his candor and told him that though no one had raised the issue of his "past" in the department, "someone higher up might, but I doubt it." [34]

Having gotten Cowley's commitment for 1950, Heilman moved to clear the appointment with the Walker-Ames Committee, a faculty body responsible for approving the allocation of funds from the endowment. In his recommendation to the chairman of the committee, Heilman recorded Cowley's scholarly achievements, and included Cowley's own assessment of his "political qualifications." Like Heilman, the Walker-Ames Committee apparently considered the latter irrelevant, for they approved the nomination and sent it on to the president. On May 13, 1949, the regents supported Allen's recommendation of Cowley over the objection of Regent George Stuntz, who warned the president that "he is not the type we need at the University." Though Stuntz later moved to rescind Cowley's appointment, the regents upheld their decision. [35]

The regents' support of Allen's recommendation is interesting in light of later controversies over similar temporary appointments. Perhaps Allen convinced the regents that the appointment would demonstrate to the faculty and concerned citizens that liberals like Cowley would be heard at the university. Cowley was not a Communist, and his appointment was a test of the recent compromise. But it should also be remembered that at the May 13 regents' meeting Allen had threatened to resign unless cleared of the auditor's allegations that the president allowed the faculty to participate in pro-Communist activities. If the regents had withdrawn support from Allen's recommendation, they would have demonstrated their lack of confidence in his judgment as well as that of Heilman. In addition, the English Department, which had suffered heavily in the recent investigations, needed the positive support of the regents to attract top scholars. Whether any of these calculations entered the discussion on Cowley is not known, but they might explain why the regents held fast during the ensuing storm.

In June of 1949, Cowley appeared as a witness for Alger Hiss at his first trial for perjury. Since his testimony alleged that Whittaker Chambers was a paranoid, conspiratorial type out to "expose" his former real or imagined comrades from the 1930s, Cowley himself came under attack from the legions who had been won over by Chambers. When the first trial ended in a hung jury, and it became apparent that Cowley would be testifying again at the re-trial, he wrote to Heilman with an offer to withdraw from the lectureship, saying he wanted to study literature with a class, not argue about the politics of ten years ago. To clear up any misconceptions, Cowley laid out his past to Heilman and asked that the letter be shown to the administration. While he had voted for William Z. Foster in 1932 and had registered as a Communist in 1934 and 1936, he denied ever joining the party. Distressed by the tactics of Hitler and Franco, he had admired the Russian stance toward them, but disavowed politics altogether after the Pact. He noted that his public resignation from the League of American Writers was recorded in the July, 1940, issue of the *New Republic*, and that he had not since engaged in politics. A self-styled "social conservative," Cowley said he believed in private enterprise and freedom of the press, abhorred the Russian policy toward the arts, but held no opinion whatsoever on Russian or American foreign policy.[36]

All during December, Allen and the regents received letters of protest from groups objecting to Cowley's impending appearance on the campus. Pro-America, a national organization of Republican women dedicated to the protection of churches, schools, and the government from Communism and Socialism, expressed concern over the "marked trend to the left in the outside talent brought to your university. . . ." Singer Burl Ives and Margaret Cole of Britain's Labor government were singled out in addition to Cowley, who was reputed to be an undercover member of fifty un-American groups. The Daughters of the American Revolution, the American Legion, VFW, and various PTA groups joined in the rising chorus against Cowley's appointment. Regent Stuntz declared himself against Cowley's "awful" poetry, but particularly "his association with Communist front organizations." A member of the state's legislature, who was also on the House Appropriations Committee, wanted to know why "another lecturer who more truly represents the ideals of our country could not have been selected." Allen assured him that Cowley had arrived at his opinions freely, and therefore had a right to be heard. A representative on the House Judiciary Committee commended Allen for his stand, contending that most people agreed with it. He likened the reaction to Cowley's appointment to the uproar over Harold Laski ten years before. Allen reminded one and all that his attitude on Communism was a matter of public record.[37]

In an effort to clear the air, Cowley issued a statement about his past politics, which appeared in the Seattle press on December 23, along with a statement from Allen affirming his belief that Cowley was not a Communist. However, university support of Cowley was berated by *Times* columnist Ross Cunningham, who wrote that the appointment was like "rubbing salt in a healing wound." The admirable January dismissals had apparently set no policy, he wrote, since once again there was evidence that "pinks and reds receive more than ordinary consideration at the University of Washington." Heilman protested that Cunningham was distorting the facts of Cowley's life by measuring them against current attitudes and ignoring his competence as a literary critic. Confident that the general public would recognize the "real truth," Heilman cited Cowley's criticism of the suppression of the arts in Russia, and his denunciation of the American Writers League in 1940 for following the Communist line. Allen issued a similar reprise, and together with Heilman discussed the situation with the American Legion. Heilman convinced them that Cowley had written his single volume of poetry as a youth, and that he was not being brought to the university to teach poetry anyway. The offensive strategy paid off; the "Americanism Commission" of the Legion agreed not to protest his appointment further. In its report to the chairman, however, the subcommittee wrote: "the general publicity which has accompanied the questioning of Mr. Crowley's [sic] employment has been such that the Board of Regents and responsible officers of the University will be most active in the future in acquainting themselves with the background of those employed," and vowed to continue its "vigilance" to assure such a result.[38]

Cowley arrived in January, told the press that he agreed with President Allen that Communists should not be allowed to teach in public schools, and voiced his disapproval of the mistaken notions of people "that think they must fight Communism with Communist methods." Cowley's winter quarter stay was happily placid; one of Heilman's favorite memories was of Cowley and the commander of the American Legion trading stories at a cocktail party. However, as will be shown later, the Legion was undaunted in its "vigilance" concerning the university, and its battle against subversion. For its part, the university became more wary, more perspicacious during the fifties.[39]

The University during Allen's Final Two Years

A subtle, creeping paralysis of freedom of thought and speech is attacking college campuses . . . limiting both students and faculty in the area traditionally reserved for the free exploration of knowledge and truth.
   —*New York Times*, May 11, 1951

The fifties began auspiciously for Allen and the University of Washington. In December, 1949, the Association of American Universities announced the election of the University of Washington to its ranks. Since the days of Henry Suzzallo, the university had been pursuing this honor; membership was a signal recognition of excellence in teaching and research at the graduate level. At last the university ranked on a par with other prestigious members of "the club"; on the West Coast only Stanford, the University of California, and the California Institute of Technology had been so feted. In January, 1950, Raymond B. Allen was chosen "First Citizen of Seattle for 1949" by the Real Estate Board. But the University of Washington, like higher education elsewhere, was on the defensive for the rest of Allen's tenure due to two interrelated factors: the economy and foreign affairs.[40]

The inflation throughout the American economy occasioned by the Korean conflict wiped out the gains of a slight June, 1950, salary increase for University of Washington faculty, and placed the institution at a disadvantage in competition for personnel. As the mobilization for war stepped up, the student population dropped, and current and prospective faculty found that other universities, government, and industry paid much higher salaries for their talent than the University of Washington. The military obligations of faculty members, especially in the health and physical sciences, exacerbated the situation.[41]

In November, 1950, state voters rejected Referendum 90, which would have set aside money for the University of Washington hospital, and the legislative appropriation for 1951 fell two million dollars short of what the university asked. Administrators and faculty members met to exchange ideas about what had caused the "disaster." The catalogue of reasons they came up with for voter "hostility" to the university is revealing: an unfavorable coalition of Republicans and Democrats in the senate; favoritism toward Washington State College; the university was seen as a "King County school"; the new medical school was variously seen as a move toward socialized medicine by some, and an AMA plot by others; the university's buildings and lands made it appear wealthy; too much research and not enough teaching. These findings were confirmed by a survey conducted in September, 1950, which also showed the university's image was that it served the wealthy, radical, sports-minded minority. The regents came up with a reason of their own: "Welfare programs in the State of Washington in the past four (4) years so disrupted the State finances that the program of capital construction has had to be delayed." [42]

Over the protests of the faculty, the board moved to eliminate 320 positions in the lower ranks of the faculty and staff, and curtailed university-sponsored research and nonacademic services. As a result, the Faculty Senate reported, the University of Washington fell behind comparable institutions such as California, Michigan, Wisconsin, and Minnesota in competition for faculty members due to lower salaries, a deteriorating library, and other faculty support deficiencies. [43]

Besides cutting back on expenditures, the coalition of Democrats and Republicans in the 1951 legislature demonstrated its conservatism by renewing its interest in un-American activities legislation. Shortly after succeeding Democrat Mon Wallgren to the governor's office in 1949, Republican Arthur Langlie had urged continuation of the legislative committee that had been chaired by Canwell, but the bill died in conference after some criticism of the tactics and methods of the 1947–48 Interim Committee. In 1951, however, the Korean War and the deepening fear of domestic subversion caused Governor Langlie to propose again the means to assure unity and to keep criticism down so as to "clear the decks for action," in the event of a national emergency such as World War III, which he considered to be "perilously close." [44]

Accordingly, the legislature enacted the Subversive Activities Act, modeled on Maryland's Ober Act, which made it a crime to be a member of an organization listed as subversive by the U.S. attorney general (Senate Bill 379). It also considered House Bill 305, introduced by former Canwell Committee member Grant Sisson, which would have created a new fact-finding committee to investigate persons and groups with Communist membership. Said Sisson, "We haven't finished the job at the University of Washington and we still have Commies teaching there, and we want to finish the job." House Bill 305 died in conference, as had its 1949 predecessor, but not before

University of Washington *Daily* editor Leonard Saari lost his position.[45]

Len Saari, a senior in Journalism, became editor of the *Daily* on February 2, 1951, after being elected by his fellow journalism students. Beginning on February 6, Saari wrote a series of articles and editorials questioning the merits of both Senate Bill 379 and House Bill 305. He successfully urged the Student Organizations Assembly to pass a resolution calling on the legislature to reject the bills as "invasions of civil liberties." He reminded readers that Grant Sisson was one of those "anxious little men" who had "tried to crucify [Melvin] Rader. They virtually suppressed evidence to do it."[46]

Saari was dismissed by the faculty of the School of Journalism on March 6 for "neglect of editorial duties," and for promoting the views of only a small segment of the campus. H. P. Everest, director of the school, denied that the action was occasioned by outside pressures. Saari's lack of "constructive" activity was an "embarrassment" to the school, he said. "Faculty censorship was not an issue. We dismissed Saari, feeling it was useless to ask him to resign."[47]

In subsequent days, Legislators Ed Henry (attorney for Eby, Ethel, and Jacobs), A. R. Paulsen, and David Roderick announced that they would conduct an inquiry into "thought control" at the university, and would call Allen and Everest to testify before the House Education Committee. There, Everest told legislators that he and Allen were within their rights. Saari protested that he had never been warned that he might lose his job. That Everest was a Republican and Saari a Young Democrat was also a factor, noted Saari. Allen and Everest called attention to Saari's poor judgment in other editorial affairs. Though the Seattle-King County chapter of Americans for Democratic Action and the ACLU urged further investigation of the incident, the matter faded from public concern.[48]

Saari's determination was further tested when he was asked by Everest and Allen to recant his editorials in return for reinstatement as associate editor of the *Daily*. He refused. He reminded the president that his own position was analogous to Allen's on the Institute of Pacific Relations. He told Allen of his fear of being blacklisted from a career as a journalist and asked how the president's actions squared with his statements that a goal of the university was to prepare students for positions in society.[49]

Meanwhile, a group of concerned students appointed a committee of seven to conduct an investigation of Saari's dismissal. Members of this Independent Students' Committee included Andrew Brimmer (who eventually served on the Federal Reserve Board), Thomas Foley (current Chairman of the House Committee on Agriculture), and Byron Coney (later active in other campus civil liberties actions, currently a Seattle attorney). On June 15, 1951, the committee delivered its findings and recommendations to President Allen: "Leonard Saari should be reinstated as editor of the *Daily*. The reasons for his dismissal, as given, were insufficient to warrant the action." The committee also urged a thorough investigation of the incident and establishment of safeguards to ensure the freedom of future *Daily* editors to express themselves "without qualification." The report was not released to the public until August, 1951, when "it made a three-paragraph ripple in the back pages of the *Seattle Times*." By then, Saari was already at work as a reporter for the *Aberdeen World*, a position he believes President Allen helped him attain.[50]

While Allen's role in the Saari affair seems to have been that of a president upholding a decision of faculty members, it also illustrates the compromises he had learned to make with a suspicious legislature. On the other hand, Allen showed himself willing to do battle for his faculty in the national arena, where he had won a reputation for being both an anti-Communist and a "scrupulous believer in a fair trial for those accused." In April of 1950 Allen, who had defended the crass tactics of Al Canwell, rebuked Senator Joseph McCarthy's "circus performance for partisan political purposes."[51]

What prompted Allen was the senator's attack on the Institute of Pacific Relations (IPR), an organization of "men of affairs"—businessmen and scholars—interested in promoting trade with and the study of Pacific nations and cultures. Because of Seattle's ties with the Pacific, leading Northwest citizens had formed a local chapter of the organization in 1929. This town-gown group faded somewhat during the war. But Professors Charles E. Martin and George Taylor had gotten Allen to help solicit new support, and by 1948 Regents Dave Beck and Thomas Balmer, Attorney Herbert Little, and other influential businessmen and faculty members were contributors. Allen became a member of the national Board of Trustees, and director of the Northwest Division. Alger Hiss was also on the board when the IPR became embroiled in the China controversy. Along with certain "China hands" in the State Department, IPR leaders Phillip Jessup and Owen Lattimore were accused by McCarthy of supporting the Maoists. Allen's attitudes toward the IPR's problems was typical; he wrote to the president of the Rockefeller Foundation, a financial backer of the IPR and of the university's Far Eastern Institute: "The poor old IPR is getting quite a kicking around, and considering phases of the history of the organization this is perhaps to be expected. It will

be too bad if it caves in now under fire, just as it would have been too
bad if the University of Washington had caved in because we har-
bored a few termites up until last year."[52]

Though the Northwest IPR had been critical of the national group
headed by Lattimore for some years, the loyalty of Professors George
Taylor and Karl Wittfogel of the university's Far Eastern Institute was
impugned by several local groups. There were, of course, some ker-
nels of truth behind the allegations. Taylor had succeeded Lattimore
as deputy director of the Office of War Information during the war,
and certain OWI documents had turned up in the offices of
AMERASIA, the house organ of the IPR. Wittfogel had been a member
of the Communist party from 1920 to 1939, but had escaped to the
United States from a Nazi prison camp to warn the world of all forms
of totalitarianism. Both these men eventually testified before the
McCarran Committee which investigated the IPR in 1951–52. Both
disputed Lattimore's view of Mao as an "agrarian reformer." They
were heavily criticized, however, and Wittfogel volunteered to resign
from the university, but Allen stood by them. The Northwest IPR
dissolved in 1950 and became part of the World Affairs Council.
When attacks on the university continued, the regents severed all
connections between it and the university.[53]

Allen's willingness to defend faculty members in this case stands in
constrast to his actions in 1948–49. The press of events was different,
as were the personalities involved. Taylor was a valued member of the
faculty and a friend of Allen and many in the business community.
Taylor's State Department security clearance was never affected; in
1950 he was offered the Psychological Strategy Board position which
Allen later filled. Though Wittfogel had been a member of the Communist party and involved in political activities, he was not placed "on
probation" as were Eby, Ethel, and Jacobs. Taylor and Wittfogel were
on the "correct" side of the Cold War, as Phillips and Butterworth
were not. The exhortation to "dispassionate objectivity" which Allen
had so firmly urged in his inaugural address was largely forgotten.

The Cold War eventually drew President Allen away from the University of Washington. In May, 1951, Allen removed his name from
consideration as the successor to Alexander Ruthven, president of the
University of Michigan. After serving as chairman of the Salary
Stabilization Board during the summer, he declined the position of
head of the Economic Stabilization Program. But on November 22 the
president suddenly resigned to coordinate the information efforts of
the Departments of State and Defense and the CIA as chairman of the

Psychological Strategy Board. Though the University of Washington *Record* pronounced the university community "shocked" at the announcement, many people had realized that Allen was a restless man searching for a new niche for his abilities. When he came to the university, Allen had spoken of the need to create conditions for world peace. Like many Americans, his hopes were frustrated by the Cold War; his work with the Eberstadt Committee on National Security and other government positions helped shape the direction of his ambition. In his "On Leaving the University" statement, Allen enunciated his determination to "help win the war on the psychological, political, and economic fronts," and to prevent World War III through positive action.[54]

Allen was an academic whose philosophy of administration reflected his own energy, optimism, and self confidence. He saw himself as an integrator shaping policy, supporting the advice of the Faculty Senate, encouraging faculty participation in the selection of deans and department chairmen, and expanding programs to meet postwar needs. Yet Allen's abilities were best suited to a period of expansion. When legislative cutbacks curtailed the hiring of the best faculty, the building of the hospital, and the innovative spirit Allen had fostered among faculty members, he moved on.[55]

In December he accepted the election of the University of California regents to the first chancellorship of the Los Angeles campus. Allen told a *Daily* reporter that he was eager to meet the challenge and to work with President Sproul. He expressed his belief that he had given all he had to offer to the University of Washington in areas of organization and personnel administration. At the last meeting of the senate attended by Allen, J. B. Harrison (English), who had bitterly opposed him on matters of academic freedom, introduced a resolution of "faculty satisfaction" with the president; it received a standing ovation. The *Seattle Times* pronounced the Allen years the "Most Progressive in University History," during which had occurred "a veritable renaissance of research in the arts, the sciences, and technology." Noting that Californians had expressed misgivings on Allen's ability to handle the chancellorship, the *Times* assured any doubters that they were receiving a man of talent and a man whose national stature rested on his handling of the tenure cases and of federal government positions. But *Time* magazine detected only mild regrets among the regents, one of whom said: "Allen is one hell of a good man, but my God, he is never here." A year later, after Allen had taken up his duties at UCLA, the *Daily Bruin*, citing his eloquence in defending the

"Allen formula" of academic freedom and in opposition to subversion, pronounced him "The Obvious Choice" of the California regents.[56]

When Allen left the University of Washington, two years had passed since the controversial rulings on Communist party membership. The probationary period for Eby, Ethel, and Jacobs was almost over, but the impact of the hearings was felt by each in the years to come. Before Canwell, Eby had been a member of the Faculty Senate, active on its committees. Afterwards such activities ceased; he was avoided by most of his old friends on and off campus. He felt the need to be evasive with persons who asked his opinion about political or social issues. Both he and Ethel mentioned that they were never sure they did their students a favor by writing recommendations for them, especially if they were seeking jobs locally or with the government.[57]

Since Eby was already a full professor, he was not sure if probation affected his salary, but Ethel told of being kept at the lowest scale for assistant professors until he became an associate professor through the intercession of friends on the College Council. Ethel remains convinced of the validity of his Marxist views and is bitter about Allen's claims to protection of the intellectual integrity of the faculty. Ethel likens probation to the position of Russian intellectuals after 1905: "Lenin told Gorky to quit trying to be a politician and to go on writing novels . . . if I was going to make a living here in the U.S., I had to shut up—that was the price of the job. I didn't think I could accomplish any wonders by making a couple of speeches when I couldn't even pay for my next meal." Campus friends of thirty years seemed afraid to be seen speaking to him, he said, and new members of the faculty soon learned to avoid him.[58]

Melville Jacobs remained especially bitter about the fact that Allen singled him out for lying, when he had done the same thing as Eby on the advice of attorney. Always an active scholar, Jacobs told how he could not concentrate enough to write during his probationary years, and his anger intensified because he received no raises or promotions. Finally, he forced himself to eat daily at the faculty club and eventually found a good deal of reward in the form of faculty support. Throughout the remainder of his teaching years he would not sign anything even remotely political.[59]

None of the three dismissed faculty ever got jobs in higher education again. Butterworth wrote to two thousand members of the Modern Language Association, but though there was a demand for Old English specialists in the 1950s, he never got an offer. Without severance pay from the University, he subsisted on odd jobs and eventually went on public assistance. Phillips spent the year after his dismissal traveling to colleges and universities around the country trying to rally suppo.t for the cause of Communist party faculty members and looking for jobs. Though the Pacific Division of the American Philosophical Association expressed confidence in his competence and he had many influential friends such as Herbert Schneider and Ashley Montague, he never received any job offers. His debate with Merritt Benson at UCLA in 1949 was one of the catalysts that precipitated the loyalty oath controversy in that system, and as he later bitterly said, "That was no way to get a job." After a period of years as a building laborer, and several legal battles in the 1950s, Phillips retired in San Francisco, where he remembered his twenty-nine years as an admired teacher of philosophy as "a nice job."[60]

For his "uncooperative" stance toward the Canwell Committee in 1948, Ralph Gundlach was convicted of contempt of legislative committee, fined $250, and sentenced to thirty days in jail, which he served in June, 1949. After selling their Seattle home "at cut price," he and his wife Bonnie Bird settled in New York, where she taught dance. Gundlach was accepted as a trainee by the Postgraduate Center for Mental Health, achieved the status of diplomate in Clinical Psychology, and did individual, group, and family therapy. He had published extensively in psychological journals. He had also continued to work for what he termed "lost causes." In 1952 he and fellow social psychologists filed an *amicus curiae* on pre-trial publicity with the Supreme Court in the Julius and Ethel Rosenberg appeal. In the period following his dismissal, Gundlach received strong support from his colleagues in the Society for the Psychological Study of Social Issues, the Consumers Union, and the American Psychological Association. Such support was forthcoming because he had denied any Communist party membership, and because his case was perceived as a deliberate provocation to American leftists. Though Gundlach expressed some dismay over the lack of protest from his colleagues in the University of Washington Psychology Department, he realized that the only way he could vindicate himself was to discredit Dean Guthrie, who he felt was chiefly responsible for his dismissal. Consequently, he and Colston Warne, his friend from Amherst, prodded the AAUP for a speedy investigation of the University of Washington dismissals.[61]

The Report of Committee A for 1948, however, implied that such action would not only be slow, but doubtful. On one hand, the committee affirmed its support for Communist party faculty who had not been deceitful; on the other, the group cited the need for "judicious consideration of the facts," especially since two committee members objected to "a general pronouncement on the issue of communism at this time." One member of Committee A who made his views known was a former member of the University of Washington faculty, Ralph Lutz. The Stanford historian said that he would vote to throw out Communist professors on the grounds that they were propagandists, not free agents in teaching. Though he admitted to Charles Martin that his remarks could be construed as prejudgment of the Oregon and Washington cases, he did not remove himself from Committee A.[62]

In its 1949 report, Committee A indicated that it was still considering the facts, but Colston Warne wrote Gundlach that Himstead was worried about rumors that Sidney Hook and his faction intended to propose a "resolution to prejudge the Washington cases" at the 1950 AAUP convention. Later, in a letter to Gundlach's wife, Warne reported that the March 25–26 Cleveland convention had been "militant." Since Hook was absent, a resolution by St. Johns University to eliminate all Communists from college and university faculties received no support, he said. In addition, W. T. Laprade of Committee A had told the assembly, "We wish to make the University of Washington case a landmark of the association," and promised a report by summer. Warne wrote that he had talked with G. P. Shannon, E. C. Kirkland, and Laprade and found out that the report would "condemn the University of Washington for the discharge of Butterworth and Phillips," and would have "harsh things to say about the 'probationary arrangement.'" He also told Mrs. Gundlach that the committee would "probably uphold Ralph" because "they are aware that no charges were brought against him in the complaint on grounds of his teaching." But Warne also cautioned that Gundlach's dismissal might be upheld to "demonstrate the fairness of the appraisal."[63]

Though it is obvious from Warne's letter that a report had been drafted by the spring of 1950, several questions arise. Why was no formal investigation on the University of Washington campus mounted by the AAUP according to their standard practice? Himstead told Warne that he had talked with Allen and wanted to talk with the complainants, but that never happened; was the draft report written only on the basis of the hearing transcript and what Allen said to Himstead? Gundlach later reported that Himstead told him in September, 1952, that the report would appear in "3 months" and that the delay was caused by the "general climate which was adverse to

academic freedom and made a strong statement inadvisable."
Himstead's statement, of course, reflected the deep division within the
academic community over Communist faculty members. The University of Washington cases met that issue directly; Allen and the regents
had finessed the AAUP. The report was issued only after Ralph
Himstead's death in 1955, along with the reports on other institutions
that had undergone Cold War-related difficulties since 1948. Though
it indicated that the actions of the University of Washington administration were censurable at the time, it called for no redress of grievances such as reinstatement of Gundlach, Phillips, and Butterworth,
because Allen and the responsible regents were no longer in charge of
the university.[64]

What would have happened had the AAUP firmly upheld its 1947
statement with an immediate investigation will never be clear. What is
clear is that an organization preeminently qualified to articulate the
role of academic freedom and tenure in a period of crisis failed to
assert its principles. Its silence lent credence to the Allen formula. By
stepping aside, the AAUP became victim and aggravator of the "subtle,
creeping paralysis of freedom of thought and speech" which spread
through higher education in the 1950s. In the years after President
Allen left the University of Washington, a minority of its faculty
would work to restore the integrity and reputation of the university
which they deemed damaged by the 1949 decisions.

V

Retrenchment or Reaction?

The Schmitz Administration, 1952–54

The University of Washington should value sensible speech at least as highly as freedom of speech. I do not believe in academic freedom in a vacuum.
—Henry Schmitz, Inaugural Address, October 3, 1952

Within two weeks of Dr. Raymond Allen's resignation, the regents' actions indicated that they had already chosen his successor. On December 2, 1951, they discussed the University of Washington presidency with Henry Schmitz, 1915 graduate of the university and scion of a pioneer Seattle family. Schmitz's career in forestry had led to prominence at the University of Minnesota. In his position there as dean of Forestry, Agriculture, Home Economics, and Veterinary Medicine, he built a reputation as a capable administrator and spokesman for the university before the Minnesota legislature. Schmitz was well known among the Washington regents. In 1946 he was, with Allen, a prime candidate to succeed President Lee Paul Sieg. But for the emerging medical school, he would probably have been chosen then. Popular among University of Washington alumni, he was elected "Alumnus Summa Laude Dignatus" in 1949. Schmitz was also a familiar figure to Seattle's business community. His brother Dietrich was a prominent banker and member of the Seattle School Board. Though Allen noted some hesitancy among the faculty, he thought Schmitz was "a good choice" and believed "the climate is quite good for him." At a time when the university's belt was being tightened by inflation and the legislature, Schmitz's qualifications as a mature and responsible academic administrator made him a natural selection to succeed the more peripatetic Allen.[1]

The regents, however, were sensitive to the idea that the faculty should have voice in the selection of their chief executive officer, and appointed a liaison committee consisting of Deans H. P. Everest (Journalism), Lloyd Woodburne (Arts and Sciences), and Harold Wessman (Engineering) to solicit faculty views on presidential candi-

President Emeritus Lee Paul Sieg (left) and Governor Mon C. Wallgren. Photograph by Cliff McNair, courtesy of the Photography Collection, Suzzallo Library, University of Washington

University of Washington *Daily*, March 2, 1948. Student cartoonist Wing Luke later was elected to the Seattle City Council.

Canwell Committee hearing, 1948. Back, left to right: Sen. R. L. Rutter; Rep. Sydney Stevens; Sen. Thomas Bienz; Rep. Al Canwell; Rep. Grant Sisson; Sen. H. Kimball. Testifying in the foreground is Louis Budenz. Courtesy of the *Seattle Post-Intelligencer*

University of Washington regents and President Allen at the final hearing on Communists at the university, January 22, 1949. Rear, left to right: Dave Beck; Winlock Miller; Clarence Coleman; George Stuntz. Front: Thomas Balmer; Joseph Drumheller; Allen; John King. Courtesy of the *Seattle Post-Intelligencer*

Left: Professor Herbert Phillips; *right:* Professor Joseph Butterworth. Courtesy of the *Seattle Post-Intelligencer*

Regents' hearing, January 22, 1949. From left: Professor Ralph Gundlach; attorney John Caughlan; Clayton van Lydegraf. Courtesy of the *Seattle Post-Intelligencer*

Left: Professor Harold Eby; *center:* Professor Garland Ethel; *right:* Professor Melville Jacobs. Courtesy of the *Seattle Post-Intelligencer*

Former Rep. Al Canwell, President Allen, and Professor Melvin Rader discuss evidence which disproved charges that Rader was a member of the Communist party. Courtesy of the *Seattle Times*

Professor Robert B. Heilman. Photograph by James O. Sneddon, courtesy of the office of Information Services, University of Washington

Laying the cornerstone of the University of Washington Health Sciences building. Left to right: Governor Arthur Langlie; President Allen; Dean of Nursing Elizabeth Soule; Dean of Pharmacy Forest Goodrich; Dean of Medicine Edward Turner. Photograph by James O. Sneddon, courtesy of the Photography Collection, Suzzallo Library, University of Washington

Top: Vice-President H. P. Everest; *bottom:* Donald K. Anderson; *right:* President Henry Schmitz. Photographs by James O. Sneddon, courtesy of the Office of Information Services, University of Washington

University of Washington Board of Regents, 1953–57. *Rear*, left to right: Grant Armstrong; Thomas Balmer; Donald Corbett; Winlock Miller. *Front:* Charles Harris; Charles Frankland; Mrs. Herbert Gardner. Photograph by James O. Sneddon, courtesy of the Office of Information Services, University of Washington

Above: Professor Abraham Keller testifying before the House Committee on Un-American Activities during the hearings on Communism in the Pacific Northwest, held in Seattle in 1954. Courtesy of the *Seattle Times.* *Above, right:* Professor Edwin Uehling. Photograph by James O. Sneddon, courtesy of the Office of Information Services, University of Washington. *Right:* J. Robert Oppenheimer learns of Albert Einstein's death, April 18, 1955, during a stopover at Seattle-Tacoma International Airport. Courtesy of the *Seattle Post-Intelligencer*

President John Kennedy and President Charles Odegaard at the convocation celebrating the university's centennial, November, 1961. Photograph by James O. Sneddon, courtesy of the Photography Collection, Suzzallo Library, University of Washington

Below: Professor W. Stull Holt. Photograph by James O. Sneddon, courtesy of the Office of Information Services, University of Washington

Professor Giovanni Costigan. Photograph by James O. Sneddon, courtesy of the University of Washington *Daily*

Left: Professor Howard Nostrand; *below, left:* Professor Max Savelle; *below, right:* Professor Arval Morris. Photographs by James O. Sneddon, courtesy of the Office of Information Services, University of Washington

dates. The Faculty Senate, in turn, suggested that the regents appoint an interim president to allow time "to canvass all promising candidates." The regents concurred; accepting the advice of the deans, they named Everest acting president and chairman of the special Executive Committee consisting of Deans Gordon Marckworth (Forestry), Edward Turner (Medical School), Wessman, and Woodburne. This group managed university affairs for the next seven months. Meanwhile, the Presidential Search Committee reached an early decision on a successor to Allen. On March 16, 1952, Henry Schmitz was named twenty-second president of the University of Washington, and H. P. Everest was named vice-president for financial affairs.[2]

Everest's vice-presidency was only the second position like it in the history of the university (Professor David Thomson had been academic vice-president under Acting President Hugo Winkenwerder, 1933–34). The creation of a vice-presidency represented both the regents' acknowledgment of the growing complexity of university affairs and their satisfaction with Everest's administrative accomplishments as acting president. Everest brought a unique background to his position. Because of his work as administrative assistant to Governor Langlie in 1944 and 1949, he was politically acceptable and familiar with the workings of the legislature. As past president of the Washington Newspaper Association, he knew and was known by editors across the state. His work on faculty committees involved with athletics and public relations lent him familiarity with alumni. His involvement with local banking and investment firms gave him experience with the local business community. A former district commander of the American Legion and member of two prestigious local clubs, the Washington Athletic Club and the Rainier Club, he was on good terms with groups usually critical of the university. In the months before Schmitz took office on July 16, Everest did much to shape the course of events to come.[3]

The most important task facing Everest and the Executive Committee was to close the gap between university salary scales and those of competing institutions. As discussed at the end of the last chapter, Allen had already eliminated three hundred faculty and staff positions in the wake of the 1951 legislative cutbacks. Now further reductions in expenditures were achieved by reducing community services and university-funded research. Nonteaching positions in interdisciplinary bureaus of Business, Economics, Sociology, Engineering, and Arts and Sciences were also cut back. In combination with an appropriation from Governor Langlie's Emergency Fund, these retrenchments resulted in a general salary increase. By March, Everest was receiving kudos from legislators. When one suggested that he become the permanent tenant of the president's office, Everest professed no interest.[4]

But if legislators were happy with Everest's surgical skills, many on campus were not so enamored of the prospect of a bare-bones budget. Though there was consensus on the need for salary increases, there was disagreement on where the money should come from. Some felt that Everest's budget request for 1953–55 was inadequate, others that certain areas were paying a bigger price than others. Dean Lloyd Woodburne, who came to the university during the halcyon Allen days, protested the Arts and Sciences budget: "I regret very much that the University officials seem to feel that the needs of the College, and perhaps of the whole upper campus, are not more urgent than is represented by the general decisions of this biennial request."[5] Thus, Woodburne gave expression to old faculty fears about the Medical School siphoning funds from older "upper campus" enterprises. Retrenchment was the dominant mood of the university during the first years of the Schmitz administration, and the resulting tensions lent impetus to the academic freedom issues of the early 1950s.

Caution in the appointment of faculty and guest lecturers on the part of the University of Washington administration, which increased after 1951, was not solely due to fears of legislative retaliation via the budget. The 1951 legislature demonstrated its continuing concern for the loyalty of public employees by requiring signed statements from faculty that they were not "subversive persons." It also directed that administrative procedures be set up to determine in advance whether prospective employees were members of organizations advocating alteration of the constitutional form of government. This legislative action followed Truman's revision of his 1947 Loyalty Order which stiffened the test of loyalty for federal employees by excluding them if there was "reasonable doubt" about their loyalty. This had the effect of placing the burden of proof on anyone who appeared to be connected with groups on the notorious "attorney general's list" of subversive organizations and activities. As many persons discovered during the fifties, the burden of their past activities was crushing and difficult to throw off. While it is not entirely clear what procedures were used by the University of Washington administration to insure the "integrity" of prospective appointees, the attorney general's list was part of the process, as is indicated by the incident concerning Harry Elmer Barnes.[6]

Harry Elmer Barnes, a social scientist of some note, was an editor of the *Encyclopedia of the Social Sciences* and a member of the New School of Social Research during its early years. An advocate of James Harvey Robinson's New History, he was attacked during the 1920s for his revisionist position on World War I, and for his views on secular morals, criminology, birth control, and educational reform. In the late 1930s his stand against U.S. entry into World War II drew further opposition, and since the end of the war he had taken a revisionist view of Hitler's National Socialism and Roosevelt's role in the events leading to the war. Politically, he was an ardent supporter of Herbert Hoover and Senator Robert Taft, and was an outspoken critic of Truman's foreign and domestic policy toward Communism.[7]

In March, 1952, Acting President Everest reported to his fellow Executive Committee members that Harry Elmer Barnes had been contacted by the Sociology Department to give lectures on penology. But Everest's "routine check" of such appointments revealed that Barnes either belonged to or had been a member of forty-seven "subversive organizations." The committee unanimously agreed that Barnes's contract should be canceled. Exactly what organizations Everest was referring to is not clear; however, Barnes had been named twelve times by the 1938 House Un-American Activities Committee as a supporter of Communist front groups such as the American Friends of Spanish Democracy, the National Council on Freedom from Censorship (of the ACLU), and the American League for Peace and Democracy, to list a few. As a columnist for the Scripps-Howard newspapers, he was especially supportive of the organizations working for freedom of speech and press in the late 1930s.[8] Other such references to Barnes throughout the forties and fifties bolstered Everest's objections to Barnes's appointment.

George Lundberg, chairman of the Sociology Department, received word of Everest's decision through the office of Professor Vernon Frost of the Committee on Lectures and Concerts. Lundberg agreed to withdraw his invitation to Barnes "out of consideration for the difficult position in which the interim administration finds itself" but demanded to know who objected to Barnes and what "alleged affiliations" were involved. Citing Barnes's record as a scholar and lecturer, as well as the university's policy on Communists, Lundberg was dumbfounded: "The Barnes incident constitutes an abrogation of a policy which the University has recently proclaimed on such matters . . . I should consider it a disservice to the University to permit that policy to be abandoned at the behest of any petty pressure group who may protest . . . I thought the membership list business had been sufficiently discredited by this time as a reliable index of personal views." Lundberg noted that Barnes had been originally invited to Seattle by a "leading industrialist" to speak at the Rainier Club on "un-American activities" and that the audience included Canwell Committee members. "I know," he concluded, "these people will be interested to learn from the University's publicity department that they are promoting Communism by their warm support of Dr. Barnes' ideas and writings."[9]

This incident sufficiently troubled Everest that he investigated the speakers' policy of other universities. President Howard L. Bevis of Ohio State commented that though only "Real Communists" were proscribed, the faculty were "expected" to keep the "interests of the University at heart."[10] However, faculty and administration views of the "best interests of the university" were often divergent, especially since few faculty seemed to realize that a more stringent standard of "acceptability" was being applied to their recommendations. When the Philosophy faculty recommended that Melvin Rader be made acting executive officer, Everest reluctantly approved, under condition that it would not lead to Rader's being made permanent chairman. Everett Nelson, the resigned chairman, objected to this condition as "a violation of elementary principles of justice . . . [and] a blow to the intellectual integrity of a great university. . . ." Since Rader had been cleared of the Canwell charges, and since President Allen had allowed him to be acting executive officer in 1949, noted Nelson, the present hesitancy was baffling.[11]

Taken together, the Barnes and Rader incidents illustrate the unease with which administrators moved in the early fifties. In part this was due to events on the national scene: the Korean War, the rampages of McCarthy and various Congressional investigations, and the verbal battles over foreign policy occasioned by an election year heightened popular awareness of subversives, potential and actual. At the University of Washington it was further caused by Everest's own political inclinations and reluctance to make decisions that might evoke protest from pressure groups who made it their business to watch educational matters. In an era marked by financial constraints and the ambiguities of the 1951 anti-subversive legislation, conformity and caution reduced the incidence of potential friction between legislators and educators.[12]

The Kenneth Burke Incident: Schmitz Sets His Course

Henry Schmitz formally assumed his duties as president of the University of Washington on July 16, 1952. In the five months since his appointment, Schmitz had taken part in guiding some of the projects that were to become hallmarks of his administration: the solicitation of private contributions to the University of Washington's endowment and the clarification of areas of authority within the university. Schmitz's experience as an administrator and legislative lobbyist for the University of Minnesota led him to emphasize efficiency, economy, and responsibility in the face of the financial and ideological strictures of the time. A self-styled "incorrigible optimist," Schmitz believed that orderly administration and the avoidance of extremes evoked the confidence and support of the people. He urged academic responsibility as a prerequisite for academic freedom. The controversies over Professors Joseph Weinberg and Frank Oppenheimer at Minnesota in the late 1940s no doubt alerted him to the difficulties surrounding faculty appointments.[13]

Schmitz's caution in this area is illustrated by his handling of the English Department's recommendation that Kenneth Burke, a noted philosopher of language and literature, be appointed to a Walker-Ames Lectureship. In April, 1952, the Burke appointment was approved by the graduate faculty committee and sent to the president's office. There, Donald Anderson, director of university relations, began a routine perusal of Burke's political background. He found that in 1937 Sidney Hook had dismissed Burke's *Attitudes Toward History* as "propaganda," a mere vehicle for Burke's "undisguised animus against critics of the Communist Party and Russia." Hook accused Burke of "moral nihilism" and of being an "apologist for Stalin" who was "fearful of letting the authority of party dogma or metaphor meet the authority of the scientific method."[14]

Anderson also found that Burke had been a member of a dozen organizations that appeared on the attorney general's list of subversive organizations, and went to great length in describing each and listing the names of officers involved in the past. Of the League of American Writers for instance, Anderson wrote: "a communist front for the International Union of Revolutionary Writers with headquarters in Moscow, which uses 'art as an instrument in the class struggle.' Others involved: Earl Browder (expelled Communist), M. Cowley, Theodore Dreiser, Langston Hughes (admitted Communist), Richard Wright (admitted former Communist), and Anna Louise Strong." Organizations listed by Anderson also included the American Committee for the Protection of the Foreign Born, and the Book Union. At the end of this six-page dossier, Anderson noted that Burke "undoubtedly knew of the company he was keeping."[15]

The sources Anderson consulted gave no clues, however, concern-

ing Burke's activities and associations after 1940, so he called his
former chief, Raymond Allen, asking him to inquire of Sidney Hook
concerning the author's current situation. In a memo dated June 16,
Anderson reported Allen's telephoned reply: "Sidney Hook reports
that he [Burke] is a mildly confused leftist and fellow travellor [sic]—
was probably gotten into that line by Malcolm Cowley—is a very poor
teacher—very obscure—terribly exaggerated (his ability)—is not
a Communist and has not been active politically recently."[16]

Anderson also contacted Fred Woltman, an editor of the *New York
World Telegram*, concerning Burke's political affiliations. Woltman
could find nothing in clipping files concerning Burke since the
Hitler-Stalin Pact, but in a postscript he reported a conversation with
an editor of the *Partisan Review* who described the author as "mild,
hard to pin down, and terribly confused . . . acts as though he's
trying to get off the hook, but isn't sure he knows how to do it or really
needs to get off the hook . . . since the '30's has had no known
Communist front connections." Burke was further described as "not a
dangerous fellow-traveler, but a screw-ball . . . a great double-talker
and can spin around a subject without touching it."[17]

Acting President Everest, in an effort to discern Burke's current
attitudes, wrote to Burke asking his comments on the nature and
extent of his involvement in the organizations and publications in
question. "They are questions I would prefer not to ask," wrote
Everest, "and I would not do so except that I know it is in the best
interests of all concerned to anticipate them now rather than to have
them raised later by others under less favorable circumstances." Noting that "certain influential friends of the University" would be concerned if Burke were a member of such groups, Everest assured him
that "we have insisted that the fears and tensions of the times not
interfere with the freedoms of those whose minds are free of outside
dictation."[18]

Everest also warned Heilman that the appointment was likely to run
into questions from the Board of Regents unless rebuttal material
could be gathered. Heilman solicited the aid of department members
in reviewing Burke's writings since 1945 to garner evidence that he
was neither a Communist nor a sympathizer. The result of this
"cooperative venture" was a compilation of the literary analyst's efforts on such topics as "Communist Self-Deception," "The Fallacy of
Communism," and "Inconsistency in Russia." Though there was a
strain of Marxism in Burke's philosophy, Heilman suggested, the
body of his writing showed him to be anti-authoritarian and anti-
Communist.[19]

Burke himself drew much the same picture. From Indiana University where he was teaching that summer, Burke replied to Everest's inquiry. Denying any Communist party connection, he acknowledged that he had lent sponsorship to some of the organizations mentioned, but pointed out that sponsoring was taken lightly in the 1930s. With regard to the American Committee for the Protection of the Foreign Born, for example, Burke wrote that he might have been a sponsor but could not recall for sure. He added: "I am, as a confirmed liberal, for the protection of the foreign born. . . . Is there some approved organization for the protection of the foreign-born that I might join?" Professing no connection with the Book Union, he wrote: "I am in favor of printing any serious-minded book. I feel that a conscientious educator should not suppress books, but should teach how to read them, and discount them for their excesses."[20]

The one organization that Burke admitted actively supporting was the League of American Writers, even though he was often scolded for deviating from its "line": "I will say frankly that, so far as organization went, I took it for granted that the League was under communist domination. We writers had never before had an organization: it was pleasant to think of ourselves as a group rather than as wholly isolated individuals."[21]

Attempting to answer Everest's question about his editorship of *Science and Society*, Burke noted: "At one time I was nominally an editor. This was before the shift of the line (around the time of the Finnish issue), when my name was dropped from the masthead." Subsequently, one of its editors, who was pro-Stalin, attacked Burke's *Attitudes Towards History*—this at the same time Hook accused it of Stalinism in the pages of *Partisan Review*. "What a tangle!" he concluded.[22]

Burke's humorous ripostes concerning past involvements ended with a serious exposition of the importance of Marxism, as a timeless ideal, to his philosophy of dialectics:

> Frankly, I treat Marx as one notable voice in the dialogue that we should equip ourselves to be at home in. There are two primary ways of cheating oneself, where Marxism is concerned. One way is by making it everything. The other is by trying to make it nothing, by thinking that one is 'loyal to one's country' by merely failing to understand what Marx is saying, or even by refusing to try to understand.[23]

With respect to his current attitudes toward Russian Communism, Burke expressed hopes for a modus vivendi: "I think we should have enough confidence in our own powers and ideas as a nation to relax a little, as regards present world tensions." In closing, he asserted that if

appointment of a left liberal would be dangerous to the administration, "then I should certainly be dropped by the wayside."[24]

This was the evidence that President Schmitz found on his desk
when he assumed office July 16. A perspicacious administrator in a
new position, Schmitz naturally leaned on the counsel of Anderson
and Everest, both of whom were aware of the climate of opinion. In
addition, his close ties with the Seattle business community—the
"influential people" referred to by Everest—affected his own perceptions of what was the "prudent" course for him to take to assure the
good of the whole university. It is doubtful that the tone of Burke's
letter furthered his cause; his casual approach to past activities and
present tensions contrasted with the current climate of unease about
unconventionality. Burke's continued espousal of the Marxist "ideal"
did not reassure Schmitz, to whom "sensible speech" was important.

Perhaps Heilman realized that Schmitz would be distressed by
Burke's letter, perhaps he was warned by Everest and Anderson that
the appointment was in trouble. For whatever reason, he presented
Schmitz with additional evidence concerning Burke's success as a
teacher at Bennington. Heilman also noted his colleagues' enthusias-
tic anticipation of the philosopher's presence in the department: "I
think one reason there is so general agreement upon him within the
department is that many critical points of view are represented in the
department, and that Burke uses many critical approaches. He is not
a 'party line' man for any one kind of literary study but uses every
kind of idea and method he can."[25]

Heilman also attempted to ease Schmitz's mind concerning Burke's
desirability as an academic person by quoting from a letter Burke
wrote the chairman on the occasion of his "apologia" to Everest:

> I agree with you, that there is no sense in merely bristling, when prob-
> lems of academic freedom come up. If we really believe in ourselves as
> educators, we must go through at least two stages: (1) the bristling; (2) the
> long suffering revision. On the other hand, we must not merely give.
> And I do most earnestly hope that you will judge me to have kept some-
> where within the realm proper to our particular discipline (for we, *as
> educators*, are entitled to be free, only insofar as we abide by the resources
> and restrictions of our specific fields). I claim no rights to be absolutely
> free, as a teacher, in some particular institution.[26]

In conclusion, Heilman urged that the Burke appointment not be
jeopardized by the English Department's political past: "I fear that in
some quarters our department is looked upon as an especial center of
'radical' appointments, a suspicion which I do not think is justified but
which nevertheless we are uncomfortably aware of and would like to

change." The department's solution, Heilman said, was to avoid the suggestion of persons for appointment whose "past might be un- favorably scrutinized . . . because they *had once had* leftist interests." Describing departmental discussion surrounding a current vacancy, Heilman noted that the top four names were ruled out in favor of someone

> entirely safe in these terms. . . . The thing I don't like about this is that because of fear of repercussions we did not attempt to appoint the men that we thought would be strongest. On the other hand, I hope that this decision will help convince any interested parties that we do not appoint people because they are leftist in point of view and that we are making a positive effort to avoid the difficulties which may arise in connection with such appointments.[27]

On August 19, a month after assuming the presidency, Schmitz informed Heilman that he had withdrawn the Walker-Ames Commit- tee recommendation of Burke, rather than present it to the Board of Regents. He assured Heilman that the decision was "not capricious" and had been made "only after serious and extensive consultation on and off the campus and after attempting to establish . . . the best interests of the total University." Burke immediately asked to know "explicitly, publicly, and in detail" the reasons behind the decision. Heilman also asked for a bill of particulars. Noting Burke's profes- sional reputation and the fact that he had signed the required state oaths, the chairman asked what more was required, what explanation could be made to the department and to Burke?

> Finally, how can we explain this action acceptably to the informed larger world—to the world of universities (including those in which Mr. Burke taught and will teach), to the world of literature and criticism (in which Mr. Burke is an outstanding figure), to the world of intelligent, stable, responsible Americans who are seriously concerned in conserving the principles that free expression is essential to our way of life and that a man is innocent until proved guilty?[28]

Answering Heilman, Schmitz laid the burden of his decision on his anxiety about "the reputation of the Department of English. This is a concern that has been shared by friends of the University far beyond the Department of English . . . [and] colors the reputation of the University as a whole." The president readily accepted Burke's denial of Communist party membership, but expressed his opinion that "there is room for doubt as to how far he has actually withdrawn" from its fringes. "Mr. Burke's appointment, particularly under the conspicuous banner of the Walker-Ames Professorships, could scarcely be interpreted as other than a page out of the past by those

who are inclined to regard the Department of English as 'leftist.'"
Returning to his concern about the "total welfare of the University,"
Schmitz wrote:

> I shall consider it my obligation as President of the University to achieve
> the kind of balance that will make the attachment of partisan labels to the
> University as difficult as can be.
>   If the University is to fulfill its mission of seeking out and keeping alive
> the truth, it must be a place where all points of view can be heard, and in
> the context of contemporary thought, these points of view should include
> the radical and the non-conformist. The maintenance of an atmosphere
> wherein this kind of freedom of expression is possible is one of the
> primary and, incidentally, one of the most difficult tasks of the University
> and of all its departments. In performing this task, it is of the utmost
> importance that all of us remember that freedom does not exist in a
> vacuum. It cannot exist without the corollary responsibility of presenting
> all sides of any given question and providing for our students the oppor-
> tunity to hear all points of view.

Finally, Schmitz noted that the university did not exist in a social
vacuum; its interests "are the concern also of the people of the State of
Washington who created and sustained the University for nearly a
hundred years." Pointing to the tensions of the time which were
grounded in the threat of Communism, Schmitz concluded:

> The reputation of your Department and of the whole University, about
> which you and your colleagues and I are all disturbed, is the product of
> the attitudes and opinions of all these people. If we are to maintain the
> kind of a University of which we can be proud, we shall not do so by
> feeding the doubts and fears and suspicions of those we seek to serve and
> who, in the last analysis, are the proprietors and trustees of the institu-
> tion. It is an easy error to belittle the interest and concerns of the people
> in an institution such as the University, but it is a betrayal of essential
> democracy to deny them.[29]

Schmitz also sent copies of his letter to Heilman to Graduate School
Dean Harold Stoke and Professor Robert Van Horn. As principals
on the Walker-Ames Committee, they had approved Burke's appointment in May. This letter thus became a major statement of his
position on appointments, particularly Walker-Ames Lectureships.
The Walker-Ames Fund had been established in 1931 by bequest
from one of the Pacific Northwest's prominent lumbermen, E. G.
Ames. Given his Seattle and forestry background, Schmitz understood the close attention the local community gave to persons who
came to the university under such a "conspicuous banner."
    Before Burke received Schmitz's letter explaining his decision, he
wrote the president with a proposal that he meet the Board of Re-

gents and Schmitz personally to discuss the theory of language course he had expected to teach during his ten-week lectureship at the university. Burke expressed his certainty that all this stir was unnecessary, and assured Schmitz that his loyalty had never been questioned when he taught at the Universities of Illinois and Indiana, and at Ohio State. Heilman quickly seconded this suggestion and urged Schmitz to reconsider, rather than earn the contempt of the academic world. The president refused to change his decision, but agreed that Heilman had the right to appeal to the board.[30]

Given the set of Schmitz's mind, and with the realization that the board rarely overturned presidential recommendations, Heilman and the members of his Executive Committee decided to sidestep the suggestion that the department appeal Burke's appointment directly to the board. They surmised that such a course would embarrass Schmitz and provoke a sympathetic reaction from the board which would divert attention from the real issues. Alternatively, the group composed yet another letter asking the president to be their spokesman before the board "as an interpreter of academic objectives and methods to those who by the nature of their lives are at some distance from the academic . . . and even when you yourself may have some question as to the complete desirability of a given proposal."[31]

Abandoning tactics for principles, the group then argued that Schmitz's decision on the Kenneth Burke appointment was made on considerations that ignored his professional qualifications and actual security status, and undertook a refutation of "suspicions" concerning the leftist character of the English Department. Noting the "tactic of pressure groups to pretend to speak for 'the people,'" Heilman and his colleagues asserted their belief that beyond such limited circles there was confidence in the university and willingness to accept "leadership in resisting groundless fears":

> The one way in which we can really "belittle" the people of the state is to regard them as so sunken in irrational fears that all we can do is soothe them, prevent them from having to make judgments, and protect them against our most gifted thinkers—to regard them, in a word, as children, which is the character you seem, unintentionally we are sure, to confer on them in your final paragraph.[32]

Further, the Executive Committee members urged Schmitz to combat suspicions by a formal investigation of the department's personnel policy to discover for himself its diverse views and professional quality, and to publicize his findings. "Surely something besides passive acceptance of these suspicions is called for." Only active pursuit of excellence in appointments would serve the interests of the people, they stated; without the trust of the president, the department would be reduced to "seek complete innocuousness and conformity . . . [and] yield to pressures which do not reflect on the real nature of our interests." Finally, they asked, "what is the role of the university in a time of unusual fear and tension?" Courageous leadership could substitute understanding for fear by confronting suspicion with fact, and could restore a measure of tolerance for nonconformity to society. "This is not a matter of 'freedom' in the abstract; it is a very concrete context. And what is finally at stake in the Burke case is the direction which the university is going to take in doing something about our immediate world." [33]

Turning aside the notion that he was reacting to "pressures," Schmitz replied that the real point was a difference of opinion about what was good for the university. Schmitz agreed to present the case to the regents by means of the last four months' correspondence and his own recommendations. The regents supplemented their deliberations by listening to Heilman at their September meeting, but finally rejected the appointment of Burke as "not in the best interests of the University at this time." [34]

Thus, by the time of his inauguration a few days later, Schmitz's notions about managing the university's reputation had been reinforced by the regents' decision. With the Burke issue fresh in mind, Schmitz reiterated these ideas to those assembled for the ceremonies:

> On the matter of the freedom of the University, I believe that the institution has a deep commitment to itself. The University must be a place where controversial issues may be discussed, objectively and with reassuring intelligence. It must be tolerant of widely varying opinions. It must resist partisanship and propaganda, since neither is related to scholarship or wisdom. The University should value sensible speech at least as highly as freedom of speech. I do not believe in academic freedom in a vacuum. I strongly believe that we must accept the responsibilities, as well as the benefits, of academic freedom.

Clearly, Schmitz felt that the faculty should be more critical of the thinking of their colleagues. In the absence of such self-censorship, he wrote to Regent Grant Armstrong, "university administrators find themselves in the unhappy position of making judgments the faculty itself should be making." [35]

But the controversy did not end quietly. Heilman noted the distress within the university over the lack of content given such terms as "the good of the University." "Many other departments," he argued, "are seriously worried about an appointments policy which it is believed will lead us to reject good men and good men to reject us. In the educational world generally we will run into serious adverse criticism, and the University's shaky reputation in the realm of free speech will receive another setback."[36] The Seattle papers eventually reported on the Burke affair. In an interview with the *Post-Intelligencer*, Burke suggested that the university's screening of him had been unjustified on purely educational grounds. The paper also quoted Schmitz as saying that he had blocked the appointment because he feared the reaction of the legislature with respect to the biennial budget, despite the fact that Burke had signed the loyalty oaths.[37]

Arthur R. Paulsen, member of the state House Committee on Colleges and Universities, took sharp exception to the university's departure from its "liberal" stance of the past. Recalling the Laski affair of the 1930s, Paulsen noted that adverse criticism was overridden by admiration of the university's determination to bring the best minds of the age to the campus. The legislator also lauded former President Allen's "commonsense" approach to academic freedom. Upset by Schmitz's implications that the legislature would interfere with internal university affairs, Paulsen averred that this "unfortunate departure" would win no friends for the university, and would only encourage those who were first to deny funds to the institution under any circumstances. Nineteen students signed a letter protesting Schmitz's decision as "ill-conceived, unnecessary and unwarranted . . . [since] students don't need to be protected from ideas."[38]

From other quarters, Schmitz received praise for his action. Charles F. Clise, Seattle businessman, assured him that "countless numbers feel as I do," when he applauded the president's "courage" in stopping English Department plans to persist in "feeding our students a continuous radical propaganda line." The *Educational Guardian*, organ of Allen Zoll's right-wing National Council for American Education, trumpeted the news of Schmitz's "pigeon-holing" of the Burke invitation. Though critical of the president's reasoning (the budget rather than the "effect on students"), Zoll wrote: "our Red-ucators report played an active part in President Schmitz' decision." When Heilman urged Schmitz to repudiate Zoll and assume leadership in fighting misinformation "that keeps local groups distressed," the president declined out of unwillingness to give Zoll's statements more prominence than they deserved.[39]

Malcolm Cowley surmised that since Burke's political past was "hardly worth mentioning," he was the target of one of the widely circulated blacklists, and "I was greatly disturbed—not for Kenneth . . . but for the University and for this evidence how the situation had deteriorated since I came out there three years ago," he wrote. "Kenneth is irreplaceable; he has something to give the liveliest students that no one else in this country or the world could give them, and that's a fact which the regents didn't even consider." In his own postmortem on the controversy, Burke reflected on the ideological battles of the 1930s, such as had taken place between himself and Sidney Hook. In light of the current situation, he wrote, "the sort of thing that can make this business morbid has begun. . . . If things get into that groove, they are about as capable of rational solution as adolescent arguments about religion. Those old haggles are fun to look back on, and to discuss as part of the human comedy. But they are damned dismal, if rehashed in the atmosphere of spy scares and treason trials. *And fantastically unreal*." [40]

While the unrealities of ideological recriminations were lost on Schmitz, the realities were not. The Burke affair illustrates the pragmatic considerations that determined the course of events during the Schmitz administration. Kenneth Burke's repudiation of his political past was dubious; moreover, his appointment was important to only a small group which had caused difficulties for the university in the past. As its first alumnus president, Schmitz was interested in making the university great, a project which demanded popular support and which left little space for unsavory commentary, such as might have occurred had Burke appeared on campus. For Schmitz, the most important point about the Burke affair was that somehow the administrative process had broken down, resulting in embarrassment for the university. It was to this aspect of the matter that the president turned. [41]

Schmitz as Chief Executive:
Formalization of Relationships

"When tradition serves our ends we shall abide by tradition. Where it falls short, we shall change it. Our one objective is to make the University virile, and to make it a forceful and dependable instrument in the efficient and democratic America that is coming."
—Inaugural Address of Henry Suzzallo, 1916, as quoted by Henry Schmitz, Inaugural Address, 1952

During his six-year tenure as president of the University of Washington, Henry Schmitz gained a reputation as a "caretaker." His protective loyalty toward his alma mater is legendary, and his administrative style reflected the practical conservatism of his forestry background. In his inaugural address he stressed the lush beauty of the campus, invoked the memory of great men who had been his teachers forty years past—Meany, Smith, Haggett, Condon, Padelford, Parrington—and pledged his commitment to maintenance of the university as a "virile, dynamic and democratic instrument" in training youth "for the higher responsibilities of American life." A warm person, he roamed the campus greeting faculty and students by name, taking prideful interest in their activities, mentally cutting and pruning, and planning for the future.[42]

One of Schmitz's major efforts was toward the ordering and clarification of organizational relationships within the university. In contrast to Allen, who had loosely delegated authority, Schmitz was uneasy about the lack of clearly delineated responsibilities. The appointment of Everest as vice-president had doubled the administration and the confusion about who made decisions. The reorganization of the Faculty Senate under Allen had theoretically given the faculty more self-governance, but the exclusion of the deans from membership, and replacement of the president with a faculty member as chairman of the senate had produced a gap between the faculty and administration which Schmitz sought to close. Working with faculty committees, Schmitz devised an organizational chart, codified university regulations, and secured the regents' formal recognition of the responsibilities of the president and faculty, and faculty rights to tenure. Through this process of "formalizing relationships," Schmitz reasserted the authority of the administration over all aspects of decision-making, and simultaneously reassured the faculty about the regents' acceptance of the tenure principle. The major problem with this kind of tinkering, important though it was, was that it increased the pressure on an already overburdened, underorganized administration.[43]

The situation is illustrated by faculty criticism of the administration's handling of the budget. Cognizant of "the acute financial problems facing the 1953 Legislature," the university presented a "hold-the-line budget" for the 1953–55 biennium which placed precedence on basic instruction and modest salary increases. Instead of the 33 percent salary increase recommended by the faculty, the administration requested a 17 percent increase to be offset by further reductions in services and operations despite inflation. An unexpected influx of Korean War veterans in the autumn of 1952 increased the student-faculty ratio to seventeen-to-one, an improvement over post-World War II levels, but higher than the fifteen-to-one figure recommended by President Eisenhower's Commission on Higher Education.[44]

In November and December of 1952, Vice-President Everest met with members of the faculty to discuss the ways in which the budget was determined, and to hear faculty concerns about the university's loss of "competitive edge." Though these meetings were designed to improve faculty-administration relations, the legislature's failure to appropriate even the trimmed budget focused renewed faculty discontent on the administration. In April, 1953, Schmitz and Everest attempted to meet criticism that the budget was not aggressively presented. Acknowledging no errors of calculation, they pointed out that the legislative appropriation was larger than the previous biennium. Faculty salaries would be increased, but at the cost of even larger reductions in services and research. Inflation took its toll.[45]

As part of their effort to gain more control over university resources, Schmitz and Everest instituted the line item budget and the President's Reserve Fund. This system cut down on the power of deans and departments to pad their budgets; when funds allocated for a specific purpose were not used, they reverted to the reserve, giving the president more flexibility in meeting unexpected costs elsewhere. Lloyd Woodburne, dean of the College of Arts and Sciences, the largest unit in the University, protested to Schmitz that he no longer had control over his own budget, and that most department heads realized his powers had diminished: "I find it difficult to believe that you intend to act as your own Dean of the College." Schmitz replied that in view of the current "snugging up" of resources the new system was the only practical solution, short of adopting a central system of control: "I cannot delegate to others decisions for which the Regents hold me responsible."[46]

With Schmitz urging responsible management of the state's money, and Everest emphasizing "realism" in the face of lagging state revenues, Woodburne and others feared that the balance in the administration had shifted toward those less sympathetic with the academic goal of building a great university. The line item budget meant that whole research units could be cut back or dropped rather than being juggled within the colleges as had formerly taken place. George Lundberg resigned as chairman of the Sociology Department in protest of the irregular manner in which the Public Opinion Laboratory was virtually discontinued. Urging a publicly defensible process, Lundberg voiced his concern that accountants were making decisions on what should be cut. Knowledgeable considerations of the academic merits of programs, he judged, was being lost.[47]

In part, the attitude Lundberg expressed sprang from a general faculty belief that the administration and the regents were too comfortable with legislative and gubernatorial notions about the adequacy of the university's budget in a time of retrenchment. Since Republican Governor Langlie's election in 1948, appointments to the Board of

Regents had been in the more conservative Republican mode. Mrs. J. Herbert Gardner, who replaced Dave Beck, was the wife of a prominent insurance executive, was a daughter of Charles Gaches (a regent during 1914–17), and was active in alumni affairs. Charles F. Frankland, a member of the Seattle banking community, had taken a large hand in Schmitz's election to the presidency. He had been Governor Langlie's longtime political confidant and campaign treasurer. Charles Harris, a certified public accountant and Wenatchee orchardist, replaced John King in 1953. He was a graduate of the University of Washington School of Business. Grant Armstrong, Chehalis attorney and city police judge, was a 1929 University of Washington Law School alumnus. Donald G. Corbett, a Spokane urologist, was president of the Washington State Medical Association. Regents Winlock Miller and Thomas Balmer, board members since the 1930s, had been reappointed by Langlie. These regents were responsive to business and economic conditions and less likely to press Olympia for money the university did not absolutely need, according to faculty theory.[48]

Indeed, a version of that theory received an airing in the 1952 gubernatorial campaign. The campaign, which pitted Langlie against former senator Hugh B. Mitchell, ran concurrently with the early months of President Schmitz's term and at the same time as the Kenneth Burke affair. Attacking Langlie's "good government image," Mitchell observed that university Vice-President Everest had twice served as the governor's administrative assistant, and that Regent Frankland was his campaign treasurer: "I tell you, the university will never take its rightful place in the top rank of America's schools of higher learning while the governor uses it as a dumping ground for personal friends and 'campaign helpers.'" Langlie countered by pointing to Mitchell's connections with the Americans for Democratic Action, which in 1949 had opposed the regents' firing of Phillips and Butterworth: "I am fed up with all this compromise with Communists in our educational system under the guise of academic freedom. . . . Mitchell and his ADA crowd defend the Communists' right to infiltrate our free institutions." A Mitchell administration, he warned, would be one "in which our youth would be tossed into a vice where subversive learnings and unrealistic teachings would have the upper hand."[49]

While Mitchell was not a member of the ADA, he did receive the group's support. Accordingly, James B. Wilson, president of the King County ADA, tried to clarify Langlie's attack. The ADA, he stated, had protested the regents' overruling of the faculty Tenure Committee in 1949 because it "seriously jeopardized faculty tenure at the university." He charged Langlie with "loading the university with his own political favorites. The spirit of free inquiry that is basic to a great university is on the defensive and retreating under the Langlie administration." In rebuttal the governor asserted pride in his appointments of persons who would "stop these left-wing activities on the campus." The *Seattle Times* applauded Langlie's reasoning and demanded to know what kind of regents Mitchell proposed to appoint. Would his advisors on the faculty be "the group in the university faculty which has fought every move to rid the university of the Communist line of thinking which has damaged the institution and swayed many of its students in past years?"[50]

Did such political maneuvering vitiate serious discussion of university appropriations? Or were administrators, regents, and legislators inured to faculty warnings of the university's deteriorating academic position? Despite their predictions of decline, the excellence of faculty achievement seemed to be increasingly acknowledged in important circles. The Graduate School received continued recognition; in 1954, when Theodore Roethke won the Pulitzer Prize for Poetry and seven faculty members received Guggenheim Fellowships, the regents acknowledged these and other distinctions in an unprecedented "Resolution of Pleasure and Pride in the Faculty." However, despite the surge of contract research and grants in the health and physical sciences, appropriations for the teaching hospital failed, and the university lost matching federal and private grants. Edward Turner, the Medical School's first dean, resigned in dismay at the apparent lack of understanding within the administration of the importance of the hospital to the future of the health sciences teaching program. When the legislature began to use regular university appropriations for the Medical School, the worst fears of its campus opponents were realized: the tail was beginning to wag the dog. Even Schmitz's enlistment of private businessmen, including his brother Dietrich, in a drive for private gifts, trusts, and bequests, was seen as a means of applying increased pressure for university conformity to local ideas.[51]

Schmitz's relationships with faculty members were marked by the same conservatism that he displayed in budgetary matters. His belief that faculty tended to exaggerate salary needs paralleled his view that faculty members were uncritical of their peers and insensitive to the ramifications of unfavorable public criticism. Schmitz made little distinction between the academic and political lives of faculty members; bad publicity in either area reflected on the university. On the other hand, he realized that at least two department chairmen and numerous faculty were distressed by the administration's "over-sensitivity" to public opinion in the wake of the Barnes and Burke affairs. George Lundberg, for instance, continued to press for a "more defensible policy" with regard to appointments. Objecting to the secret character of the investigation of Barnes' past associations, Lundberg urged open evaluation of such evidence and collaboration among department heads, deans, and the president when the personal qualifications of a prospective appointee were in question. Above all, most weight should be given to evidence collected by those who knew the academic competence of the prospective appointee, not to that collected by nonacademic administrators. However, Lundberg noted, such a process was necessary only when government or military secrets were involved, not merely "unusual ideas":

> In this connection I venture to suggest that among the University's functions is the broad function of educating the public regarding what a University is and what it is for. There is bound to be, especially in an institution emerging recently into a first class university, a considerable number of people both on the faculty and on the administration who still look upon the university as primarily a glorified high school in which about the only important considerations are that classes meet regularly and that parents do not complain. . . . May we not as well face the fact that a university cannot properly go about its business and do the things for which it primarily exists without incurring a certain amount of cross-fire from all kinds of pressure groups and special interest aggregations, as well as occasionally from the public at large? . . .
>
> Indeed, everyone renders lip service to the idea of a university as a place in which especially qualified and privileged people fearlessly explore the most forbidding realms in pursuit of new truth and in response to the creative urge. A leaflet has recently come to me [sic] desk regarding the Walker-Ames Fund. It repeats over and over again the desire of the donor to bring to the University "unusual minds." Is it not vain to assume that the University can attract these minds unless it is also willing to put up with a good deal in the way of personal idiosyncrasies, political and social affiliations, and other characteristics quite frequently associated with "unusual minds." [52]

Lundberg's pleas echoed those of Heilman and the Executive Committee of the English Department. Even though they came from a fellow conservative, however, Schmitz was likely to regard them with a wary eye since a major concern in the matter of appointments was the elimination of future embarrassments.

As a consequence of the Burke affair, the regents asked the president to set up procedures to insure the propriety of appointees. Late in November, 1952, Schmitz announced the formation of an administrative committee to assist him in the formation of policy "relative to the appointment of persons whose political backgrounds raise questions as to the appropriateness of University sponsorship." Chaired by

Dean Emeritus Edwin Guthrie, the five-member committee consisted
of Professors H. Stanley Bennett (Anatomy), Alfred Harsch (Law), J.
Richard Huber (Economics), and Sargent Powell (Chemistry).
Though the results of their deliberations were not known for six
months, the *Seattle Times* took editorial note of the approval of the
state press regarding Schmitz's decision to check up on prospective
faculty members, urging the university to continue its vigilance. In
conclusion, the *Times* endorsed the assessment of J. B. Matthews,
HUAC's chief information gatherer, who had asserted: "Only one institution in the United States, namely the University of Washington at
Seattle, has taken any effective steps to remove Communists from its
faculty."[53]

While the Guthrie Committee worked to formulate a policy, Everest
and Schmitz took interim steps to assure themselves of the loyalty of
prospective appointees. Everest first sought the advice of R. E.
Combs, chief counsel for the California Tenney Committee, on the
methods used to investigate possible subversive activities in the
backgrounds of present and prospective members of California colleges and universities, indicating the need to combat "the same problems at this University." This "California plan" had gained national
attention when Combs testified to its effectiveness before the Senate
Internal Security Subcommittee in March, 1953. According to Combs,
trained investigators of the Tenney Committee gathered information
on faculty members and passed it on to administrators in educational
institutions.[54]

In March Schmitz began requesting four letters of recommendation for each faculty appointment. J. H. Manley of Physics protested
to Dean Woodburne that this put the university in a "slightly ridiculous light," and doubted these cold, uniform formalities would accomplish anything since departments would consider the competence of
the individual before hiring. Heilman pointed out that such letters
would reveal little about unknown men, while asking for letters of
reference on distinguished men would make departments a "professional laughingstock. . . . Surely we must take for granted those
matters which are taken for granted in good professional practice,
and one of these is that a major professor in a major university is a
suitable short-term visitor at another university." Schmitz replied that
as president he was responsible for every appointment, and underscored the importance of the personal qualifications as well as the
professional reputations of prospective appointees.[55]

But on the same day that Schmitz exhibited this defensive posture
toward the judgment of his faculty, he lent his support to legislative

opponents of a measure backed by state women's clubs and the American Legion that would have required students in all Washington institutions to enroll in American and Washington history courses. To the chairman of the House Committee on Colleges and Universities, Schmitz wrote that curricular matters were the province of the faculty, and that the study of American institutions was an integral aspect of many courses. Such defenses of university integrity were, of course, comparatively unknown to the faculty, but they fit Schmitz's style as a cautious man who chose his allies carefully. The academic world of the early fifties was treacherous; potential for controversy—which Schmitz sought to avoid—lurked around every corner.[56]

On the national scene, Senator McCarthy was enjoying a vintage year; as chairman of the Committee on Government Operations and of the Sub-Committee on Permanent Investigations, he kept critics at bay by initiating 445 preliminary investigations and 157 investigations, and by holding seventeen public hearings. Though his attacks were directed mainly at the State Department, many academics were implicated. The House Un-American Activities Committee under former F.B.I. agent Harold Velde, and Senator Jenner's Senate Internal Security Sub-Committee were the chief purveyors of the "red infiltration of colleges and schools" message. In 1953, 280 persons either invoked the Fifth Amendment or admitted Communist party activity before these committees; of these, 97 were teachers and 57 taught in colleges and universities. None of the teachers admitted current Communist party membership.[57]

The activities of these committees produced little legislation on the national level, but they gave impetus to the states' inclinations to institute loyalty oaths for employees. The Washington legislature, which had passed a loyalty oath in 1951, refined it in 1953. The investigations of congressional committees also inspired the executive branch to continue its search for subversives. In September, 1952, the Justice Department indicted seven Northwest Communist party leaders for violations of the 1940 Smith Act: they were charged with conspiring to overthrow the government by force. During their trial in Seattle, Herbert J. Phillips, who had been dismissed from the university in 1949, invoked the Fifth Amendment. Phillips was not on trial, but had been called by the defense to give expert testimony concerning Marxism. His refusal to name his associates in the party during cross-examination by Special Prosecutor Tracy Griffin (counsel for the university in 1948–49) caused the *Post-Intelligencer* to recall the events of four years before. Jailed for eighty-one days during the trial, he was eventually convicted of criminal contempt and sentenced to an extraordinary three years in prison.[58]

In the midst of this dark year, the Guthrie Committee submitted its report on "Faculty Appointment Policy." Reflecting the tensions of the era, the report accepted the university's unwillingness to hire active members of the Communist party. The proscription against Communists in the wake of the regents' 1949 actions was by now pervasive throughout U.S. higher education, and the state's 1951 Subversive Activities Act forbade employment of "subversive persons." The report endorsed thorough investigation of every prospective faculty member's scholarship and political background, but it also urged careful study and evaluation of adverse rumors and warned of the unreliability of the attorney general's list as a criterion. In the case of acting or temporary appointees such as Walker-Ames Professors, however, "the qualifications . . . may often be evaluated in a somewhat different context from those of regular permanent appointments, for the former do not achieve positions of lasting influence in University affairs, and hence some personal characteristics regarded as disqualifying in a permanent appointee might be acceptable or tolerable for the brief duration of a temporary appointment." The committee also urged that no "crippling restrictions," such as the requirement of an advance exhaustive study of background, be placed on the approval of transient lecturers.[59]

The Guthrie Committee report was hailed by Schmitz for its wisdom in recognizing the impact of the "whole man," and in urging joint consultation between the faculty and administration. Implied criticism of the administration's oversensitivity in appointments also pleased some faculty members. Acceptance of the report by the Faculty Senate and the regents seemed to presage improved understanding about the nature of free expression within the university. Because of the general acceptance of the committee's report, Schmitz called upon its five members to clarify the university's stand on another prominent issue of the era: faculty members who invoked the Fifth Amendment before congressional investigating committees.[60]

In March, 1953, Schmitz had endorsed the position of the Association of American Universities (AAU), which not only stated that "membership [in the Communist Party] extinguishes the right to a University position," but also warned that a faculty member who invoked the Fifth Amendment assumed the "burden of proof of his fitness to hold a teaching position and lays upon his university the obligation to re-examine his qualifications for membership in its society." Since the UWAAUP, of which H. Stanley Bennett was president, expressed no objection to the AAU statement, the Guthrie Committee recommended that the senate adopt it as university policy. If one recalls that in 1948 the Tenure Committee decided that faculty refusal to answer the questions of a legislative committee required no university action, the impact of events of the intervening four and a half years becomes clear.[61]

The Fifth Amendment policy was formulated to warn faculty members of their obligations, but ignored the awful dilemma faced by those who had long since left the Communist party but did not choose to implicate past associates. One University of Washington professor who soon met this situation was Abraham Keller of the Romance Languages Department. In the spring of 1954, the House Un-American Activities Committee under Chairman Harold Velde visited Seattle for the purpose of taking testimony concerning Communist party activities in the Pacific Northwest. One of those subpoenaed was Keller. Because he had been a member of the party while in graduate school at Berkeley (1938–46), Keller realized that questioning would center on his friendship with Joseph Weinberg.[62]

Weinberg and Frank Oppenheimer had been physicists at the Berkeley Radiation Laboratory during the war. After Los Alamos itself, the Radiation Lab had been the installation most critical to the U.S. atomic bomb project. Shortly after the detonation of the U.S.S.R.'s first A-bomb in 1949, when HUAC investigated the loyalty of physicists, both had lost their positions at the University of Minnesota. Oppenheimer told HUAC of his past Communist party membership. Weinberg, accused of being the "Scientist X" who had allegedly passed atomic bomb details to the Soviets, denied membership. He was indicted for perjury in 1951 after denying that he attended a Communist party meeting at the home of J. Robert Oppenheimer in 1941. Weinberg was acquitted in March, 1953.[63]

In the summer of 1953 the Russians exploded what was thought to be the world's first H-bomb, well in advance of the day in March, 1954, when the U.S. announced a similar feat. The Russian success again focused attention on the loyalty of physicists who, like J. Robert Oppenheimer, had opposed development of the H-bomb. In June, 1954, Robert Oppenheimer, the "Father of the Atomic Bomb," was being scrutinized by the Atomic Energy Commission on charges that he was a security risk. Like his brother Frank, Robert was destined to lose this contest with the investigators. That same June, HUAC's Chairman Velde came to Seattle to search the recollections of Abraham Keller for more links between the Oppenheimers, Weinberg, and the Communist party. Above all, he was hopeful that Keller might supply information that would enable HUAC to reopen its case against Weinberg.[64]

And so in the days immediately following the Faculty Senate's endorsement of the AAU statement, Keller went to President Schmitz to discuss his dilemma: he would try to avoid invoking the Fifth Amendment, which would endanger his job and embarrass the university. But he warned that he had no intention of implicating innocent persons. Schmitz, who had apparently been contacted by the Velde Committee, thanked Keller for his frankness and told him to do whatever he and his counsel thought necessary. Having been a key administrator during the Weinberg incident at Minnesota, Schmitz expressed regrets that Weinberg had not been so open as Keller with the administration, thereby leaving no alternative except dismissal. After much searching, Keller found attorneys who would counsel him before the Velde Committee: John Harlow and Benjamin Asia (who had been Garland Ethel's counsel before the Tenure Committee in 1948–49). As they discussed the case, Keller realized that invocation of the Fifth Amendment would be unnecessary because he was unable to affirm certain knowledge of Weinberg's Communist party membership.[65]

The Velde Committee hearing room was packed with American Legion Auxiliary and Pro-America members, and bright with the glare of television cameras. At his request, Keller himself was not televised; during his two-hour testimony Seattle viewers saw only the questioners and the audience. With what the *Seattle Times* described as "an air of determined imperturbability," Keller denied knowing anything of Frank Oppenheimer beyond passing acquaintance. He parried persistent questions about his physicist friend Weinberg. He also revealed that one consequence of his Communist party activities in California, and of his refusal to give the F.B.I. and the State Department information about his former Bay-area friends, was that in 1951 he had been denied a passport to teach and do research in Europe. Although congressional inquirers threatened him with contempt citations for his "clear and direct evasion," they were ultimately frustrated in their search for new names or evidence to add to their files. Keller later told reporters that the committee just did not understand his scruples about saying under oath things of which he had no certain knowledge.[66]

Though some faculty members shunned Keller after his "noncooperative" performance before the Velde Committee, President Schmitz stood by him. Keller was never indicted for contempt, and when the committee again contemplated subpoenaing him on its second swing through the Northwest in March, 1955, he was not asked to testify. Keller attributes this to a letter he wrote to HUAC outlining his intention to publish his account of the investigators' questionable tactics. But he also believes that Schmitz's refusal to fire him, or even to pressure him to cooperate, saved him from further harassment. Since several other former university employees had been called by the Velde Committee, Schmitz was undoubtedly discomfitted by the hearings and the attention they drew to the university. On the other hand, Schmitz's conservative reputation was unquestioned, and the university's position on Communists was clear.[67]

Schmitz's willingness to defend a member of his faculty in a difficult situation did not extend to transient lecturers who made "casual and accidental" contributions to the university. When Schmitz discovered that Rolfe Humphries, a proposed speaker for the English Department, had been active in support of the Spanish Loyalists in the 1930s, he refused the appointment. There was, after all, no reason to *invite* difficulties that might arise from such an appearance. Regardless of the vaunted Guthrie report, which had decried "crippling restrictions" on temporary appointments, Schmitz believed this was not a question of academic freedom. As he wrote to the Dean of Arts and Sciences, Lloyd Woodburne: "Are there really many demonstrable cases in first class universities where a scholar is unable to carry on unfettered research in his field of scholarship?" Though Chairman Robert Heilman and the English Department did not contest Schmitz's decision on the Humphries matter, the president soon found himself embroiled in a test of his opinions on academic freedom. By the autumn of 1954, the stage was set for the controversy over the appointment of J. Robert Oppenheimer to a Walker-Ames Lectureship.[68]

VI

The Oppenheimer Controversy

and Aftermath

It is unfortunate that this incident has created doubts in the minds of some, concerning the sincerity with which the University adheres to the principle of academic freedom.
— Faculty Senate Resolution on the Oppenheimer Matter, April 7, 1955

On February 14, 1955, the *Seattle Times* carried a small news item which heralded a major crisis for the University of Washington. President Henry Schmitz had vetoed the proposed appointment of J. Robert Oppenheimer, the "Father of the Atomic Bomb" and director of the Institute for Advanced Study at Princeton, to a Walker-Ames Professorship. Regarding the Physics Department's request for the week-long lectureship, the president stated that "bringing him here at this time would not be in the best interests of the University." By this single action, Schmitz drew the university into the momentous debate, then centered on Oppenheimer, concerning scientists, the national security, and the development of thermonuclear weapons.

Misgivings about the loyalty of scientists were awakened with the espionage of Alan Nunn May in Canada (1946) and Klaus Fuchs in Britain (1950), and were further stirred by House Un-American Activities (HUAC) investigations and the trial and execution of the Rosenbergs (1953). The U.S.S.R.'s explosion of its first atomic bomb in 1949, and its announced detonation of a hydrogen bomb in 1953 (claimed to be the first in the world), heightened the suspicions of those who believed the Russians could not have developed such devices so quickly without access to the secrets of U.S. scientists. The value of scientists to the national security in a nuclear age was paralleled by the threat, implicit in their international language of symbols and equations, of their loyalty to science above nation.

Oppenheimer's background had been a source of concern to security officers from the moment he was proposed as director of Los Alamos in 1942. His wife and his brother, Frank, had been Communist party members, as were some of his friends and students, and he had often

126

allied himself with "front groups" in his years at Berkeley. During each period of his employment in public service, however, he met the increasingly stringent standards of loyalty imposed on those with access to secret information. His brilliant contributions to the atom bomb project, both as a theoretician and as an administrator, were unquestioned. But his arguments for international control of atomic energy and his opposition to the development of the H-Bomb after the war gained for him the enmity of Edward Teller and other scientists, Atomic Energy Commissioner Lewis Strauss, and Pentagon and congressional leaders.[1]

Robert Oppenheimer's thinking on atomic energy was influenced by his deep horror over the atomic bombings of Hiroshima and Nagasaki. He worked to remove its control from the military and to develop an international agency for its peaceful use. His qualms about the "Superbomb" were both practical and moral. Along with Hans Bethe, Enrico Fermi, and other atomic physicists, he doubted the feasibility of the physics involved in building a hydrogen bomb, and doubted that it would ever be deliverable "except by ox cart." But he also opposed production of a bomb so devastating that its use would be tantamount to genocide, and tactically useless. Oppenheimer advocated a more balanced defense strategy that would include air power and an arsenal of tactical nuclear weapons. He urged open discussion, in the arena of Congress, of the moral dimensions of thermonuclear development. The people, he believed, should understand the implications of the H-bomb before scientists, the military, and the weapons industry committed the nation to an irrevocable escalation of the arms race. His efforts to forestall H-bomb development were successful because most scientists on the General Advisory Committee to the AEC, of which Oppenheimer was chairman, supported that position. In January, 1950, following the Russian A-bomb and Klaus Fuchs incidents, President Truman overruled the advice of the GAC and ordered a crash program to produce the "Super."[2]

By the time Eisenhower took office, proponents of the H-bomb controlled the AEC, and Oppenheimer was on the margins of power. The climate of opinion in the midst of the Korean War urged scientists to subordinate private scruples to the national security. Secrecy was paramount as the U.S. moved to secure its hegemony in the nuclear race. On May 28, 1953, the new president again tightened the test for public employees. Loyalty alone was insufficient. Now the employment or retention of persons depended on their ability to prove that they were not detrimental to the national security. In the months following the U.S.S.R.'s H-bomb proclamation, William Borden, former executive director of the staff of the Joint Committee on Atomic Energy, wrote J. Edgar Hoover that Oppenheimer's criticism of U.S. H-bomb development had jeopardized national security. Hoover's report to Eisenhower on the matter led the president to order suspension of Oppenheimer's security clearance in December, 1953. The president's action placed the matter in the hands of the Personnel Security Board of the AEC, forestalling any possibility of its being captured by Senator Joseph McCarthy's Committee on Government Operations, which had direct contact with Hoover. By the time McCarthy addressed the nation on the subject in April, 1954, he was in trouble over his hearings on the Army, the U.S. was testing thermonuclear devices, and the AEC hearings on Oppenheimer were about to commence.[3]

After nineteen days of hearings, the AEC's Personnel Security Board voted two-to-one to revoke Oppenheimer's security clearance, a decision upheld by the AEC in late June, because "his conduct and associations reflected a serious disregard for the requirements of a security system." Though the atomic energy commissioners did not question his loyalty, they noted that he continued to see and advise persons whom he knew were suspected of Communist backgrounds. The hearings disclosed other indiscretions on Oppenheimer's part, including lies to a security officer to protect a friend, and associations with his ex-fiancée after his marriage in 1941. Most telling, however, was the finding that Oppenheimer's conduct over the H-bomb was "sufficiently disturbing as to raise a doubt as to whether his future participation . . . would be clearly consistent with the best interests of security."[4]

Reaction among Americans was intense, commensurate with the enormous prestige and admiration Oppenheimer had enjoyed prior to the hearings, and with the tensions of the Cold War. Physicists like Bethe and Fermi issued statements in his defense; they too had advised against H-bomb development. Were brilliant minds to be lost to public service through partisan prosecutions? Fourteen University of Washington physicists, ten of whom had worked with Oppenheimer at Los Alamos, protested the decision in a telegram to Eisenhower. They urged the president to speak out against those who could not tolerate differences of opinion. Casting aside the "Father of the Atomic Bomb," they said, was "damaging to the national defense." Other scientists argued that the security system had gotten out of hand; because the burden of proof lay with suspected individuals, a foreign agent might shut down a project simply by planting false information against key persons. In the popular press, Oppenheimer was portrayed either as a naive, misguided mystic whose guilt feelings paralyzed U.S. defense efforts, or as a victim of AEC Chairman Lewis Strauss's personal vendetta. On another level, outrage centered on Oppenheimer's affinity for left-wing causes and his less-than-puritanical personal life. The disquiet among Americans over the troubling issues raised by the Oppenheimer matter was reflected in the bitterness of the controversy over President Henry Schmitz's decision to refuse to extend him a Walker-Ames Professorship at the University of Washington.[5]

Efforts by the university's Physics Department to bring Oppenheimer to Seattle began in April, 1953, when department Chairman John H. Manley explored the possibility that his old friend would conduct a symposium at the American Physical Society meeting in the summer of 1954. Manley had been Oppenheimer's associate director at Los Alamos, and secretary to the GAC while Oppenheimer was chairman of that body. When Oppenheimer expressed interest in Manley's invitation, Manley formally nominated him to the Walker-Ames Committee, and on December 8, 1953, Schmitz informed the committee chairman, R. B. Van Horn, of his approval. Since Oppenheimer's security clearance was suspended secretly by Eisenhower on December 14, and he was probably engaged in marshaling his defense, Manley received no word from the physicist confirming his intention to attend the July meeting. Schmitz later told the Faculty Senate that he learned of Oppenheimer's difficulties with the AEC "some time before the story broke in the press," and obtained Manley's agreement that "it was not unreasonable of the University to withdraw the approval and to review the situation, if desirable, after the case had been settled." The American Physical Society meeting took place without Oppenheimer within weeks after the revocation of his security clearance. However, Schmitz never withdrew the university's invitation, and it was allowed to "lapse."[6]

In October, 1954, Edwin Uehling, acting chairman of the Physics Department while Manley was on leave, renewed the effort to bring his old teacher and colleague to campus. (Uehling had been a post-doctoral fellow under Oppenheimer from 1934 to 1936.) Negotiations with Oppenheimer revealed that he would be available for a week in May, 1955, after completion of the Condon Lectures for the Oregon university system. With the agreement of his department and Dean Woodburne, Uehling's request for Walker-Ames funds was again approved by that committee and sent on to President Schmitz. After a week's deliberation, in which he read the published record of the Oppenheimer hearings and consulted "members of staff, members of the professional staff as well as deans," Schmitz notified Graduate School Dean Harold Stoke on December 10 that he could not consent to the Oppenheimer appointment. As winter quarter began, Uehling and Stoke attempted to work out a way to get Oppenheimer appointed, suggesting, among other avenues, a source of funds other than Walker-Ames to finance the lectures. Despite assurances that Oppenheimer would be lecturing only on physics, the negotiations failed to change the president's mind: though he respected scientists who still admired Oppenheimer, he believed public reaction to Oppenheimer's appointment would be unfavorable. On February 9, Uehling broke the news to the members of the Physics Department, many of whom had worked with Oppenheimer in the past. In the next few days it became a general topic of campus conversation. The Executive Committee of the university chapter of the AAUP inquired, but their efforts to change Schmitz's mind also failed. After the news was published in the *Seattle Times* on February 14, the controversy assumed a life of its own which lasted the better part of three months.[7]

Attorney Kenneth A. MacDonald was among the first to express his frustration with Schmitz's decision. In a letter to the *Seattle Times*, the ACLU state board member urged voters to ask the legislature to withhold university building appropriations "until this act of fear and this assault upon free inquiry and scholarship by Dr. Henry Schmitz be reversed." Fear of public reaction indicated, he wrote, that Schmitz was "not interested in the educational process," and that "students are not encouraged to respect the value of scholarship." What good are new buildings, he asked, when "a free and vital education is made more difficult to obtain at the university under such timorous top leadership as exists today."[8]

Organized opposition to Schmitz's decision on Oppenheimer's appointment first came from the Student Organizations Assembly, which urged the president to reconsider in the name of academic freedom. Various groups, including the YMCA, Campus Veterans, and the campus chapter of the ACLU, sponsored an open forum to discuss the issues involved. On the day of the forum, Schmitz elaborated on his decision, saying that it was reached "after long and careful study of his [Oppenheimer's] governmental relationships . . . I do not plan to reconsider. . . ." Oppenheimer's competence as a physicist was not in dispute, said the president, "nor does it involve the question of academic freedom nor his right to express a view point." The only question was the "best interests of the University."[8] Students scoffed that such "protection" would result "in our becoming not only the Silent but also the Deaf-Mute Generation." Challenging Schmitz about the meaning of his inaugural address, another student remarked that instead of virility, dynamism, and democracy, "the decision smacks of bigotry, of weakness, and of compromise." While Schmitz was burned in effigy, students circulated a petition to the Board of Regents, urging a courageous stand such as that taken by previous boards in controversies surrounding the Laski (1939) and Cowley (1949–50) Walker-Ames appointments. Leaders of the Students' Committee on the Oppenheimer Ban ended the forum by announcing a citizen's march to Olympia, and encouraged sympathizers to join them in asking for legislative and gubernatorial intervention.[9]

The forty students who caravaned to the state capitol the next day received a mixed reception. William Shannon (Seattle Republican), chairman of the Senate Committee on Higher Education, noted that he had sent Schmitz a letter congratulating him on his stand. Representative Andrew Hess (Seattle Democrat), chairman of the House Education Committee, pronounced himself personally "shocked" by Schmitz's decision, but said legislative interference in internal university affairs would be "improper." Governor Arthur Langlie told the press he neither approved nor disapproved the decision. Regent Charles Frankland issued a statement of support for the president. Undaunted, the students claimed that they had found little opposition to the appointment of Oppenheimer and much general support for their position, and determined to continue their efforts to gain complete information from the president as to the basis of his decision. In a letter to the faculty, the student committee emphasized that their aim was to insure adherence to policy expressed in the Guthrie report. When the president refused further discussion, forty students took their complaint to the Board of Regents, which again unanimously upheld the president's interpretation of the appointment policy.[10]

In exerting their support for Schmitz, the regents were under little pressure to act differently. The petition presented by the students had been signed by only one in fourteen (1,200), and the forum had attracted only 400. The hostility of the attack on Schmitz had shocked many students, and the *Daily* had refused to take an editorial stand on the question. Moreover, the sophistication of the student committee's attack brought charges that faculty members were directing the protest. Indeed, the state ACLU had directed its Freedom of Expression Committee to "stimulate interest in the Oppenheimer situation" shortly after news of Schmitz's decision broke, and the campus chapter had helped sponsor the open forum. Professors Melvin Rader and Alex Gottfried (Political Science) were leaders in both groups.[11]

If they were looking for further evidence in support of the president, the regents could note that faculty members generally were divided in their views of the affair, prefiguring a split that held throughout the controversy. Arts and Sciences faculty members such as Rader, Merritt Benson (Journalism), Herschel Roman (Botany), and Solomon Katz and Stull Holt (History), joined their colleagues in physics in protesting. Benson argued that the university's motto, "Lux Sit," was the imperative form: "Dr. Oppenheimer is one of the most brilliant men in the world. It would be an inspiration to the Physics Department to hear him speak." Rader pointed out that Oppenheimer's loyalty and eminence as a scientist were undisputed, even by the government, while Roman reflected on the "very deep resentment and a feeling of shame among many faculty members." Such public dissents were matched by those Schmitz received privately; on February 25, Heilman, Katz, and Phil Church (Meteorology) procured the signatures of twenty-one of their thirty-three fellow chairmen in Arts and Sciences for a letter of protest to Schmitz. Some of these same faculty, like Katz, had opposed the student "March on Olympia," fearing "a time when the Legislature will act against academic freedom."[12]

Faculty spokesmen in Engineering, Business Administration, Law, and Forestry, generally supported the president's duty to make decisions. Gordon Gose (Law), for example, told the *Daily* that "there is too much of a tendency on the part of the faculty to usurp the executive function." J. I. Mueller (Ceramic Engineering) said, "I think President Schmitz is as right as rain. I think it is his job as an executive of a tax-supported institution to see that no controversial personage is made a member of the faculty." Another unnamed faculty member asked, "Why don't you young kids drop this whole thing?"[13] Schmitz also received private assurances concerning his action. Kenworthy of Physics expressed his approval and reminded Schmitz that in previous correspondence he had warned the president of the "pro-Communist" attitudes of his colleagues who had joined the department since the war. Not only had they opposed the dismissals of the three Communist faculty in 1949, but they had also considered hiring Frank Oppenheimer after his dismissal from the University of Minnesota (1949). Although the dissension within the Physics Department was the result of long-standing disagreements between "new" and "old" physicists, it lent credence to Schmitz's view that some faculty were using the Oppenheimer affair to advance their own ends.[14] Carl

Allendoerfer, chairman of the Mathematics Department and chairman of the Faculty Senate, also registered his private agreement with Schmitz on the grounds that Oppenheimer was a poor lecturer. Since Oppenheimer's reputation as a teacher and lecturer in both technical and nontechnical areas was excellent, Allendoerfer's claims were probably suspect even to Schmitz. A few days later, Allendoerfer joined his chairmen colleagues in signing the letter of protest to Schmitz.[15]

In the face of such mixed faculty reaction, acerbic comments in the press failed to alert the regents and Schmitz to the gravity of the situation. In contrast to the editorial support given the AEC the previous summer, newspapers and journals generally recognized Oppenheimer's continued value as a physicist. The *Argus*, a small but influential Seattle newspaper, took the view that Schmitz's decision should be challenged by the regents and the state legislature on grounds that no other university had denied its students and faculty the right to hear this great thinker. Oregon newspapers took full advantage of the imbroglio to play up the wisdom of the Oregon university system in inviting Oppenheimer. The *San Francisco Chronicle* commented:

> He [Schmitz] knows Seattle and the State of Washington and he apparently felt it advisable in the words of the University's famous song, to "bow down" to the lunatic fringe in the Legislature and the citizenry. No doubt he was justified in assuming that, were Dr. Oppenheimer to speak from a University rostrum, these troublemakers could do the University real damage. . . . The ban . . . does not suppress Oppenheimer; it just keeps his brilliance in expounding modern physics and the philosophy of science from coming into direct contact with the minds of students and faculty. . . . They are the losers.[16]

During these early days of the controversy, neither the *Seattle Times* nor the *Post-Intelligencer* had commented editorially on these events at the university. The *Post-Intelligencer*, a Hearst newspaper, however, did carry the columns of Fulton Lewis, Jr., and Westbrook Pegler, who lost no opportunity to attack Oppenheimer's moral and scientific record.

Aside from the public and private commentary on the decision, the regents were indisposed to reverse Schmitz. Most of them had been appointed by incumbent Republican Governor Langlie, whose views on the matter were reported in the *New Republic*. Students who had met with Langlie during the "March on Olympia" told the magazine that Langlie said: "I don't know how many mothers of boys whose sons had fought the Communists in Korea have told me that their boys had lost their God-Fearing values at the University of Washington . . . Oppenheimer has been loose with the nation's security. And with the background of the University, you want to bring Oppenheimer here!" Langlie's use of anti-Communist rhetoric was characteristic of his style since his entry into politics in Seattle in the 1930s. In each campaign he attacked some segment of his opposition on what he perceived to be its domination by Marxism. For Langlie, the students' march on Olympia was perhaps reminiscent of similar actions by the unemployed and pensioners of years past.[17]

The legislature generally followed Langlie's initiatives on subversive legislation. In his message to the 1955 legislature, Langlie said: "Today the menace of communism looms as an even greater threat to the future of the free world than the 'isms' of the past." He then backed legislation similar to the Communist Control Act, which had been passed by the U.S. Congress in 1954. On February 18, the day of the students' march, House Bill 683 was introduced. In its final amended form, it outlawed the Communist party in the State of Washington, and required a disclaimer oath of all state, county, and municipal employees. Governor Langlie signed the bill into law on March 21, two days after Representative Velde's House Committee on Un-American Activities ended the second round of its hearings on Communism in the Northwest.[18]

The regents, then, were fairly certain that supporting Schmitz would not alienate the governor and the legislature. In addition, most of them were veterans of previous similar disagreements between the faculty and the president about Walker-Ames appointments, and assumed that the brouhaha would die eventually. However, several factors made this controversy different from those that had gone before. Oppenheimer's status in scientific and intellectual circles had not been diminished by the AEC action; he was seen as a victim of partisan politics and Cold War hysteria. Oppenheimer was symbolic of the direction the University of Washington faculty wanted to go: away from regional toward national status. If geographic isolation was to be exacerbated by intellectual isolation, the university would never become the cosmopolitan center of erudition its faculty wanted it to be. Oppenheimer was not merely a writer (like Cowley), a philosopher (like Burke), or a controversial historian and sociologist (like Barnes), he was a scientist and polymath whose appeal transcended disciplinary bounds. His rejection united Arts and Sciences and Medical School faculty members who feared that passive acquiescence to the president's decision would constitute an indictment of them among their colleagues at other institutions, jeopardize their changes of getting other quality visitors, and nullify their efforts to build the university. What good were buildings, a teaching hospital, or a cosmic ray facility without a forward-looking personnel policy which promoted free inquiry?

Physics Department member Seth Neddermeyer, whose work on implosion theory was so vital to the U.S. atom bomb project, expressed some of those sentiments in a statement to the president and his physics colleagues across the nation. Neddermeyer believed that unless he informed others of his strong disapproval of Schmitz's action the department would deteriorate and the University of Washington would be considered a "medieval school . . . concerned with preserving existing prejudice." Or as his acting chairman, Edwin Uehling, stated:

> In my opinion, the ruling of the president is most unfortunate. Not only do we deny ourselves the opportunity of contact with one of the really great minds of America, but we tell the world and we tell ourselves that we do not seek to become a great University.
>
> The framework of ideas in which the president's decision was made will build a school but it will not build a university. We will train students and their numbers will grow, but if present attitudes prevail, we are not likely to make important contributions to knowledge.

Schmitz and the regents had indeed misgauged the best interests of the university in the minds of many faculty. As the controversy moved into its second stage, the "very deep resentment and feeling of shame" among them expressed itself in bitter internal and public acrimony.[19]

Boycott

The failure of the student actions and faculty expressions of dissent to change the minds of Schmitz and the regents led the faculty to take a new initiative. On February 28, two days after the regents' unanimous expression of support for the president, the Senate Committee on Public Lectures and Concerts requested Senate Chairman Carl Allendoerfer to ask Schmitz to present to the faculty "a detailed statement of his reasons for banning the appearance of Mr. Oppenheimer on the campus, and additionally to relate the decision to his interpretation of the policy as stated by the Guthrie Committee." This was necessary, they wrote, to end dangerous "speculation," since "we are unable to reconcile the decision on Oppenheimer with the [Guthrie] report." Schmitz consented, and on March 3 appeared before the senate "sick at heart and disillusioned," but unapologetic: "I am not administratively accountable to the Senate," he said, "I yearn for fac-

ulty understanding, support, and friendship, but I refuse to buy
them at the price of the administrative integrity of the University."
Dismayed at the "carnival of public dissent," Schmitz spoke only of his
official actions, refusing to give "reasons" for his ultimate decision:
"There is nothing mysterious about my determination not to do so. I
will not, whatever the pressure, be drawn into discussion of the innocent victim of this distressing episode. . . . You, as individuals or as a
group, may disagree with my decision, but you cannot disagree with
my duty and responsibility to make it." The issue was not debatable,
he said, and after appealing for unity, Schmitz left the senate.[20]

Schmitz was followed to the podium by Professor Uehling, who
related the actions of the Physics Department in the dispute, and
emphasized again the importance of visitors such as Oppenheimer.
"There has never been any question of the desirability of the Oppenheimer appointment. At no time in the rather long period of
negotiations has any opposition to this appointment ever been expressed. Bringing Oppenheimer here has at no time been a controversial matter insofar as the Department of Physics is concerned";
Schmitz's decision had produced "consternation and incredulity"
within the department. After appointing a committee to review the
effectiveness of appointment policy, the senate voted to canvass its
members as to their personal sentiments in regard to the Oppenheimer decision. The results of the poll were to be considered at
the April 14 meeting.[21]

Schmitz's senate appearance failed to dampen the internal bicker-
ing, and led to further speculative commentary on the reasoning behind his decision. George N. Stevens, dean of the Law School, urged
Daily readers to look behind the brilliance of Oppenheimer the scientist to Oppenheimer the *man*. The whole affair was merely a difference of opinion about the man: "What a man is, what he believes,
what he feels cannot help but be reflected in what he teaches, cannot
help but affect, eventually, his judgment in every area." It is "sheer
nonsense" to say that a university cannot deny someone who disre-
gards "ethical and moral values" the right to lecture on campus, or to
contend that it is a denial of academic freedom, said Stevens. Amid
the storm of comment this letter provoked, the faculty of the History
and Philosophy departments protested that the Schmitz-Stevens code
of conduct should not be imposed on the rest of the faculty: "If the
faculty of this, or any other university, were limited to only those men
and women who have never been guilty of a falsehood or who have
never erred during their lives with respect to the law, ethics or moral-
ity, how large would the faculty be?"[22]

Since Schmitz had asked for a cessation of commentary on the issue, it is not unlikely that Dean Stevens' letter was a trial balloon to test reaction to his own views. Drafts of a statement in the president's files dated March 8 and 11, show that he was disturbed by Oppenheimer's "puzzling and contradictory personal and official record. I would not want to extend him the privilege of a Walker-Ames lectureship." On the other hand, Schmitz wrote, his position did not constitute a "ban"—Oppenheimer would be free to come to the university if he was not paid by university funds. Schmitz considered him to be "a figure whose role in our national destiny had been and continues to be, in dispute . . . he is not a man, I think, whose presence is necessary or whose possible contributions to our Physics Department cannot be matched elsewhere." But the president was incapable of saying that sort of thing in public about another man; Stevens' legalistic jargon had said the same thing, and it had provoked sharp attack. At the same time, some solution had to be found. An anonymous memo to the president pointed out that the silence policy had made "the administration seem dogmatic, aloof, indifferent to appeals of whatever caliber, weight or dignity," and has permitted "mistakes and misunderstandings of fact to assume the weight of truth" to the extent that "not even friends of the administration can explain or defend us."[23]

As Schmitz and his advisers cast about for ways to settle the matter, the university's position deteriorated further on the national level. In early March, Harvard literary historian Perry Miller refused an invitation to speak at the University of Washington due to "an egregious insult to a great scholar." Victor Weisskopf, professor of Physics at M.I.T., and a frequent visitor to the campus (he had been a Walker-Ames Professor in 1953), also refused to come: "As long as the Oppenheimer ban stands, no self-respecting physicist could go to the University of Washington." Soon after, seven prominent biochemists, including three from the University of Wisconsin and two from Harvard, wrote Schmitz of their refusal to participate in a Medical School symposium on enzyme action. By refusing to appoint Oppenheimer, who was director of the Institute for Advanced Studies at Princeton, the scientists said, "you have clearly placed the University of Washington outside the community of scholars." President Schmitz's response was a statement of regret that the scholars had misconstrued his action as a violation of academic freedom, and that by their actions they denied their knowledge to their colleagues. The conference, which had been scheduled for early April, was indefinitely postponed. The informal boycott gained new proportions when six physiologists canceled out of a symposium sponsored by the Zoology Department.[24]

Though some faculty expressed gratitude for this outside support from their colleagues, others worried that the repercussions of the Oppenheimer controversy would get out of hand and damage the university's reputation beyond repair. Anatomy professor H. Stanley Bennett warned Vice-President Everest that the American Association for the Advancement of Science and the National Academy of Science were in the process of considering censure of the university and endorsing the academic boycott. Locally, he observed, confidence and support for Schmitz among the faculty was "seriously corroded . . . [M]any of the once solid timbers of presidential support have been worn out . . . or rotted nearly through." Bennett suggested that perhaps money could be collected to offer Oppenheimer a Sigma Xi lectureship; the danger in that course being that the physicist might refuse. The best move, in Bennett's estimation, was a reversal by the regents and Schmitz. Such a course, he suggested, need not force the president's resignation, whereas doing nothing might.[25]

Meanwhile, the *Seattle Post-Intelligencer* published an article by Westbrook Pegler which rejected the idea that Oppenheimer's flirtation with Communists was the result of "boyish naivete," and attacked the sinister arrogance of scientists who defended him. Next day, the paper ventured its first editorial opinion on the Oppenheimer controversy at the university. "The plain truth of the matter, as has been suggested elsewhere, is that the collective body of scientists is suffering from a cosmic guilt complex for having unleashed the horrors of atomic warfare on an already stricken and miserable world. . . . The notion that 'academic freedom' is involved in the refusal of the University to invite Dr. Oppenheimer to lecture on the campus is emotional and juvenile balderdash." The term itself had been so "abused by the brethren of the left" that it had lost its meaning, and had become just "another cliche in the word arsenal for apologists for totalitarianism," the editorial concluded.[26]

In succeeding days the *Post-Intelligencer* used interviews with Oppenheimer and University of Washington faculty to buttress its point of view. Reporter Dan Coughlin phoned Oppenheimer and learned that he had become aware of the controversy by way of the *New York Times*, and had never been formally invited to the university. Asked if he felt the university was violating academic freedom, Oppenheimer replied, "That's not my problem." In response to the *Post-Intelligencer* inquiry, "Do you think it right that these scientists [boycotters] embarrass the University?" he responded, "The University has embarrassed itself." Such truculence did not go well with Schmitz's faculty supporters, and the next day the paper headlined the news that an "Eastern scientist" had influenced the boycotters. Quoting a Faculty Senate member, Coughlin reported that "a high ranking scientist in Washington, D.C. . . . told them 'I wouldn't go to the University of Washington if I were you.' " Though some faculty were "delighted," others were "dismayed," believing that the university was being "attacked nationally as an 'example' to other institutions" whose leaders might be disposed to "interfere with faculty desires." Coughlin concluded that faculty efforts to dissociate themselves from Schmitz's decision would result in the president's censure by the senate. The *Post-Intelligencer* editorialized that the "independence of the University of Washington is at stake here"; those faculty who supported the boycott aligned themselves with "a small group of ambitious professors" bent on wresting control from parents and taxpayers, and urged the regents to "stand fast for real academic freedom against "childish . . . petulant" scientists.[27]

This sustained attack by the area's second largest newspaper marshaled new expressions of support for Schmitz. The next day, the regents issued another statement which reemphasized Schmitz's authority: "we welcome faculty advice, but we can never abdicate our legal responsibility for final decisions." The Alumni Association came out in complete support for Schmitz as a distinguished alumnus exerting his "authority against pressures from on and off campus," and decried the insubordination that was embarrassing the university nationally. These demonstrations were given new impetus when Alfred Schweppe, president of the Washington State Bar Association, former dean of the University of Washington Law School, and member of the AAUP, distributed a statement to the press during the weekend of March 26. Pronouncing himself disturbed over the attitude of the faculty toward the "University's sound discretion," Schweppe argued that in exercising its freedom not to hire Oppenheimer the university was protecting the Walker-Ames heritage. Because he had played a prominent role in drawing up the trust, Schweppe asserted his certainty that E. G. Ames would have given "emphatic approval" to Schmitz's decision to withhold a lectureship from someone "who has been found wanting in certain important qualities in relation to the security of his country" as Robert Oppenheimer. Bestowal of the same honor on Harold Laski in the 1930s had left Schweppe "deeply disappointed." He expressed hope that Schmitz would not now give in to those faculty members who were conniving to foist Oppenheimer on the university.[28]

Coming as it did from a respected attorney who had opposed Canwell in 1948, Schweppe's attack on the faculty dissenters provoked new commentary in the media, including letters and a radio debate between the lawyer and Stull Holt of History. Holt took the position that the faculty was "more nearly 'the University' " than Schmitz and the Board of Regents, and was better qualified to pass on the qualifications of teachers. Schweppe countered that such insubordinate arrogance flew in the face of law and the history of American state universities; the boundary of academic freedom extended only to the protection of the rights of teachers already employed, not those of outsiders. To underline his view that the faculty was exerting secret pressure on the president, Schweppe revealed that the UWAAUP had voted 3-1 against Schmitz's decision a month previously. This forced chapter President Edward Ullman (Geography) to admit that this was true and to criticize Schweppe's "bad taste" in imputing conspiratorial motives to the action of the group. But the real importance of Schweppe's "informational" statements was the cogency with which they laid out for the readers of the area's two largest newspapers the major disagreements between Schmitz and the faculty, as well as adding prestige to the *Post-Intelligencer*'s campaign against the academic boycott.[29]

Though faculty members such as Joseph Kraut (Biochemistry) and Dean Worcester (Economics) countered the views of Schweppe and the *Post-Intelligencer* by positing the academic freedom of students and faculty to hear Oppenheimer, most faculty efforts, as spring quarter began, were directed toward compromise. Dr. Detlov Bronk, president of the National Academy of Sciences, told the *Seattle Times* that the organization would not take formal action on an "internal matter" of a "sister educational institution," nor would it endorse the academic boycott. Ralph Himstead's statement that the AAUP was "watching this situation and considering action," prompted University of Washington chapter President Ullman to write the national chairman a cautionary letter. Though the 300 members of the UWAAUP had voted 142-46 against the Schmitz decision, and though faculty morale was low due to this incident and "recent lack of progress in keeping our University abreast of other leading institutions," Ullman indicated that majority opinion held that Schmitz had acted honorably but not wisely. He underscored his view that most faculty wanted to keep the matter internal by stating that no one on the faculty encouraged the boycott, and that procedures would be set up to forestall future difficulties through faculty consultation with the president.[30]

For his part, the president chose to ward off an investigation by the

American Association for the Advancement of Science (of which he was a member) by couching the conflict in "internal power struggle" terms. The basic question, he wrote, was the right of the university to employ or not employ; academic freedom was not involved, since neither he nor the regents were concerned about anything Oppenheimer might have said if hired. Given the controversial nature of Oppenheimer's governmental relationships, and "the attitudes of friends of the Walker and Ames families," and past controversies over Walker-Ames appointments, Schmitz had simply decided not to approve the appointment. Once the decision became public, the "academic atmosphere" came into play—"an atmosphere produced by differences of outlook in the several colleges of the university, by cleavages within the Department of Physics, by long-standing presumptions of prerogatives by faculty groups and committees, by attitudes and responsibilities of the Board of Regents. . . ." The issue of the discretionary power of the president and the board "should be resolved within the University," he concluded.[31]

Schmitz's private correspondence thus reflected a confidence in his own assessment of the situation which paralleled his public unwillingness to elaborate on his decision. Oppenheimer's international stature attracted worldwide attention to the university, and faculty worried about the long-term effects on its reputation. Though metropolitan newspapers like the *New York Times* supported the faculty position, such moral victories were offset by local vituperations which reopened old scars. On March 30, the *Post-Intelligencer* printed Fulton Lewis, Jr.'s broadside against the boycott, in which he scorned the "mulish obduracy" of a considerable segment of the scientific world to accept the judgment of Oppenheimer a "threat to national security."[32]

In this atmosphere, Vice-President Everest arranged meetings between representative figures in both faculty factions to consider ways to achieve a truce and to avert Schmitz's censure by the university senate. The "opponents" of Schmitz were drawn from the Arts and Sciences faculty: Z. W. Birnbaum (Mathematics), Paul Cross (Chemistry), A. E. Murphy (Philosophy), J. R. Huber (Economics), and Carl Allendoerfer. Schmitz's "supporters" were selected from the professional colleges: Donald MacKenzie (Accounting), J. Corbally (Education, also a member of the Senate Executive Committee), Laurel Lewis (Electrical Engineering), J. Mueller (Ceramic Engineering), and W. Shattuck (Law). Everest's selection thus reflected the perception that Schmitz had alluded to: "differences in outlook among the several colleges" about the nature of the university and academic freedom. At its second and last meeting, the committee agreed on a statement that

might help "restore faculty-administration relations here and improve the University's position elsewhere," which was referred to the
Faculty Senate Executive Committee.[33]

At the April 7 meeting of the Faculty Senate, the Executive Committee presented its revised version of the "Everest Committee"
statement, a statement by the president that gave assurances of increased faculty consultation, and the results of the secret poll of senate members. The vote—56-40 against the decision (3 undecided, 1
nonvote)—reflected Arts and Sciences domination of the senate, as
did the debate on the resolution. As finally adopted, the resolution
acknowledged the damage done to the university by both the decision
and the resulting public discussion, accepted the president's good
intentions for the future, and deferred to the Committee on Policies
and Procedures development of new machinery for appointments.
"We believe that the President and the Regents of the University are
strong in their intent to support the right of the faculty to think, to
teach, to speak, and to write as they see fitting," it further stated.
Though the main resolution passed 66-20, a motion by Professor
Mueller to make it unanimous failed. Bitterness was further meas-
ured when an amendment that read "We are proud to be members of
the faculty of the University of Washington, and we earnestly hope
that our colleagues from other institutions will again feel free to join
us from time to time for scholarly discussions on our campus," passed
only by the slimmest of margins: 43-42.[34]

Ten days later, on his way to deliver the Condon Lectures in Oregon, J. Robert Oppenheimer changed planes in Seattle. There, he
received news of the death of his Princeton colleague, Albert Einstein.
In response to questions by *Seattle Times* reporter Ed Guthman, Oppenheimer said that he would be happy to speak at the university in
the future: "If the university wanted me to come, and it could be
arranged—certainly I would come. No one is interested in a repetition
of the events in the past four months."[35]

The Assessment

The senate meeting put an end to public faculty debate on
Schmitz's decision, but private recriminations and chagrin carried on
for years. The conflict produced no winners, and each side could
count its losses. As Oppenheimer was a symbolic figure in the debate
over the best means to achieve national security, so too did he become
the focal point in the debate over the proper means to assure the
national status of the University of Washington. Americans generally

viewed Oppenheimer as either a martyr to national anxieties or a villain who had compromised national security. President Schmitz felt that he was maintaining university neutrality on this tragic question by disallowing Oppenheimer's appointment. But an internal decision of this magnitude could never be construed as neutral to a faculty already chafing under restricted budgets and prior incursions on their judgment. Had Schmitz decided a second time to allow a Walker-Ames appointment for Oppenheimer, he would have undoubtedly met some opposition from traditional sources, but he might have retained the confidence of most of his faculty. The revelations of the AEC Personnel Board, however, precluded approval; Schmitz was incapable of moving in that direction. The president was, after all, a popular scion of Seattle and the university; the regents, alumni, state officials, and regional political and religious groups rallied to his defense. For example, James Stevens, author of *Paul Bunyan* and "Dean of Pacific Northwest Novelists," characterized Oppenheimer as a "destructive scientist," a "magnetic Valentino," a "right smart city slicker," who, though educated at Harvard and European universities, had given us Hiroshima, which "yet scares humanity." On the other hand, Stevens portrayed Schmitz as the "productive scientist," the "solid forester" schooled in public institutions, who with his "woodsman's hand gave us progressive leadership in forest rehabilitation and education. He only lacks the glamor to win the attention of an Ed Murrow. Is that bad?" Stevens' assessment of the conflict won wide approbation in letters to Schmitz.[36]

The university's reputation in conservative Pacific Northwest political circles also took its part in the decision. As Regent Thomas Balmer later told the faculty at a luncheon sponsored by the UWAAUP, "the Canwell thing" was prominent in the minds of the regents when they voted to sustain Schmitz. They feared renewed legislative suspicion of the university would jeopardize the budgetary appropriation. The legislature had enacted laws outlawing the Communist party and had imposed a disclaimer oath on public employees. But the legislature of 1955 had also offered the spectacle of Al Canwell defying an investigation of his disposal of the records of the 1947–48 Committee on Un-American Activities. Threatened with a contempt of legislature citation, Canwell refused to divulge the whereabouts of materials he had not destroyed for fear they would fall into "improper hands."[37]

Against this latent fear of Communism and suspicion of Eastern "city slicker" professors stood a growing majority of the faculty, who saw the issue in terms of their freedom as professionals to choose their colleagues. By 1953, half of the Arts and Sciences and all of the

Medical School faculties were newcomers since World War II. For the most part, their ambitions and loyalties lay with the profession, and they realized that their colleagues at other institutions would wonder if they meekly allowed Schmitz's decision to stand uncontested. As Glenn Hughes (Drama Department chairman) wrote to Alfred Schweppe, "It is simply a matter of small-town or big-league . . . for thirty-five years, I have tried to talk the University into being non-small town." Jackson Mathews (chairman, Comparative Literature) could not accept the compromise solution agreed upon by the senate; he resigned partly because of the "restrictive and negative leadership" at the university which threatened his professional future.[38]

There were other signs that the conflict had wrought mixed fortunes. When the seven boycotting biochemists announced that they were in favor of "resuming normal relations with the University," their reasons were the show of opposition to Schmitz by the faculty, and the president's agreement to cooperate in the future. But many faculty wondered about the double-edged nature of professional support. By dissenting, had they not jeopardized their own future by attracting unfavorable attention to the university? As the draft report of the Bennett Committee pointed out, some of their colleagues in other universities were advising promising prospects to go elsewhere. In supporting Oppenheimer, who publicly admitted past falsehoods, the faculty were easily portrayed as arrogant and amoral. No matter how forcefully they presented arguments based on abstractions such as "academic freedom," Schmitz's silent refusal to attack Oppenheimer won the day.[39]

For others, including many faculty members, the issue was simply the authority of the president and the regents. President Emeritus Lee Paul Sieg expounded on the historical roots of this view in the *Seattle Times Sunday Magazine*. The proper role of the faculty was teaching and research, he wrote, not administration. Through the past mistakes of President Allen, however, the faculty had become confused:

> About eight years ago, a serious error was made by the leader of our university. Through what motive this was committed, I do not know, but it was committed in spite of solemn advice to the contrary. He gave up all but the mere shell of his position. He still signed diplomas, but he abdicated his position as president of the faculty.
>
> There was much loose talk about being democratic, whatever that might have meant, in a clear and necessary division of responsibility. The result was that there was thrown to the faculty, through its senate, the job of the president.

Though Sieg's was an extreme statement of the view that the faculty should leave governance to the administration, it reflected Schmitz's view that Allen had been remiss in relinquishing the chair of the senate to the faculty, and in allowing the exclusion of the deans from its deliberations. These subtle barriers to communication loomed large in times of crisis, and, in the view of Schmitz and the deans, led to an emphasis on the rights of the faculty without due consideration for their responsibilities.[40]

Inevitably, the Physics Department bore the brunt of the blame, for in recommending Oppenheimer they had "unnecessarily" raised a question that split the faculty. The Faculty Code, some noted, made dishonesty and immorality grounds for dismissal; Oppenheimer's admission of past violations of the principles of the code made him ineligible for a post at the university. Or, as Dean Woodburne observed, "there is some belief that some of the people in Physics are not unwilling to allow the department to be used in a campus squabble sponsored by the extreme liberals under the motto that no one can turn down the recommendation of an executive officer."[41]

Still another ingredient in the conflict was the perception that numerical domination of the senate by the College of Arts and Sciences threatened to destroy the autonomy of other colleges. For instance, Forestry's twelve staff were inevitably outvoted by the forty departments in Arts and Sciences in a polarized situation. Based on this perception, members of the College of Business Administration set about offering ideas to Schmitz and Everest on the reorganization of the senate and the administration. Professor Arthur Cannon offered a plan which divided the university into eight colleges with a prorated number of votes in the Faculty Senate. Professor Stanley Bryan spent fall quarter of 1955 studying the administrative organization of other institutions of higher education and talking with university faculty and staff, and in January recommended a broadening of the president's office through the addition of at least four more vice-presidents. His "rule of thumb" was that no executive responsible for policy decisions should have more than six subordinates reporting to him. Now, he suggested, the president and vice-president were assuming too much of the burden in making policy; the administration had not grown with the university. Though the size of Arts and Sciences was troubling, he noted that most faculty did not feel communications were "abnormally obstructed." The problem lay with the administration, which many Arts and Sciences faculty felt was too distant. Lines of command made the faculty hesitant to approach the president. Persons with a pure Arts or Sciences background felt the president was too concerned with finances to hear them effectively. Those trained at the university, or those who had been at the university for awhile, or those with applied sciences backgrounds (who had more access to outside funds) were more sympathetic to the conservative concerns of the administration. Bryan also found that the deans were perceived as too powerful; cronyism in tenure and promotion still occurred. These problems pointed to the need for a dean of faculties who could bring uniformity across college lines, Bryan observed. However, with the exception of the formation of the Colleges of Architecture and Fisheries from within Arts and Sciences, the reforms he suggested were left to another administration. The real problem, as Bryan implied, and as the Bennett Committee pointed out, could be traced to the ideas that went into the Oppenheimer decision—ideas that were adequate for governance fifty years ago, but which in 1955 were "unsound, demoralizing, disruptive, and unwise." [42]

As the history of academic freedom in the 1950s makes abundantly clear, Schmitz's proclivity toward political judgments was not unique; however, the Oppenheimer affair brought renewed criticims of the university in popular and scholarly journals. Harold Taylor saw a direct line from the dismissal of Communist professors in 1949 to the Oppenheimer decision: "Once political criteria are introduced . . . academic freedom has abandoned its first line of defense and must keep retreating to various unprepared positions, no one of which can be held for long under sustained attack." Robert M. Hutchins echoed this concern: using the "standard of competence would have saved us from the excesses of the silly season, such as the refusal of the University of Washington to let Professor Oppenheimer lecture there on physics, and from the consequences of concentrating on the negative task of preventing one particular unpopular variety of infiltration." These criticisms missed the mark only slightly. While Schmitz was willing to stand by faculty members like Keller, and to appoint a person whose security clearance had been revoked by the government, his decisions depended on his determination to divest the university of its radical reputation. Persons of whatever political stripe who made themselves controversial were not likely to be appointed, since Schmitz feared adverse publicity which might jeopardize university public support. From that perspective, the faculty appointment policy did not mean the same thing to Schmitz as it did to many members of the faculty. Academic freedom did not mean that the faculty were free to hear whomever they wished if, in Schmitz's judgment, that person did not meet his "best interests of the University" standard. On the other hand, decisions on who should be invited to speak at the university provoked protest from some unexpected quarters.

In January, 1955, for example, George Lundberg began making arrangements on behalf of the Sociology Department to have Harry Elmer Barnes speak on the international situation. Schmitz, recalling the situation of three years' previous, requested the concurrence of the Political Science Department. Chairman Kenneth Cole remarked that his department would have no objections, since that would impugn the judgment of another department. In the course of this mini-tempest, Lundberg wrote to Schmitz, former Regent John King, and Alfred Schweppe, threatening to expose to the press this violation of the Guthrie appointment policy which prohibited public discussion of foreign policy "from either right or left." [44]

Schmitz had no sooner given permission for Barnes's lecture than W. Stull Holt protested to Schmitz that Barnes was also well known for his historical works, which Holt considered disreputable and dishonest; having Barnes speak on campus would imperil the reputation of the History Department. Citing a Barnes "misquotation" of a passage by Samuel Flagg Bemis on revisionist attempts to fasten war guilt on Franklin Roosevelt, Holt accused Barnes of irresponsible scholarship, and urged Schmitz to reconsider his approval. "I would like to emphasize that the issue of freedom of speech is not involved here. It is not because of his conclusions or interpretations that I wish to protest," he wrote. Lundberg's view, of course, was that Holt's indignation was caused precisely by his dislike for Barnes's interpretation of Roosevelt's role in the provocation of World War II, and by Holt's defensive posture toward his own "connections with Johns Hopkins" historians. Lundberg reminded Holt that Barnes's lectures at Columbia, California, Wisconsin and Cornell had provoked no outrage from those history departments: "May I suggest that you do your department somewhat less than justice when you imply that its reputation hangs by so slender a thread that a single lecture by *anybody* will snap it." This argument between a historian and a sociologist on the eve of the Oppenheimer controversy was somewhat bewildering to Schmitz, who in writing to Holt that Barnes would be invited, remarked: "The only consolation I can get from the affair is that we may learn something the hard way." [45]

A few days later Holt wrote Schmitz to express his wish that the university had taken the "risk involved in having Dr. Oppenheimer here," since his scholarship and loyalty were not in question. Indeed, if Schmitz learned anything from the Barnes and Oppenheimer episodes, it was that taking "risks" was a highly judgmental matter in the atmosphere of the 1950s. In succeeding months the president's magnanimity was sorely tested.[46]

In June, Dean Woodburne informed Schmitz that the National Science Foundation had asked the Physics faculty to host the International Theoretical Physics Symposium in September, 1956. Seventy-five of the world's top physicists would be attending, including Oppenheimer. Woodburne advised Schmitz to assent to the conference to prevent further damage to the university's reputation. Since the symposium was a major coup for the university, and since Oppenheimer's involvement would involve no specific outlay of funds for him personally, Schmitz supported the Physics Department request. In January, Physics Department Chairman Manley proposed that the president assure Oppenheimer's attendance by contacting him personally, "so that the campus 'ban on Oppenheimer' can be laid to rest." Schmitz called Oppenheimer to welcome him to campus, and in September he attended at least one of the physicist's lectures. In the words of the University of Washington *Daily* editor, "the University took a long step back into the educational community."[47]

Schmitz also approved the appearance of Robert M. Hutchins to lecture on higher education, though Pro-America and the American Legion mounted a letter-writing campaign against it. As president of the Fund for the Republic, these groups noted, Hutchins was squandering $15 million in Ford Foundation money on fellow-travelers such as Walter Gellhorn, Charles W. Johnson, and Helen Lynd to do studies of un-American acitivities committees, race and housing, and fear in education. They also reminded Schmitz that the fund had distributed Ed Murrow's interview with Oppenheimer to schools and church groups around the country. Schmitz resisted this campaign against one of his critics by replying that Hutchins would only be at the university for one lecture, on a topic in which he had vast expertise. While his views were unpopular, Schmitz noted, there was no reason why he should not speak. On January 16, 1956, 1,600 persons crowded the university's Meany Hall to hear Hutchins attack schools for "training" Americans for "adjustment to society," and for their failure to teach people to think for themselves about creative ways to change social conditions. Significantly, the lecture was sponsored by the campus chapter of the ACLU.[48]

In the spring, the AAUP broke its seven-year silence on the appeals of professors who believed their academic freedom had been violated directly or indirectly by administrative actions based on the "Communist issue." A Special Committee of the association examined the public record concerning cases at eighteen institutions and issued a comprehensive report on "Academic Freedom in the Quest for National Security." The committee reiterated the 1947 position of Committee A that, in itself, past or current membership in the Communist party was insufficient grounds for dismissal. Likewise, refusal to testify before an official investigative body or to take a loyalty oath, in themselves, were not reasons for dismissal.

Regarding the actions of the University of Washington regents and administration in 1948–49, the Special Committee concluded that rejection of the Tenure Committee's recommendations regarding Butterworth and Phillips, and the probationing of Eby, Ethel, and Jacobs were censurable actions. Ralph Gundlach's dismissal was based on a "fictitious majority," the committee decided. In addition, it noted approvingly that President Schmitz's refusal to appoint Oppenheimer to an honorary lectureship had been offset by the current invitation to him, and by supporting "the admissibility to this country and the worthiness of a place on its faculty of a resident of Canada who is a philosophical anarchist." Because the personnel of the university administration had changed, the committee recognized that "it would not be appropriate to censure the present Administration on the ground of the 1949 dismissals." [49]

Although the AAUP's report gave no reasons for its protracted period of silence on the University of Washington cases, the evidence indicates that dissension within the association was responsible. Ralph Lutz, a former University of Washington faculty member and member of Committee A, considered the decision a personal triumph. In a letter to Charles E. Martin (Political Science), Lutz wrote: "As I expected, one wild man in spite of the special commitee's report, did still want to censure the university but he was ignored." Forwarding Lutz's letter to Schmitz, Martin noted: "Ralph Lutz of Stanford has stood by all along in this. Without his aid we would have been censored." [50]

In April, the members of the UWAAUP accepted the recommendation of its "Committee on Academic Freedom," which included Hans Neurath (Biochemistry), J. H. Manley, and Solomon Katz, and expressed "general approval of the Report of the Special Committee." Its adoption by the membership at the annual national convention, however, provoked a good deal of criticism in the press, and from inside the association. Columnist Raymond Moley reported that four thousand members had left the AAUP recently, and noted, "Good Americans will hope that this loss will now be accelerated. For its so-called 'principles' not only damage the dignity but reproach the intelligence of the profession which the association professes to represent." Moley himself had dropped out of the AAUP, he declared, because of the "anti-anti-Communist obsession" of its leadership.[51]

Sidney Hook decried the "basic evasion" of the special committee's emphasis on the "red herring" of national security. "The problem of Communism, and Communist teachers in colleges and universities has little or nothing to do with national security," he wrote. "It has everything to do with the question of professional ethics and professional integrity." He warned that the report would be damaging to the AAUP and to the cause of academic freedom, and accused the AAUP of failure to allow internal debate on the dangers posed by Communism. Hook's polemic revealed the depths of the divisions within academe created by the Cold War. In succeeding months, Ralph Fuchs, the new general secretary of the AAUP, undertook a dialogue with Hook. Though it did not settle the differences between them, it opened the door to understanding and eased longstanding resentments.[52]

Thus, time and compromise had averted the two-edged sword of AAUP censorship from the University of Washington. By making its stand late in the difficult years, the AAUP seems to have gained and lost membership. The University of Washington chapter, for example, which boasted 345 members in 1953, steadily lost members after that date. Between 1955 and 1958, chapter rolls dropped from 321 to 236. Such numbers are ambiguous, because the urgency of membership declined as the Cold War eased and the prestige and prosperity of the profession increased. On the other hand, the AAUP's silence during the fifties reduced its credibility with some professors.[53]

In the midst of the spring controversy over the AAUP's report, Schmitz approved the appearance of Kenneth Burke before an advanced English class, provided there was no publicity. Burke, who was lecturing at Reed College, did not accept the invitation. Meanwhile, at the urging of students, faculty, and Vice-President Everest, the regents unanimously agreed to a modification of the Speakers' Ban. For the first time since 1911, students were allowed to invite members of recognized political parties so long as provisions for equal representation were observed. Since the Communist party had been "outlawed" by the 1955 legislature, Communists were not allowed, nor were members of subversive organizations (those so designated by the attorney general's list). In May, the regents adopted the Revised Faculty Code, and in July, Henry Schmitz announced his intention to resign the following year at age sixty-five, though he was later persuaded to remain on until August, 1958.[54]

During the final two years of his presidency, Schmitz devoted his considerable prestige and skill at working with legislators to efforts to gain higher appropriations for higher education in the state. In December, 1957, he was named by Democratic Governor Al Rosellini to survey Washington's contributions to education in the wake of Sputnik. But Schmitz was never able to overcome the barriers between himself and a majority of the faculty created by his stands on academic freedom and the recession of the 1950s. One appraisal of his image as president was projected to the nation by *Time* magazine: "He was a kindly man who meant well and did well for the University in his own way." Despite increased biennial appropriation and quadrupled research and development funds, "few tears were shed" at his imminent retirement. *Time* also quoted a professor who said, "We've had an IBM-type administration, uncreative, and insensitive to what it is that attracts people to the academic life." Though the Board of Deans and Dean of Students Donald Anderson protested this judgment, many faculty agreed that Schmitz and the regents had given too little weight to their ideas and interests. Though the senate had been formally recognized by the regents, for instance, the board bypassed the advice of the senate in selecting faculty members who would help choose the successor to Schmitz. This fact was duly noted by Arnold Stein, president of the UWAAUP. Expressing gratitude that the board had included six deans and four faculty in the selection committee, Stein noted faculty disappointment that the faculty representatives had been appointed, not elected by the Faculty Senate; it is important, he said, for human beings to feel represented.[55]

And, he might have added, it was important to the faculty to be active participants in the destiny of their university, to clarify for the future a few of the ambiguities surrounding academic freedom in an age of conformity. As J. B. Harrison in his "Appreciation of J. Allen Smith" had written:

> Whatever may be the outcome of the current dialectic in such matters, it is the function of a university to participate in the discussion. The making of a university is far more importantly the accumulation of such a record of such participation than the accumulation of bricks or the proliferation of courses. Though the study of atomic physics may possibly contribute to the destruction of modern society, the prohibition or abandonment of this and other dangerous studies would soon reduce modern society to a state of "innocuous desuetude" which would make its demise a matter of indifference. Similarly, the demise of a university which was content to have its faculties doing only "what they were paid for" in terms of dogmatizing the true and the beautiful and the good would be a good riddance. If the University of Washington continues to deserve existence,

whether or not for its advertised "thousand years,"[14] it will be because it continues to foster among its personnel those who see to it that their institution does not stand on the outside looking in upon conflicts in the world's arena.[56]

In the months following its enactment, a small group of faculty determined to assert their opposition to the 1955 loyalty oath. Thus began a nine-year struggle to throw off the overt vestige of the Cold War limitations on academic freedom at the University of Washington.

VII

Denouement:

The Speakers' Ban and Loyalty Oath Issues, 1955–64

> The rest of the nation may now associate the University of Washington with this fight for freedom rather than with the repressions of the Canwell Committee.
> —Arval Morris, June, 1964

During the 1940s and 1950s, the impact of federal security measures on state lawmakers and educators was enormous. From Truman's Loyalty Order in 1947 until 1956, forty-two states and over two thousand county and municipal subgroups required affidavits of loyalty from teachers, lawyers, doctors, voters, and recipients of public welfare and housing. But it would be incorrect to state that the federal government alone caused this manifestation of American insecurity; loyalty testing has accompanied virtually every period of social unrest or war since colonial days. In the State of Washington, the affirmation of loyalty to state and national government required of all teachers after 1931 was brought about by pressure groups concerned with the erosion of allegiance to capitalism and democracy in the midst of the Depression. Strikes, internal unrest, and Cold War tensions following World War II caused the legislature to attach a no-strike, anti-subversive oath for state employees to the 1947 appropriations act, which was reaffirmed in 1949 in the wake of the Canwell Committee report. Though attempts to revive the State Un-American Activities Committee (1947–48) failed in 1949 and 1951, the Korean conflict and related developments won support for a more comprehensive loyalty program for state employees. At the prompting of Governor Arthur B. Langlie, the 1951 legislature passed the Washington State Subversive Activities Act.[1]

Like many other states, Washington patterned its legislation on Maryland's Ober Act in providing criminal penalties for persons found to be "subversives" or members of foreign or domestic subversive organizations, and in requiring every individual suspected of

153

being a subversive person to declare that he was not. Refusal to sign the statement of loyalty resulted in immediate dismissal. The 1953 legislature, in response to a Supreme Court decision on such actions by the states, further refined its definition of "subversive organizations." In 1955, at the suggestion of the vFW and American Legion and again with the governor's support, the legislature outlawed the Communist party and amended the 1951 act specifically to include the party as a subversive organization. It also required employees to swear that they were not members of "subversive organizations" as defined by the U. S. attorney general's list.[2]

Shortly after President Schmitz discussed the newly defined oath with the faculty on June 1, 1955, Vice-President H. P. Everest began distributing oath forms to all university employees for signature. In succeeding weeks, a steering committee of faculty and staff who were ACLU members (Ronald Geballe, Alex Gottfried, Joseph Kraut, Abraham Keller, Melvin Rader, William Reed, and Philip Wilcox) called meetings to discuss a challenge to the 1955 disclaimer oath with ACLU attorney Solie Ringold. The group that responded was small due to a number of factors: normal faculty dispersion for the summer, the realization that anti-Communist legislation was popular and that opposition would be unpopular, and the continuing divisions among the faculty in the aftermath of the Oppenheimer controversy. Many professors were disinclined to fight the oath. The strategy of those who chose to dissent was a result of all these factors.[3]

Professors Howard L. Nostrand (chairman of Romance Languages since 1939) and Max Savelle (an American history scholar of national reputation, at the University of Washington since 1947) volunteered to be complainants in the suit against the university because their backgrounds were comparatively free of prior "subversive activities" and because they were senior, tenured faculty members. The ACLU agreed to assume the costs of the proceedings and supplied free legal counsel. With the help of attorneys Solie Ringold, Francis Hoague, and Byron Coney, Nostrand and Savelle secured a temporary restraining order against signature requirements in August. They made it clear that this was a "friendly test" of the 1955 oath on grounds that it violated the First, Fifth, and Fourteenth Amendments to the U.S. Constitution. The heart of their argument was that the organizations listed as "subversive" by the attorney general had never been given a hearing, and that the law went too far in restricting liberties of thought and association in the name of security. They also argued that the state statute constituted a bill of attainder by providing for punishment without benefit of trial, a direct violation of Section 10, Article 1, of the Constitution.[4]

Nostrand and Savelle carefully informed the university administration of their intentions, emphasized that their action was not a protest against either the state or the university, and declared that they would sign the oath if it were found to be constitutional. However, some citizens refused to acknowledge their right to contest the disclaimer oath. B. J. Dahl, editor of the *Chewelah Independent* and veteran state legislator, wrote that "the professors should realize that the mere fact they object to taking such an oath condemns them in the eyes of the public as enemies of our nation, or at least undesirable citizens." Dahl urged the regents to dismiss Nostrand and Savelle immediately. A University of Washington *Daily* editorial deploring such "flag-waving" tactics provoked Dahl to threaten that the legislature "may take a long look at the University budget . . . if that is the type of student-thinkers we are spewing at our University." Savelle responded that "it is the teacher's job to criticize the government," and decried the loss of faith in civil liberties rampant in society. However, he knew that his actions were considered dangerous on campus as well as off. Though the Faculty Senate voted its "thanks" to Nostrand and Savelle "for assuming leadership and setting into motion an investigation of the constitutionality of the loyalty oath of 1955," neither the faculty nor the campus chapter of the AAUP united solidly behind their efforts. Some faculty worried that threats such as Dahl's might be acted upon by the legislature. Coming so soon after the Oppenheimer affair, the suit could be seen as another expression of faculty unwillingness to abide by the decisions of authority.[5]

When Nostrand informed President Henry Schmitz of the suit, Schmitz expressed the wish that the challenge to the oath had come from state employees other than the university faculty. However, the president accepted the Nostrand-Savelle action in a spirit of amicable neutrality, respectful of their right to contest the law. When a local organization canceled a Savelle speaking engagement, Vice-President Everest defended him. Savelle, he wrote, "is a highly respected member of the staff." The suit "is a perfectly proper action by men who, as private citizens, have moved to obtain a clarification of the issues involved in a statute affecting all state employees. . . . Security measures establishing the loyalty and integrity of public officials, including University staff members, are accepted as fundamental necessities in the public interest." But, he noted, such regulations should stand the test of law: "In performing this service Doctor Savelle, as has been demonstrated, ran the risk of misunderstanding. But his willingness to proceed in the public interest would seem to be in the tradition of sound American citizenship." Both Schmitz and Everest contributed to the ACLU's oath case fund.[6]

Meanwhile, Nostrand, Savelle, and their attorneys marshaled arguments against the oath. Nostrand asked those who were supporting the suit to set down their thoughts "relating the oath to the basic questions of the kind of character and kind of human relations we want the laws of our land to help to create." He noted that citizens had been calling the Seattle office of the F.B.I. "to ask whether it is all right for them to take part in the Freedom Agenda group discussions organized by the League of Women Voters!" Nostrand attributed such episodes to the influence of using the attorney general's list to define subversiveness and "the extension of its influence through oaths." Laws requiring investigation of citizens' private lives, he asserted, would do nothing to advance national unity. On the contrary, "to bring about the needed degree of cultural cohesion in a modern pluralistic society requires nothing less than a deliberate cooperative effort of humane synthesis and education."[7]

Among those who set down their thoughts on the oath were William H. Matchett (English) and Abraham Keller. Matchett, like other faculty members, had not heard of the oath suit during the summer and had signed the oath. After reading of the temporary restraining order in August, he sent Nostrand a copy of the statement he had attached to his oath explaining why he had deleted the words "undivided allegiance." Matchett based his distaste for oaths on William Penn's statement: "He that fears untruth needs not swear, because he will not lie . . . and he that doth not fear untruth, what is his oath worth?" Above all, Matchett declared, his first allegiance was to God. As a member of the Society of Friends, he would refuse to join any secret society such as the Communist party that advocated force and violated his religious pacifism. The a priori nature of the oath also offended him since "everyone must be assumed guilty unless ritualistically authenticated." Keller's objection was that "it would put a premium on uniformity and would put in jeopardy the critical spirit which is at the heart of the academic process and which, even more than reverence, it is our duty to teach in a democracy."[8]

By the time their case was heard in December, 1955, the plaintiffs had already won a victory of sorts. Their background claims to tenure were not disputed by the court or the attorney for the university regents. This first legal recognition of tenure in Washington State was formally acceded to by the regents in May, 1956. On April 29, 1957,

Thurston County Superior Court Judge Charles T. Wright declared the 1955 portion of the Subversive Activities Act unconstitutional on grounds that it illegally delegated authority to the state attorney general. Wright permanently enjoined the regents from imposing the oath. Nostrand, however, expressed disappointment that the judge had failed to rule on the constitutional issues, and Savelle warned about the "Age of Conformity" which was brought on by the vagaries of oaths, and which defrauded both students and the public. But the Washington State attorney general was also unhappy with Wright's decision and, in February, 1959, won its reversal in the state supreme court on grounds that it fulfilled the constitutional intent of protecting the security of the state's citizens. The incorporation of the attorney general's list of subversive organizations in the 1955 legislation was, however, declared unconstitutionally vague as an indication of a person's subversive character.[9]

Nine months later, the United States Supreme Court agreed to hear arguments in Nostrand and Savelle's appeal from the state supreme court, but during oral arguments on March 30, 1960, the court seized upon a point: did the Washington State Supreme Court believe that the law provided a hearing at which the respondents could explain or defend their refusal to take the oath? The state court ruled, in reply, that though the 1955 law provided for no such hearing, tenure provisions of the university did require such proceedings before dismissal; however, such an inquiry would have the limited purpose of determining only whether the professors executed the oath, since the law brooked no excuses for failure to do so. On January 22, 1962, the U.S. Supreme Court again disappointed Nostrand and Savelle by refusing to rule on the substantive constitutional issues. Over the dissents of Justices Douglas and Black, who felt the respondents deserved the opinion of the court, the majority ruled there was nothing to decide until after a hearing and dismissal were actually accomplished. The regents were now free to apply the oath; Savelle and Nostrand conceded they would sign the affidavit they had spent seven years contesting. For them and for the one hundred University of Washington professors who had contributed to the ACLU effort, a partial victory had been won, but the dilemma presented by the oath remained.[10]

Part of the victory, of course, had been the declaration of unconstitutionality rendered against state misuse of the attorney general's list of subversive organizations. In itself, this ruling reflected changes in the national climate since 1955. The easing of the Cold War to lukewarm temperature was signaled by Russian-American summit conferences and Khrushchev's visit to the United States in 1959. Except for such instances as the Russian suppression of the Hungarian revolution and the explosion of a 50-megaton bomb, Americans generally became more preoccupied with domestic concerns. Though the CPUSA was still seen as part of an international conspiracy, the demise of Senator McCarthy (1954) had helped reduce the intensity of national anxiety about internal subversion. However, groups such as the Minutemen and the John Birch Society (founded in 1958), persons such as Dr. Fred Schwarz, organizer of the Christian Anti-Communist Crusade, and events such as the launching of Sputnik (1957) continued to exert pressures on political and educational institutions to stand fast against subtle Communist borings from within. This "New Right" agitation concerning education was abetted by the Eisenhower administration's determination to alert the public to the menace of Communism. While the struggle for the allegiance of men's minds spread to outer space, military and business groups gave a "broad aura of authority and legitimacy to such propaganda and to such pitchmen of the radical right as the Rev. Dr. Schwarz and the Rev. Billy Hargis." As the nation moved into the 1960s American insecurity was easily focused on specific issues by those who warned of "moral decay, political apathy, and spiritual bankruptcy." During the 1960 campaign, for instance, opponents of Kennedy darkly asserted the existence of a "Kremlin-Harvard-Vatican Axis," revealing the anti-Communist, anti-intellectual, nativist roots of traditional American anxiety.[11]

Coincidentally, liberals were regaining some of the voice they had lost during the early 1950s, but they did not yet have the common rallying point that would be later presented by opposition to the Vietnam conflict. Fragmentary opposition to the right focused on such issues as civil rights of Negroes, the House Un-American Activities Committee, disarmament, and civil defense maneuvers. In the Pacific Northwest, as in the rest of the nation, skirmishes between the right and left were generally around such well-defined issues as the "proper" way to educate citizens about Communism. In meeting the academic freedom issues of the late 1950s and early 1960s, the University of Washington faculty responded to new leadership among its members, to a new president, and to a changing Board of Regents.[12]

The election of Charles E. Odegaard to the presidency in 1958 came at the beginning of the third great era of expansion in the history of the University of Washington. Like President Suzzallo and President Allen following the two world wars, Odegaard was faced with rising enrollments, an inadequate physical plant, and nationwide shortages of qualified faculty and personnel. Unlike Presidents Sieg and Schmitz, who assumed the presidency in time of financial stringency, Odegaard could look forward to a future of steadily increasing revenues from state and federal sources. An alumnus of Dartmouth (1932), he had received advanced degrees at Harvard in medieval history; after teaching at the Universities of Illinois and Michigan, he became dean of the College of Literature, Science, and the Arts at the latter institution. In his inaugural address, he challenged the people of the West to build an educational system to rival that of the East.[13]

During the first two years of his presidency, Odegaard succeeded in gaining faculty and regent acceptance of his statement on the "Role of the University in Higher Education in Washington," which defined the university's function as providing education for undergraduates in certain areas and graduate, postdoctoral, and professional training programs. In developing long-range policy for controlling the growth of the university, Odegaard relied heavily on faculty committees in a kind of "seminar approach" to administration. At the same time, however, he expanded the central administration and improved informal internal channels of communication as had been urged during the Schmitz administration. Faculty confidence in Odegaard's general approach to university affairs was an important element in responding to challenges to university integrity during the 1960s.[14]

One such challenge was the disclaimer oath required of recipients of National Defense Education Act funds. In 1958 Congress responded to Sputnik and the resulting concern about science education with an appropriation of $826 million for student loans. Before receiving the loans, however, students were required to sign an affidavit that they held no subversive beliefs nor belonged to subversive associations. Universities such as Harvard and Yale refused to participate in the program on grounds that it discriminated against students who, though in need of NDEA funds, found it conscientiously impossible to sign such an oath. The American Association of University Professors (AAUP) mounted a national campaign aimed at removal of the oath. Senator John F. Kennedy introduced bills for the same purpose.[15]

Meanwhile, the University of Washington chapter of the AAUP urged the Washington State congressional delegation to support repeal of the oath requirement. Although some state representatives were noncommital, Senators Warren Magnuson and Henry Jackson declared themselves opposed to the affidavit. In April, 1959, a university Faculty Senate resolution protesting the oath was sent to the Department of Health, Education, and Welfare. The University of

Washington, however, did not join the ranks of the AAUP's "Non-Participating Universities." President Odegaard stated that even though the oath was a "misguided" interference with the rights of students, it would be even more foolish for the university to withdraw from the program. Unlike well-endowed institutions, the university had no funds to replace the $300,000 that students at Washington received through NDEA. Though some grumbled, most students and faculty realized that the best course for the University of Washington was to join the AAUP's list of "Disapproving" colleges and universities. In October, 1962, President John Kennedy signed a bill abolishing the loyalty oath as a condition for government loans to students.[16]

Placed in the context of the postwar era, when national security had become a pervasive concern, the NDEA affidavit illustrates the threat to the integrity of the educational process that President Eisenhower warned of in his 1961 farewell speech: "The prospect of domination of the nation's scholars by Federal employment, project allocations, and the power of money is ever present—and is gravely to be regarded." In the State of Washington, for instance, Eisenhower's "military-industrial complex" was very influential. By 1963, 28 percent of Washingtonians employed in manufacturing were engaged in the war contracts industry; half of those so employed were in Seattle-area concerns such as the Boeing Airplane Company. Concern among Washingtonians about the best way to educate citizens about Communism was often translated into "courses" developed by conservative groups such as the John Birch Society and Reverend Billy James Hargis' Christian Crusade and subscribed to by civic groups and corporations such as Boeing.[17]

Early in 1961, a local high school teacher asked University of Washington History Professor Giovanni Costigan to assess a filmstrip called "Communism on the Map," which was being widely distributed to schools, PTA and church groups, and military installations. Costigan judged it to be a "gross distortion of historical events" emphasizing the worthlessness of NATO and distrust of democratic institutions. On January 24 he showed it to members of the faculty, ninety-two of whom signed a statement protesting its "irresponsible mingling of fact and falsehood." In later debate about the filmstrip, the Boeing Company management admitted it was distributing "Communism on the Map." Costigan received threats and a local member of the John Birch Society put out a "fact sheet" of Costigan's past activities. These included his support for the Spanish Republic in the 1930s, ACLU membership, opposition to the Dies Committee and Senator Joseph McCarthy, and his stand in favor of the recognition of the People's

Republic of China and closer relations with the Soviet Union. The controversy died away with various groups either supporting or denouncing Costigan's activities. Letters to President Odegaard reflected about 50 percent approval of Costigan's "exposure" of "Communism on the Map" and related right-wing "educational" programs.[18]

Both the NDEA oath and "Communism on the Map" episodes illustrated the increasing concern shown by students about the impact of Cold War thinking on their academic freedom. The University of Washington Speakers' Ban, a remnant of an earlier era, presented another opportunity for students to demonstrate their views on their role in the educational equation. The process of reevaluating old policies in the light of current circumstances, however, did not always go smoothly.

Since 1956, when the regents began allowing public addresses by political speakers, the rule excepting representatives of subversive groups and the Communist party had not been changed. Though faculty and student groups could invite persons belonging to such groups to speak before classes or closed campus meetings, the regulations did not allow alleged subversives to address public, open meetings. Meanwhile, the Communist party was trying to gain platforms to air its views on the difficulties it was meeting as a result of the 1950 Internal Security (McCarran) Act, which required its members to register. In January, 1962, a group of students agreed to sponsor a public address by Gus Hall, former general secretary of the Communist party. In advance of university approval, a Communist party spokesman announced that an invitation had been extended. Subsequently, the student-faculty Advisory Committee on Political Speakers recommended that the request for Hall's appearance be denied for lack of conformity with the regents' policy. The Advisory Committee's recommendation was upheld by Dean of Students Donald K. Anderson and President Odegaard. The president commented that the university should not provide a public platform for the Communist party, which was flouting the mandates of Congress and the United States Supreme Court. With regard to the report that Hall had been invited by the university, Odegaard stated, "The false announcement may have been an effort by a Communist spokesman to make it appear that the University of Washington first issued an invitation and then withdrew it. This was not the case." The incident provoked protests from students, faculty, and the campus ACLU chapter; it also netted a larger audience for Hall when he spoke at the nearby YMCA.[19]

The Hall incident also resulted in the regents' reassessment of the speakers' policy. On April 12, President Odegaard explained the changes in policy to the Faculty Senate. The attorney general's list would no longer be used as a criterion for the acceptability of speakers appearing at meetings open to the public. Representatives of the Communist party, however, would still be excluded from university podiums in compliance with the law.[20] Odegaard defended this aspect of the policy in terms of the educational goals of the university:

> The University recognizes a distinction between discussion in an educational context of communism as a social and political movement and the provision of a platform for the advocacy of the communist conspiracy. In particular cases the decision about an individual may not always be clear but again the University will have to make its own decision as to the qualifications of the speaker for a campus appearance. . . .
>
> If the University of Washington is to perform its proper function in our society, then it should not permit itself to be bullied and pressured into standing for partisan opinions of a majority or of a minority. And, equally, it should not permit itself to be bullied and pressured into acting in a way which gives the appearance of standing for the indiscriminate sponsorship of everything—in other words, of really standing for nothing.[21]

In response to Odegaard's statement, five hundred faculty signed a petition urging that the policy be further altered to allow for invitations to any speaker by any faculty or recognized student group, since "the appearance of an invited speaker on the campus does not involve an endorsement of his views by the University."[22] Professor Robert Heilman elaborated at length the views of himself and others who opposed the Odegaard-regents policy, concluding: "I think we have lost some ground professionally." New and younger faculty, he noted, worried that this was another indication of the lack of tolerance and breadth of view they had heard about before joining the University of Washington, due to past events such as those associated with Canwell and Oppenheimer. In addition, he related an experience at a Carnegie Tech English Conference, where the speakers' policy was discussed: "I was very sorry to find them thinking of this as one more evidence of an ailment that they think of as having plagued the University of Washington for a long time. . . . They remember the Canwell investigation, and, in later years, the Cowley, Oppenheimer, and Burke cases, and their whole tendency was to commiserate with me about our unfortunate lot." What such persons said to young Ph.D.'s was important, and Heilman concluded with the hope that Odegaard would find a way to moderate "local pressure of the wrong kind" by projecting the style of "a first class university winning confidence from its peers, and strengthening its own self-respect."[23]

Odegaard's response was another statement to the faculty in which he urged them not to obscure the liberality of the policy, which restricted only speakers who would appear at meetings open to the public. In October and November the issue flared anew when Ben Davis, national secretary for Negro affairs of the Communist party and a Harvard Law graduate, spoke before a closed meeting of the Law School faculty and students; he was denied permission to speak at an open meeting. The controversy eventually reached the state legislature when Spokane Representative Margaret Hurley urged the house to adopt a resolution commending Odegaard's stand. In the course of a heated debate on the resolution, Seattle Democrat Wesley Uhlman declared that state universities were the proper place to compare philosophies. Uhlman also said that President Odegaard told him that he and his administrators had denied Gus Hall a platform because of fear the legislature would cut university funds. "We're starting again the same old story of chest thumping, the old Tarzan method of 'Me better American than you,'" the *Post-Intelligencer* quoted Uhlman as saying. Though others warned that Communism had proven itself a bad philosophy, no longer debatable, others felt Odegaard had taken the easy way out and endangered the free speech of all. Everett Democrat Jack Dootson declared, "This is one of the few occasions I'm in agreement with Mr. Uhlman. The people who wanted to keep Hall off campus are the same kind of people who wanted to keep Einstein out of this country—the American Legion, a super patriot organization." The Hurley resolution was tabled when an attempt was made to amend it with a commendation for the president of Gonzaga University (Spokane) who had condemned "ultra right extremist groups known as the so-called 'freedom groups' " which had distributed derogatory leaflets about Henry Steele Commager when he spoke there.[24]

For their part, the regents and President Odegaard cautiously watched developments in other universities and privately expressed misgivings as to the wisdom of their policy. In August, Regent Herbert Little talked with some California regents who reported only slight opposition to their June relaxation of the ban on Communist speakers. "This was indeed a surprise to me," he wrote, "but quite heartening, particularly in view of some of the extreme rightist elements, especially in southern California."[25]

Meanwhile, the senate had appointed an ad hoc committee to explore possible alternatives on the speakers issue, and in November it recommended elimination of the ban on any specific group, such as the Communist party. Treading a path between "complete free speech" advocated by some faculty and the "controls" of the past, the committee urged a policy of "affirmative responsibility" consistent with the goals of the university to acquire and disseminate knowledge. In order to help students understand their responsibility toward this goal, the committee suggested that requests for speakers be cleared through the dean of students, who would consider the educational value of the speaker. In this manner, representatives of extreme groups least likely to respect the purposes of the university could occasionally be allowed to speak.[26]

Subsequent debate on the proposal of the ad hoc committee revealed that a majority of the faculty opposed its vague widening of criteria to include groups from both the right and left, subject to the discretion of only one person. Instead, this majority favored adoption of a policy such as the universities of Oregon and Harvard had of allowing any individual to speak that anyone wanted to hear. A minority of the faculty continued to argue for a "governing policy," which would admit the university's responsibility to judge the validity of certain points of view. At the January 6, 1964, meeting of the senate, Odegaard placed the debate of the previous two months in the context of the "struggle to define whether there is anything special about a campus in relation to a Hyde Park." The president reminded the faculty that in the last six years only two speakers had been denied: "We shouldn't obscure the spring for two swallows." Since the senate had failed to resolve the issue, Odegaard recommended to the regents a policy that he felt was consistent with both free exchange and the educational objectives of the university. At meetings likely to provoke extreme emotional response, the regents declared, "the President . . . may prescribe conditions for the conduct of the meeting, such as requiring a tenured member of the faculty as chairman, or requiring permission for comments and questions from the floor . . . or the appearance of one or more additional speakers at the meeting in question or at a subsequent meeting so that other points of view may be expressed."[27]

Though this policy met the approval of the faculty, members of the legislature deplored the regents' action. Representative Hurley demanded to know what pressures had been exerted: "The odious designation 'The Soviet of the State of Washington' appears more and more justified. I can understand how communist front organizations can manipulate control of the legislature . . . but I cannot understand how their influence can penetrate and find expression in the actions of the Board of Regents of our State University." Representative Michael Odell, also of Spokane, and a member of the John Birch

Society, called for a probe of subversion at the university and for the resignation of the regents. State Senator Martin Durkan called on the board to reconsider in light of state and federal laws concerning the CPUSA: "It seems quite obvious that to lend known Communists the facilities of the university to promote their subversion is clearly illegal." Favorable correspondence and editorial positions of regional newspapers, however, outweighed unfavorable reaction which came in the form of petitions from predictable sources such as American Legion posts. In March the regents reaffirmed their new policy, and in subsequent months Governor George Wallace, Gus Hall, George Lincoln Rockwell, and Al Canwell spoke on campus without undue incident.[28]

The dynamics of the speakers' policy change demonstrated the subtle shifts in attitude that had occurred in the university, in the legislature, and in the general population in the years since the Communist party had been outlawed in 1955. Basic to this change was the renewed sense of self-confidence that came with a relaxation of international tensions. The abatement of internal anxieties allowed renewed recognition that repression of views held on either the right or left served no real purpose except to insulate their proponents from the moderating influence of open debate. In asserting their support for students' freedom to learn, faculty members demonstrated their willingness to concern themselves openly with the restraints that had been placed on their freedom to teach and to do research. And, during the early 1960s, the Washington State loyalty oaths continued to occupy their attention.

The Supreme Court's refusal to hear the appeal of Nostrand and Savelle in January, 1962, cleared the way for imposition of the oath on all state employees. But on the University of Washington campus the determination to resist was broader and deeper than it had been in 1955. On February 6, Professors Geballe, Gottfried, Nostrand, Rader, Savelle, and Wilcox of the ACLU repeated their action of seven years before by calling a meeting to consider the current status of the oath. Within the week, the UWAAUP sponsored a speech by attorney Francis Hoague on the same topic. As the strategy unfolded, the UWAAUP and the ACLU combined their efforts to contest the loyalty oath, with the UWAAUP assuming most of the organizational work. In April the UWAAUP informed the faculty of the risks and legal questions involved in further tests of the oath, and outlined possible courses of action. The major question was whether or not the Supreme Court would hear a new case, since no faculty member had yet been dismissed for refusal to sign. Yet the only way to delay imposition of the oath was by new litigation. The second course would be similar to that used at the University of California—refusal to sign, a hearing before the Faculty Tenure Committee, dismissal, and suit for reinstatement. And, warned UWAAUP President John Maki, "such litigation may mean a long and trying experience . . . as long as five years, during which the plaintiffs must remain here or drop from the case. It will mean appearance in court to testify and an exposure to the public eye which may or may not be pleasant. It will mean time lost from teaching and research. For some it could mean nervous strain adversely affecting both personal and professional life." Potential challengers would need strong personal motivation.[29]

In May the Board of Regents amended the Tenure Code to include failure to sign as a reason for dismissal, as required by state law, and notified the faculty that they would be requested to execute the oaths of 1931 and 1955 by October 1, 1962. Employment of persons not protected by tenure, they stated, would be terminated within thirty days of failure to comply. Sixty-four faculty, staff, and students then announced plans to seek a temporary injunction to prevent administration of the oath. UWAAUP President John Maki urged those who supported the effort to refrain from signing, emphasizing that such action would provide a means of measuring concern among the employees, and would not constitute defiance of the law or of the regents and president.[30]

That spring, the UWAAUP conducted a poll to ascertain the range of opinions among faculty members. Of 1,200 voting members of the faculty, 541 responded to the ten-item questionnaire; 260 agreed that "for the good of the University, the oath should be eliminated"; 126 indicated that they approved the oath and would sign immediately; 217 said they would not immediately sign the disclaimer oath in hope that the courts would issue an injunction. Seven expressed resentment strong enough that they would resign from the university, and ten faculty members indicated they were seeking positions at institutions that did not require an oath. Although some of the respondents checked more than one question, the poll indicated a good deal of support for a test of the oath in the courts. Though there was still some faculty resentment of "ultra-liberal" ACLU involvement in the suit, and some feeling that the loyalty oaths were unimportant, the campus was not seriously divided due to a wide recognition that the president and the board did not favor the oaths because of the problems they presented for recruitment of the diverse personnel needed for a growing university.[31]

This diversity was illustrated by the variety of employees represented among the sixty-four plaintiffs: Lawrence Baggett (first on the alphabetical list) was a teaching assistant; Rocky Bauer was an undergraduate; Joost Businger was a citizen of Holland and a professor with tenure; Isabel Caro was an assistant professor (Anthropology); David Eaves was a research assistant and graduate student (Mathematics); John Emlen was a teaching assistant (Zoology); Ronald Geballe was chairman of the Physics Department; W. Mary Griffiths was an acting assistant professor (Zoology); Arnold Hansen was a micrometeorologist; Arthur Kobler was a research associate professor (Electrical Engineering); Robert MacDonald was a visiting associate professor (Social Work); Annick Smith was assistant editor of the University Press; and Leslie Warner was a secretary-typist. Almost every category of university employee was represented in this broadened test of the constitutionality of both the 1955 disclaimer oath and the 1931 oath of allegiance for teachers.[32]

Mere enforcement of the oaths presented difficulties for the administration; after the Boeing Airplane Company, the University of Washington was the largest employer in the city of Seattle. At the June hearing concerning the restraining order sought by the plaintiffs, Provost Frederick Thieme supported the injunction request because of the magnitude of the task of reaching 13,000 employees and 1,400 teaching faculty with the proper oaths by October 1. While all employees were bound to sign the 1955 oath, teachers were required to sign the oath form which included the 1931 oath. Thieme pointed out that some employees were not paid by the state, but by grants; some were part-time teachers supported by grants; some were on sabbatical or already absent for the summer; some who were newly hired might decide not to come to the University of Washington because of the oath; those who were citizens of foreign nations might feel forced to resign if the oaths were imposed before a court decision. Thieme's points were reinforced by Gordon Griffiths, acting chairman of the History Department, who said he could not conscientiously enforce the oath on members of his department; he cited the grave problems involved in recruiting and asserted the justice of putting off the oath for those who were newly hired and in transit to the university. On the basis of these arguments, the restraining order was granted, and only twenty academic and ninety-two nonacademic staff signed the oath.[33]

For Gordon Griffiths, who had been involved in the California oath controversy (1949–50), the lack of bitterness between the faculty and administration was a source of pleasure: "There is no [Regent] John Francis Neylan exploiting the oath to unseat the president, and pro-

moting political ends at the university's expense, while accusing the
faculty of being the party which was wrecking the university. This
administration knows that we want to get rid of the oath for the good
of the University." Several dozen citizens and groups such as the
Daughters of the American Revolution wrote the president and the
regents about the "traitorous" faculty who were working to thwart
democracy and Christianity, but there was no serious opposition from
the public. A UWAAUP fund-raising committee was formed to support
the legal efforts of Professor Arval Morris (Law) and ACLU attorneys
Byron Coney and Kenneth MacDonald. The costs of the suit eventually totaled $17,000; monetary assistance was received from the facul-
ties of Washington State University, Western Washington State College, Everett Junior College, and Whitman College.[34]

The Final Challenge

The case presented by the UWAAUP-ACLU attorneys reflected the
myriad concerns of its diverse plaintiffs. The basic constitutional arguments were similar to those raised by Nostrand and Savelle. The
decision to challenge both the 1931 affirmation of allegiance to the
U.S. and Washington State governments and the 1955 disclaimer oath
broadened the arguments, but did not change them. The plaintiffs
contended that both oaths violated the rights guaranteed to all citizens
by the First, Fifth, and Fourteenth Amendments in that the vague
terms of the statutes were a deterrent to free speech and conscience,
and failed to provide due process, except for a "sham hearing" for
tenured faculty, at which the only point to be decided was whether or
not the oath had been executed. The faculty and staff also argued, as
had Nostrand-Savelle, that violation of the constitutional provision
against bills of attainder was implicit in the vague language of the
oaths. The addition to the challenge was that the oaths violated Article
VI of the U.S. Constitution because, in attempting to regulate sedition
against the U.S. government, the state was interfering in an area
preempted by the U.S. Congress, as illustrated by the Smith Act
(1940), the McCarran Act (1950), and by the federal loyalty-security
program. Furthermore, the plaintiffs contended, the oaths were imposed without the state showing sufficient evidence to warrant such
severe laws.[35]

The heart of the argument for all the plaintiffs was that the vague
language of the oaths was a prior restraint on their freedoms. Baggett
et al. projected no less than 51,000 variations of speech, association,

and publication that could be construed as "subversive activities"; persons swearing to the oaths could be tried for perjury unless they understood all the ramifications of their past, present, and current activities. Central to the claims of the faculty plaintiffs was the issue of academic freedom: the vague language of the oaths was antipathetic to open inquiry. Depositions by Professors Z. W. Birnbaum (Mathematics), Robert Fleagle (Meteorology), Boris Jacobsohn and Isaac Halpern (Physics), and A. C. Keller (Romance Languages), were presented to show their fear that their interactions with members of Communist nations in research and conferences could be construed as giving aid to persons engaged in the overthrow of the U.S. government, even if (as some did) they held security clearances from that government. Depositions from President Odegaard and Vice-Provost Glenn Leggett were presented to show that the oaths were superfluous to the existing recruitment and personnel procedures practiced at the university. Evidence that the faculty and administration were cognizant of the importance of screening Communists and other subversives out of prospective faculty was deduced by presentation of Allen's actions in 1948–49, and the 1953 faculty appointment policy. Such selective vigilance was preferable to the wholesale infringements on First Amendment freedoms entailed by the oaths, plaintiffs argued.[36]

Understandably, faculty who were citizens of foreign nations such as Joost Businger (Holland), Paul Dietrichson (Norway), and Kenneth Read (Australia) felt jeopardized by the new tenure requirement, because they could not conscientiously sign the oaths. All stated that they would never have accepted employment at the university if the oaths had been in effect when they were recruited, bolstering the claims of Odegaard, Leggett, Griffiths, and Geballe that the university would suffer harm from the oaths. Melvin Rader cited his past and current difficulties with "Communist hunters," and asserted his apprehension that he would be indicted for perjury if he signed the oaths. Stull Holt objected to the 1931 oath of allegiance and to the 1955 disclaimer oath because, as a teacher of American History, he often criticized past improper actions of the government. "Various superpatriotic societies, like the John Birch Society," he commented, "collect from students statements made by professors in their classes." Similarly, Professor Rhoads Murphey (Geography and Far East) wondered about the harassment and threat of prosecution for perjury he would experience as a result of free discussion of U.S. involvement in the Far Eastern nations, such as Formosa and Vietnam. Two faculty, William Matchett (English) and Gordon Orians (Zoology), refused to sign the oaths because they violated their Quaker beliefs. The record is replete with such specific complaints that the vague language of the oath violated the academic and constitutionally guaranteed freedoms of the employees of the University of Washington.[37]

State Attorney General John O'Connell argued, in support of the law administered by the regents, Odegaard, and himself, that both the 1931 and 1955 oaths were fair and necessary for the state's duty to insure the loyalty of its employees. Citing the record of the Canwell Committee, he showed that there was evidence of danger from within. Plaintiffs' "refusal to sign" was specious, since through court action they had not yet had the opportunity to do so; until someone had been dismissed, he argued, the case was improperly before the courts. He further contended that all employees would receive a hearing before dismissal whether they were tenured or not, due to laws governing state employment practices.[38]

In February, 1963, a three-judge panel of the U.S. district court agreed with the plaintiffs that there were substantial constitutional issues raised by the 1931 oath; they agreed that loyalty oaths do not create loyalty, and that teaching and research personnel should be free of "secret restraints on their individual intellects," but they declined to rule on the oaths until the Washington State Supreme Court had done so. They also upheld the 1955 oath law over all constitutional objections, since it was designed reasonably to test the loyalty of employees.[39]

On appeal to the United States Supreme Court, the decision of the district court was reversed by a 7-2 margin. In reaching their decision, the justices cited only the contention of the appellants that the language of the oaths was "unduly vague, uncertain and broad," and thus a violation of the Fourteenth Amendment, and through it the First:

> The State may not require one to choose between subscribing to an unduly vague and broad oath, thereby incurring the likelihood of prosecution, and conscientiously refusing to take the oath with the consequent loss of employment, and perhaps profession, particularly where "free dissemination of ideas may be the loser."

With regard to the district court's ruling that the four undergraduates had no legal interest in the suit, the Supreme Court took no stand, but noted that "the interests of the students in academic freedom are fully protected by a judgment in favor of the teaching personnel."[40]

Thus for the first time since 1931, the University of Washington faculty and students were free of overt restrictions on their academic freedom. The successful prosecution of Baggett v. Bullitt laid the foundation upon which other academics could contest their freedom, and helped reverse the "sinister chain reaction" which began at the University of Washington in 1949. An epitaph on those difficult years was written by Arval Morris, "The rest of the nation may now associate the University of Washington with this fight for freedom rather than with the repressions of the Canwell Committee." [41]

Epilogue

The University of Washington's odyssey through eighteen Cold War years reveals the tensions that can arise between education and a society in crisis, and the impact of those complex interactions on public and professional perceptions of academic freedom. At the outset of this study, academic freedom was defined as the right of teachers, researchers, and students to an atmosphere in which they may freely investigate and disseminate ideas that interest them. Such an atmosphere is ideally characterized by a lack of inhibiting pressures or restraints from colleagues, administrations, the state, or public opinion. Although the ideal of academic freedom is organic to the nature of the university, the adequacy of its defense depends upon the consensus within the group of professional educators, which enables them to articulate the ideal to the society they serve. When concerns among academic colleagues about the acceptability of certain actions or beliefs reinforce doubts in society, there is less likelihood of concerted defense of the freedom of individuals. This situation is exacerbated, especially in public institutions like the University of Washington, when the academic community is engaged in efforts to improve salaries and working conditions, and public scrutiny is heightened by social crisis.

Such was the state of affairs at the University of Washington during the Cold War years. The factors that inhibited civil liberties in society permeated the university and limited academic freedom. President Raymond Allen's decision to fire Professors Joseph Butterworth and Herbert Phillips came at a time when academics and nonacademics alike were searching for a solution to the dilemma of Communism.

That his solution met little effective resistance from individuals and organizations such as the AAUP is a measure of the effectiveness of his argument and of the turmoil the issue caused within academic circles. In emphasizing the monolithic, conspiratorial qualities of Communist party membership, Allen disarmed those who argued that he was undermining the integrity of the educational process and preempted the idea that in a democracy free expression of ideas moderates radical solutions. During the ensuing debate, Butterworth and Phillips lost their identities as well as their futures in the academic community. Phillips' reputation as a teacher of integrity and distinction was forgotten. He and Butterworth were remembered not for their contributions to the university and to the debate of the era, but as symbols of the threat presented by their beliefs.

In times of tension, societies are less interested in principles than in results, and academic freedom has never been a good armor against the power of public opinion. The idea that disinterested scholarship is beneficial to society was submerged in the struggle to bring the force of U.S. know-how to bear against the U.S.S.R. The Allen formula was soon applied to those who associated with Communists or other "subversive" groups on the attorney general's list, or who refused to cooperate with authorities. Those who attempted to refute the views of the majority, both in and out of higher education, received little support. The threat of attack by "patriotic" pressure groups silenced potential critics. Tenure, which is today an accepted safeguard for those who dissent, was not formally recognized by the University of Washington regents until 1956. Ralph Gundlach, who never admitted Communist party membership, had been fired with the consent of his peers for conduct that would have passed undisciplined but for the Canwell hearings. His case illustrated the position of the dissenter:

> After I was fired in mid-year by the University Regents, I obtained endorsements and positive evaluations of my work as a scholar and psychologist by the State Psychological Association, the Western Psychological Association, the Society for the Study of Social Issues, and a special committee of investigation of the American Psychological Association which made a thorough study and reported favorably. I then moved for reinstatement at the University of Washington. No attorney would take my case. I contacted over a dozen firms, some in Seattle and some in the State Capital. They would not take it because there was no case. "Tenure is illusory." "I still have not found any sound legal basis upon which to build a possible law suit against the University." One attorney thought that since the Regents went through the form of the Tenure hearings, there might be a case, but he changed his mind; "When a Board of Regents is given the power to remove faculty members at pleasure, such a statutory provision is a 'part of every contract of employment.'"

Gundlach concluded that "there really is no academic freedom at the University of Washington."[1]

The fortunes of Professors Harold Eby, Garland Ethel, and Melville Jacobs illustrated what could happen even to those who had tried to cooperate with the administration. Again, their successes as teachers and scholars were submerged beneath the stigma of "probation." They became walking warnings to their colleagues. The realization by individuals that no one could help them if they "got into trouble" led some faculty to devise strategies to protect themselves from suspicion. They warned their students against "radical activities"; they stopped subscribing to the *New Republic* and similar journals of the left; they dropped out of the ACLU; they took care about what they wrote in journals and what they discussed in class.[2]

Although students and faculty generally supported the basic tenets of Cold War thinking, individual students and faculty did not. Despite the widespread fear, significant numbers were willing to resist encroachments on civil and academic liberties. They urged their presidents to speak up against pressures from local pressure groups with cogent arguments about the benefits to society of free inquiry. President Allen's readiness to do this was confined to a defense of individuals who were clearly not Communist party members. But for his personal inclinations, President Henry Schmitz could easily have relied on his enormous local prestige to defend the right of Burke and Oppenheimer to teach at the university. Like Sieg before them, and Odegaard who followed, these presidents relied on the consensus of opinion to guide their decisions. Allen's "successful" reading of this consensus was noted by the Bennett Committee in the wake of the Oppenheimer controversy: Allen's decision to exclude Communists from the faculty had been challenged, but its logic and validity had enlisted "a considerable base of faculty support" and had been accepted by "first-line American Universities." Schmitz's decision not to invite Oppenheimer, however, was judged to violate the pragmatic principle "Does it work?" or "What is the wisest and best course for the University to choose?"[3]

The Bennett Committee also noted that the AAUP had not challenged Allen's stand. When in 1956 the AAUP did condemn the university administration for its actions of 1948–49, Allen objected that the cases had been handled fairly; "political tests" had not been used since the Communist party was not a legitimate political party. Allen noted that that judgment of the party had been validated by the Tenure Committee and by the Supreme Court.[4] Allen was right, of course. But like many academics he was both the victim and creator of the Cold War. In the years after 1949 the university was caught up in the development of an internal security system which paralleled that of the federal government and the Boeing Airplane Company. Appointees likely to become causes célèbres were simply not considered further. There were, of course, exceptions to the dossier approach to appointments. Schmitz, in particular, was willing to go the extra mile to hire persons he could more easily have ignored. Both Allen and Schmitz were liked by most faculty members as individuals and as presidents. It is unfortunate that their academic accomplishments have been less well remembered than that they were "Cold War presidents."

The Cold War years also spelled mixed fortunes for the reputation of the University of Washington. Before 1935 the university was a regional institution characterized by small close-knit departments. The ranks of the faculty were often augmented by former students who pursued advanced studies while teaching. Old friendships and collegial relationships were destroyed when faculty members sought solutions to the Depression in political activities related to faculty unionism (AFT) and the Popular Front. New approaches to research and scholarship also put strains on departments. The Psychology Department faculty witnessed arguments among exponents of pure and "applied" research; the Physics Department found itself divided over the "new physics," nuclear weapons, and security clearances. Other departments experienced similar difficulties amidst the ideological and scholarly changes following World War II. Such divisions precluded unified support of colleagues whose academic freedom was threatened. The university gained a reputation for offering less than an optimal environment for prospective faculty members, and there was some difficulty in hiring because of it.

But despite the lack of clarity and unity concerning academic freedom which resulted from the crisis of national security and traditional regional politics, the University of Washington faculty did strengthen its reputation professionally. Though they could not agree on academic freedom, the faculty united on the necessity of forging a first-rate university. In the postwar years they were able to overcome those factors that had inhibited national recognition: geography and economics. Improvements in transportation and communications helped reduce the traditional insularity of the faculty. The influx of new students and faculty after the war combined with general prosperity, and, later, President Charles Odegaard's cultivation of federal grants and contracts allowed the university to establish a national standing. The movement toward faculty participation in university governance, which took definite form in the 1930s, accelerated after the war.

On another level, the university's "image" among Washingtonians changed somewhat with time. In 1950 the university had been perceived as serving the wealthy, radical, sports-minded minority. Fourteen years later, residents of western Washington expressed the view that the University of Washington was "rightist," politically "conventional," and academically unfree. University administrators, however, continued to believe that citizens saw the university as "leftist," and politically "unusual." They also attached more importance to the university's football team than did residents.[5] These attitudes were reflected in the legislature's reaction to the Speakers' Ban issue of 1962–64.

It might be argued that the tide of history was on the side of the "academic revolution" at the university, and that the libertarian reaction followed naturally on the excesses of the 1950s. But the role of "old liberals" like J. B. Harrison, Melvin Rader, R. G. Tyler, Edwin Uehling, and Max Savelle in rallying younger faculty members cannot be ignored. While they did not underestimate the power of the legislature, the importance of public opinion, or the basic timidity and indifference of the majority of their colleagues, their consistent espousal of the ideal of academic freedom assured it a central place in the "academic revolution" at the University of Washington. In combination with newer faculty like Robert Heilman, Ronald Geballe, Howard Nostrand, and Abraham Keller, they protested Allen's decision, pressed for institutional integrity, and spearheaded opposition to incidents such as that involving Oppenheimer. The fortunes of J. Robert Oppenheimer had focused national debate on the uses of knowledge in an era of ideological warfare, and defined more clearly the conflict faced by academics between their roles as scholars and as citizens. Schmitz's action sharpened that conflict and brought into play the faculty's growing professional power in defense of the beleaguered touchstone of that professionalism, academic freedom.

The vigor of faculty and student dissent from the Oppenheimer decision foreshadowed a new era for academic freedom at the university. During the course of the succeeding nine-year struggle against the loyalty oaths, administration and faculty members united to eliminate that common threat to institutional prestige and the integrity of the educational process. As the minority of the 1950s became the majority of the 1960s, faculty members backed student demands for academic freedom with concerted action. By the time the faculty succeeded in removing the loyalty oath and liberalizing the Speakers'

Ban, the long process of repudiating the misaligned values of the Cold War era was well under way.

Years of foreign and domestic policy geared toward the Pax Americana slowly yielded to a more balanced view of the role of the U.S. in world affairs and the function of dissent in a democracy. Animadversion on the Vietnam conflict and on the alliance between government agencies and higher education was central to the process. In part, this was a reaction to the manner in which intellectuals and academics had resolved the conflict between their roles as scholars and citizens. This reaction, which gained strength through generational, racial, and sexual politics, also damaged the integrity of the educational process. Dean Rusk and Walt W. Rostow served as examples of academics who were denied employment in major universities because of objections to their roles in the Johnson administration during the Vietnam era. In the relentless onslaught of subsequent events, the issue of Communism has been submerged, not settled: a return to the Cold War never seems far beneath the surface of American foreign and domestic policy.[6]

At bottom, the issue of the "politicization" of higher education during the 1960s and 1970s is another form of the old question about the uses of knowledge to society. One may expect in coming years to witness continued struggles between educators and government agencies over institutional autonomy and regulation. As in the past, external threats to academic freedom continue to be paralleled by internal debate about the best means to safeguard it. After thirty years, faculty unionism is again gaining adherents. After twenty years, tenure is again being seriously questioned. As the history of the University of Washington during the Cold War years shows, scholarship and citizenship, the dual roles of educators and researchers, seldom lead to neutrality or aloofness from the concerns of society.

Appendix A: Chronology

1911 Political Speakers' Ban imposed by U.W. regents amid turmoil of Populist, Progressive, and Socialist debates on social problems and role of U.S. government

Early attempts to organize U.W. faculty and define duties of regents and administration

1913 President Thomas Kane dismissed by regents; regents, in turn, dismissed by Governor Lister; a central issue is Kane's failure to control outspoken faculty and students

1915 AAUP chapter formed at U.W.; Prof. Frederick M. Padelford is member of committee on academic freedom and tenure which draws up national organization's "Declaration of Principles"

Henry Suzzallo becomes president of U.W.; AAUP investigation of his dismissal of "radical" education professor reveals no wrongdoing by Suzzallo

1917 World War I—dissenters from the war and some faculty of German origin resign, are riffed, or take leaves of absence for the duration

1919 Instructors' Association formed at the U.W. to improve wages, working conditions, and governance

Seattle General Strike; national "round-up of Reds" organized by Attorney General Palmer

1926 President Suzzallo dismissed after political changes among regents; U.W. comes into period of close gubernatorial management

1930s Depression revives national debate on U.S. economic and political structure; Washington legislature imposes loyalty oath on teachers

178

Hard times at U.W.—salaries lowered, faculty reduced; AFT formed on campus; many faculty members active in organizing unemployed and opposing Fascism; student strikes for peace and against compulsory R.O.T.C.

Regents uphold Political Speakers' Ban; legislature threatens investigation of "radicalism" at U.W. after appointment of British socialist Harold Laski to Walker-Ames Lectureship

1938 U.W. Faculty Senate formed; Faculty Code adopted by President Lee Paul Sieg and faculty

1939 Nazi-Soviet Non-Aggression Pact alienates many U.S. supporters of Russia and U.S. Communist party

1943 Legislature enacts Regents' Tenure Law (no arbitrary dismissal)

1946 U.W. doubles size (to 14,000) in wake of G.I. Bill; Raymond Allen appointed president

1947 Revision of Faculty Code: senate and tenure regulations strengthened; regents decline formal adoption of code; legislature refuses to adopt state tenure law

"Cold War"—U.S. and U.S.S.R. disagree over postwar arrangements; Truman inaugurates containment policy abroad and loyalty program at home; U.S. Attorney General Clark draws up list of subversive organizations

Washington legislature appoints committee to investigate un-American activities in Washington State

1948 AAUP's Committee A asserts the right of professors to be members of the Communist party

Regents uphold Political Speakers' Ban

July: Canwell Committee investigation of subversive activities at U.W.

September: President Allen and regents bring charges against six tenured U.W. faculty members after Canwell Committee finds they are current or past members of Communist party; UWAFT ejected from national organization for "unprofessional [political] activities"

October–December: Faculty Committee on Tenure and Academic Freedom hears arguments; decides Communist party membership not a violation of current Faculty Code

1949 January: Allen recommends dismissal of two avowed Communists on grounds that they are not "free to objectively pursue truth"; regents concur; those dismissed appeal to AAUP for redress; national debate on "Allen formula"; AAUP silent

Russians explode atomic bomb; China "falls" to Communists

Professor Melvin Rader proves Canwell Committee witness lied about him

1950 Korean War; Joseph McCarthy, his colleagues, and House Un-American Activities Committee compete to find subversives in and out of government

1951 U.W. *Daily* editor dismissed for opposing pending loyalty legislation; Allen resigns to head Psychological Strategy Board, is named to chancellorship at U.C.L.A.

1952 President Henry Schmitz's refusal to appoint Kenneth Burke to Walker-Ames Lectureship due to his "past associations" leads to adoption of appointment policy

1954 U.W. faculty adopts position of Association of American Universities concerning professors who invoked the Fifth Amendment

1955 Schmitz's refusal to appoint J. Robert Oppenheimer to Walker-Ames Lectureship provokes national controversy

Communist party outlawed by Washington legislature; disclaimer oath imposed on state employees; U.W. faculty members Howard Nostrand and Max Savelle appeal oath

1956 AAUP report on U.W. rejects "Allen formula"; regents formally adopt Faculty Code; regents modify Speakers' Ban to exclude only "subversive persons" and Communist party members; President Schmitz resigns

1958 National Defense Education Act requires disclaimer oath of recipients of funds

1961 Film "Communism on the Map" stirs faculty opposition

1964 Regents vote to allow Communist party members conditional right to speak on campus

U.S. Supreme Court strikes down Washington loyalty oath of 1931 and disclaimer oath of 1955

Appendix B

The charges before the Faculty Committee on Tenure and Academic Freedom are presented in this appendix as they appear in *Communism and Academic Freedom: The Record of the Tenure Cases at the University of Washington* (Seattle: University of Washington Press, 1949), pp. 115–25.

BEFORE THE FACULTY COMMITTEE ON TENURE AND ACADEMIC FREEDOM

EDWARD H. LAUER, Complainant,	)	
vs.	)	COMPLAINT
JOSEPH BUTTERWORTH, Respondent.	)	
	)	

Comes now the complainant and complaining of the respondent alleges:

PREMISE NO. 1

The complainant is Dean of the College of Arts and Sciences at the University of Washington.

PREMISE NO. 2

The respondent is a member of the faculty of said University of Washington and teaches in the Department of English, of which said complainant is the Dean.

PREMISE NO. 3

The Communist Party of the United States is not a political party in the sense that it freely and openly advocates that the form of government and social order advocated by Karl Marx should be substituted for the form of government and social order existing in the United States of America, and that such substitution should be openly accomplished by peaceful constitutional means.

181

During all of the times mentioned herein said Communist Party has insisted on the interpretation of Marxism as laid down by Lenin, and in more recent years by Stalin. It has, moreover, required that its members conceal their identity, take on assumed names, deny membership and use any means, even though considered false and fraudulent under the American conception of that term, to attain its ends, and has required undeviating compliance with the mandates of Stalin and the Soviet government in connection with the attitude to be taken and the deceptions to be made by party members respecting public issues as they have arisen in this country from time to time.

It has, moreover, required the performance of various tasks and programs assigned to the Party members, and such members have risen in Party esteem and their importance has increased in Party councils in proportion to the time given by them to the carrying out of Party policies as directed by higher Party officials, either through the Party itself or through organizations created or sponsored by them, which are large in number and are popularly known as Communist fronts.

PREMISE NO. 4

During its 1947 session, the legislature of the State of Washington took cognizance of the dangers inherent in members of the various state institutions belonging to said Communist Party, and by legislative enactment appointed a committee, legally designated as the Legislative Committee on Un-American Activities (popularly known and hereinafter designated as the Canwell Committee), which committee was charged with the duty of investigating Communist infiltration into the various state institutions and/or other agencies operating in the State of Washington. In this connection said Committee was also given the power to subpoena witnesses and take their testimony under oath. The legality of said Committee was thereafter approved by the Supreme Court of the State of Washington, in the case of State ex rel. Robinson vs. Fluent, reported in 130 Wash., Dec., page 179.

PREMISE NO. 5

In the Administrative Code of the University of Washington, the chapter on Tenure and Terms of Appointment of Faculty Members has the following provision:

Section IV. Removal for Cause

Persons having tenure under the provisions of this act may be removed from the faculty of the University for one or more of the following reasons:
  (a) Incompetency
  (b) Neglect of duty
  (c) Physical or mental incapacity
  (d) Dishonesty or immorality
  (e) Conviction of a felony involving moral turpitude
Proceedings for the removal of such person shall be conducted in accordance with the rules of procedure hereinafter described (see Chapter IV, Part II).

PREMISE NO. 6

Respondent is a member of the faculty of the University of Washington, entitled to "tenure . . . during good behavior and efficient and competent service," according to the provisions of Chapter IV, Section I, of said Administrative Code.

CHARGE NO. I

Respondent is and for many years past has been a member of the Communist Party.

CHARGE NO. II

At a general faculty meeting on May 12, 1948, the President of the University, Dr. Raymond B. Allen, explained to faculty members that the Canwell Committee would, no doubt, undertake a full-scale investigation of Communist activities on the University campus. He then and there emphasized in this connection that no member of the faculty could expect the Administration to defend any faculty member who had been carrying on in secrecy activities the nature of which was unknown. The clear meaning of his statement was that any member of the faculty so engaged and desiring the protection of the University was in duty bound not to withhold pertinent facts concerning affiliations which might embarrass the University.

Notwithstanding the membership of respondent in the Communist Party, either then or theretofore, no effort was made by him to explain his connection with said Party to Dr. Allen, or to any other responsible superior faculty member, nor did he in any wise endeavor to assist them in preparing for any hearings that might be held or charges that might be made against the University because of membership in and association with the Communist Party at any time, but to the contrary remained silent, and thereby knowingly concealed facts which it was his duty to disclose, and he particularly concealed the fact that he was or had been a member of the Communist Party.

CHARGE NO. III

Thereafter and before the Canwell hearings herein referred to, the Honorable Albert F. Canwell, Chairman of the Canwell committee, gave to President Allen the names of six (6) members of the faculty whom, he said, he was prepared to prove were either past or present members of the Communist Party. The respondent, above named, was one of the six (6) and the President of the University scheduled an individual conference with him. At that conference respondent equivocated and/or failed and refused to disclose to the President whether he then was or ever had been a member of the Communist Party.

CHARGE NO. IV

As a member of the Communist Party respondent consistently followed the so-called "party line," that is to say, the instructions emanating from Moscow, and by such membership placed himself in a position where he could not be an honest man nor a free agent in teaching the truth wherever it led. During a portion of that period the Communist line required that a member of the Party should decry the European war between Hitler and the democratic nations of western Europe as an imperialistic war, and Party members assigned to such duty picketed the White House and in their propaganda described President Roosevelt as a "war monger." After the German attack upon Russia said party line, without explanation, was immediately changed and the war against Russia became a war to save democracy, with the Communist Party, through its leaders in this country, advocating immediate help to the Western powers through the medium of war, if necessary.

Thereafter, when the U.S. became involved in the war the Communist Party, through its members and devotees, insisted upon the so-called Western front or invasion of Europe as early as the spring of 1942, and continuously thereafter clamored for such invasion, notwithstanding the fact that the Western powers, and especially the United States, were unprepared to undertake such an invasion until the early summer of 1944, and notwithstanding the fact that the United States delayed any such invasion until advised by its military leaders that the invasion had a reasonable chance of success.

Throughout these various inconsistent policies of the Communist Party, respondent adhered to the so-called party line, thereby demonstrating his dishonesty and incompetency to remain on the faculty of the University of Washington.

CHARGE NO. V

In compliance with the requirements of the Communist Party and in neglect of duty to the University of Washington, respondent has at all times during his membership spent a large part of his time attending Party meetings and meetings of various organizations sponsored by said Party and known as Communist fronts, and in assisting in the preparation of various kinds of propaganda to further the Communist cause and to assist in the establishment of Marxism, in the United States as that philosophy has been explained and determined by Lenin and Stalin, and in said Party exploited the fact that he was a member of the faculty of the University of Washington.

CHARGE NO. VI

At the conference with the President, referred to in Charge No. III above, respondent was advised that he doubtless would be called as a witness at the Canwell hearings, and that for the good of the University he should make a full disclosure of any present or former connection with the Communist Party.

Thereafter, respondent, by legal subpoena, was called as a witness to testify at a hearing of the Canwell Committee on the 22nd day of July, 1948, and then and there took and subscribed to the following oath, legally given to him:

I hereby swear that I will tell the truth, the *whole* truth, and nothing but the truth, so help me God.

Notwithstanding the taking of such oath, respondent refused to testify to pertinent matters, and especially refused to say whether he then was or ever had been a member of the Communist Party. Such refusal on respondent's part was a dishonest and an immoral act and was in defiance of the President's admonition, and again demonstrating his unfitness for membership on the University faculty.

CONCLUSION AND PRAYER

For the reasons above given respondent has brought contumely and disrepute upon the University of Washington; his behavior has been bad; he has neglected his duty; he has been dishonest and incompetent; he cannot render efficient and competent service, and he has demonstrated his professional unfitness to remain as a member of the University faculty.

WHEREFORE, complainant prays that this Committee recommend to the President of the University that said respondent be discharged of his duties and removed as a member of said faculty.

> Edward H. Lauer
> *Dean of the College of Arts and Sciences*

BEFORE THE FACULTY COMMITTEE ON TENURE AND ACADEMIC FREEDOM

EDWARD H. LAUER, Complainant,

vs.   COMPLAINT

RALPH H. GUNDLACH, Respondent.

(The complaint against Respondent Gundlach contains the same wording as that against Respondent Butterworth except in Premise No. 2 and Charge No. VI.)

* * * *

PREMISE NO. 2

The respondent is a member of the faculty of said University of Washington and teaches in the Department of Psychology, of which said complainant is the Dean.

* * * *

CHARGE NO. VI

. . . respondent . . . was called as a witness to testify at a hearing of the Canwell Committee on the 21st day of July, 1948. . . .

* * * *

> Edward H. Lauer
> *Dean of the College of Arts and Sciences*

EDWARD H. LAUER, Complainant,)
vs.)   COMPLAINT
HERBERT J. PHILLIPS, Respondent.)

(The complaint against Respondent Phillips is the same as that against Respondents Butterworth and Gundlach except for the wording of Premise No. 2 and Charge No. VI, and the addition of a Charge No. VII.)

* * * *

PREMISE NO. 2

The respondent is a member of the faculty of said University of Washington and teaches in the Department of Philosophy, of which said complainant is the Dean.

* * * *

CHARGE NO. VI

. . . respondent . . . was called as a witness to testify at a hearing of the Canwell Committee on the 21st day of July, 1948. . . .

* * * *

CHARGE NO. VII

Respondent was legally served with a subpoena to testify as a witness at the hearing of the Canwell Committee, to be held on the 19th day of July, 1948, but contemptuously and in violation of law ignored said subpoena and left the jurisdiction of said Committee, but returned to said jurisdiction after suspension by the University authorities.

* * * *

Edward H. Lauer
Dean of the College of Arts and Sciences

EDWARD H. LAUER, Complainant,)
vs.)   COMPLAINT
E. HAROLD EBY, Respondent.)

(The complaint against Respondent Eby duplicates those against Respondents Butterworth, Gundlach, and Phillips except in the premise and charges reproduced below.)

* * * *

PREMISE NO. 2

The respondent is a member of the faculty of said University of Washington and teaches in the Department of English, of which said complainant is the Dean.

CHARGE NO. I

At a general faculty meeting on May 12, 1948, the President of the University, Dr. Raymond B. Allen, explained to faculty members that the Canwell Committee would, no doubt, undertake a full-scale investigation of Communist activities on the University campus. He then and there emphasized in this connection that no member of the faculty could expect the Administration to defend any faculty member who had been carrying on in secrecy activities the nature of which was unknown. The clear meaning of his statement was that any member of the faculty so engaged and desiring the protection of the University was in duty bound not to withhold pertinent facts concerning affiliations which might embarrass the University.

Notwithstanding the membership of respondent in the Communist Party, either then or theretofore, no effort was made by him to explain his connection with said Party to Dr. Allen, or to any other responsible superior faculty member, nor did he in any wise endeavor to assist them in preparing for any hearings that might be held or charges that might be made against the University because of membership in and association with the Communist Party at any time, but to the contrary remained silent, and thereby knowingly concealed facts which it was his duty to disclose, and he particularly concealed the fact that he was or had been a member of the Communist Party.

CHARGE NO. II

Thereafter and before the Canwell hearings herein referred to, the Honorable Albert F. Canwell, Chairman of the Canwell Committee, gave to President Allen the names of six (6) members of the faculty whom, he said, he was prepared to prove were either past or present members of the Communist Party. The respondent, above named, was one of the six (6) and the President of the University scheduled an individual conference with him. At that conference respondent falsely denied to the President that he had ever been a member of the Communist Party. Thereafter, just prior to the Canwell hearing, he stated to the President that he had been a member but had withdrawn, and justified his prior falsehood by saying that his dishonest statement to the President had been made under "the advice of counsel."

CHARGE NO. III

As a member of the Communist Party, respondent consistently followed the so-called "party line," that is to say, the instructions emanating from Moscow, and by such membership placed himself in a position where he could not be an honest man nor a free agent in teaching the truth wherever it led. During a portion of that period the Communist line required that a member of the Party should decry the European war between Hitler and the Democratic nations of western Europe as an imperialistic war, and Party members assigned to such duty picketed the White House and in their propaganda described President Roosevelt as a "war monger." After the German attack upon Russia said party line, without explanation, was immediately changed and the war against Russia became a war to save democracy, with the Communist Party, through its leaders in this country, advocating immediate help to the Western powers through the medium of war, if necessary.

Thereafter, when the United States became involved in the war the Communist Party, through its members and devotees, insisted upon the so-called Western front or invasion of Europe as early as the spring of 1942, and continuously thereafter clamored for such invasion, notwithstanding the fact that the Western powers, and especially the United States, were unprepared to undertake such an invasion until the early summer of 1944, and notwithstanding the fact that the United States delayed any such invasion until advised by its military leaders that the invasion had a reasonable chance of success.

Throughout these various inconsistent policies of the Communist Party, respondent adhered to the so-called party line, thereby demonstrating his dishonesty and incompetency to remain on the faculty of the University of Washington.

CHARGE NO. IV

In compliance with the requirements of the Communist Party and in neglect of duty to the University of Washington, respondent has at all times during his membership spent a large part of his time attending Party meetings and meetings of various organizations sponsored by said Party and known as Communist fronts, and in assisting in the preparation of various kinds of propaganda to further the Communist cause and to assist in the establishment of Marxism in the United States as that philosophy has been explained and determined by Lenin and Stalin, and in said Party exploited the fact that he was a member of the faculty of the University of Washington.

CHARGE NO. V

At the conference with the President, referred to in Charge No. II above, respondent was advised that he doubtless would be called as a witness at the Canwell hearings, and that for the good of the University he should make full disclosure of any present or former connection with the Communist Party.

Thereafter, respondent, by legal subpoena, was called as a witness to testify at a hearing of the Canwell Committee on the 21st day of July, 1948, and then and there took and subscribed to the following oath, legally given to him:

> I hereby swear that I will tell the truth, the *whole* truth, and nothing but the truth, so help me God.

Notwithstanding the taking of such oath, respondent refused to tell the whole truth by then and there refusing to describe his activities in the Communist Party, his associations therein and the persons with whom from time to time he had sat in Communist Party meetings and with whom he had associated in Communist Party activities. Such refusal on respondent's part was a dishonest and an immoral act and was in defiance of the President's admonition, again demonstrating his unfitness for membership on the University faculty.

CONCLUSION AND PRAYER

For the reasons above given respondent has brought contumely and disrepute upon the University of Washington; his behavior has been bad; he has neglected his duty; he has been dishonest and incompetent; he cannot render efficient and competent service, and he has demonstrated his professional unfitness to remain as a member of the University faculty.

WHEREFORE, complainant prays that this Committee recommend to the President of the University that said respondent be discharged of his duties and removed as a member of said faculty.

> Edward H. Lauer
> *Dean of the College of Arts and Sciences*

BEFORE THE FACULTY COMMITTEE ON TENURE AND ACADEMIC FREEDOM

EDWARD H. LAUER, Complainant,)	
vs.)	COMPLAINT
GARLAND ETHEL, Respondent.)	

(The complaint against Respondent Ethel is the same as that against Respondent Eby except for the wording of Charges No. III and V.)

* * * *

CHARGE NO. II

Thereafter and before the Canwell hearings referred to, the Honorable Alfred F. Canwell, Chairman of the Canwell Committee, gave to President Allen the names of six (6) members of the faculty whom, he said, he was prepared to prove were either past or present members of the Communist Party. The respondent, above named, was one of the six (6) and the President of the University scheduled an individual conference with him. At that conference respondent equivocated and failed to admit that he had ever been a member of the Communist Party. Shortly thereafter, and sometime prior to the Canwell hearing he stated to the President that he had been a member but had withdrawn.

* * * *

CHARGE NO. V

. . . respondent . . . was called as a witness to testify at a hearing of the Canwell Committee on the 20th day of July, 1948. . . .

> Edward H. Lauer
> *Dean of the College of Arts and Sciences*

BEFORE THE FACULTY COMMITTEE ON TENURE AND ACADEMIC FREEDOM

EDWARD H. LAUER, Complainant,)

vs.   )   COMPLAINT

MELVILLE JACOBS, Respondent.   )

(The complaint against Respondent Jacobs is the same as that against Respondent Eby except for the wording of Premise No. 2 and Charge No. V.)

* * * *

PREMISE NO. 2

The respondent is a member of the faculty of said University of Washington and teaches in the Department of Anthropology, of which complainant is the Dean.

* * * *

CHARGE NO. V

. . . respondent . . . was called as a witness to testify at a hearing of the Canwell Committee on the 22nd day of July, 1948. . . .

Edward H. Lauer
Dean of the College of Arts and Sciences

Notes

Chapter I

1. *Old Truths and New Horizons: Addresses Delivered at the Inauguration of Dr. Raymond B. Allen as President of the University of Washington, May 22–24, 1947* (Seattle: University of Washington Press, 1949), pp. 15, 18.

2. *Capitols Who's Who for Washington: The State Encyclopedia, 1949–50* (Portland: Capitol Publishing Co., 1949), p. 152; University of Washington *Bulletin*, October, 1946, p. 1.

3. *Regents Journal* 9 (June 2, 23, 1945): 714, 719; (February 18, 1946): 777; Guthrie to Allen, January 24, February 8, March 4, 1946, Guthrie Papers, box 2. All manuscript collections cited in this work are located in the University of Washington Library unless otherwise noted.

4. *Seattle Times*, February 24, 1946, p. 1; *Seattle Post-Intelligencer*, August 28, 1946, p. 5.

5. University of Washington *Bulletin*, October, 1946, p. 2.

6. University of Washington *Bulletin*, January, 1947, p. 4, and February, 1947, p. 2; *Seattle Post-Intelligencer*, April 23, 1946, p. 1. The cost per student in 1946–47 was $340, a decrease from $476 in 1943–44. Unlike most institutions, the university's building fund was derived from student fees, rental of its downtown properties, and income from its lands. See *Thirty-first Biennial Report from the Board of Regents to the Governor of Washington* (1951), p. 54.

7. As summarized in "Report of the Committee on Graduate Study," *AAUP Chapter Bulletin* 4 (December, 1946): 2–4, UWAAUP Chapter Records, box 1. Correspondence relating to Padelford's efforts to gain AAU recognition is in Padelford Papers and in President's Office Records, boxes 130–31.

8. Calvin F. Schmid et al., *Studies in Enrollment Trends and Patterns, Part 1—Regular Academic Year: 1930 to 1964* (Seattle: University of Washington Press, 1966), p. 168. Schmid demonstrates the persistence of the regional character: in 1964, 63 percent of the university's students were from King County. The benchmark institutions with which the university compared it-

self were Oregon, California, Illinois, Indiana, Michigan, Minnesota, and Wisconsin. Charles Gates, *The First Century at the University of Washington, 1861–1961* (Seattle: University of Washington Press, 1961), p. 182. Gates points out that many of those faculty members were hired during the period of expansion following World War I.

9. Memo, President Henry Schmitz to the Board of Regents, "The Origin and Development of the Administrative Code," June 3, 1954, President's Office Records, box 106. William R. Wilson (Psychology) to L. P. Sieg, May 16, 1939, President's Office Records, small box 15; Wilson commented that presidential directives would not undo ingrained habits. Gates, *The First Century*, pp. 187–93. Charles E. Martin, personal interview, October 21, 1975, Seattle.

10. *AAUP Bulletin* 25 (1939): 121; 33(1947): 188. In the minds of many faculty members, however, the AAUP did not lend help when it was most needed. In 1938, Florence Bean James (English-Drama) was removed from the faculty during a "reorganization" which entailed a reduction-in-force. Not a few faculty members believed she was let go because of the political nature of plays enacted at the Seattle Repertory Playhouse, which she and her husband operated near campus. The local chapter appealed to Ralph Himstead, general secretary of the AAUP, for an investigation of the case: "It is perfectly clear, is it not, that at the University of Washington the expressed will of the faculty on matters pertaining to personnel is flatly disregarded. This leaves us without local recourse—short of forms of direct action both difficult and questionable of application in academic affairs—and requires us to seek outside support as it would seem to be the responsibility of the AAUP to offer." Himstead replied that the national organization was too busy to look into cases as minor as that presented by Mrs. James. UWAAUP to Himstead, March 28, 1939; Himstead to Ralph Gundlach, August 23, 1939, Gundlach Papers, box 1.

11. William Edward Eaton, *The American Federation of Teachers, 1916–1961* (Carbondale: Southern Illinois University Press, 1975), pp. 79–83, 93–94, 107. *Seattle Post-Intelligencer*, January 29, 1937, p. 3.

12. *The American Teacher*, March–April, 1937, p. 12; September–October, 1937, p. 5; March–April, 1938, p. 26. Personal interviews: Edwin Uehling, November 12, 1974; W. Stull Holt, October, 1974; Melvin Rader, October, 1974, all in Seattle.

13. "Academic Freedom at the University of Pittsburgh," *AAUP Bulletin* 15 (1929): 578–91; "Academic Freedom in Pittsburgh," *New Republic* 58 (May 22, 1929): 21–22; Gates, *First Century*, pp. 180–83.

14. *Seattle Post-Intelligencer*, January 29, 1937, p. 1; University of Washington *Daily*, June 4, 1936, p. 1.

15. *Seattle Star*, March 18, 1936; Sieg to Thomas Balmer, April 20, 1939, President's Office Records, box 81.

16. *Seattle Post-Intelligencer*, June 18, 1935, p. 1; June 19, 1935, pp. 2, 3. Gundlach to Elton Guthrie (secretary of Local 401, AFT), February 24, 1937, Gundlach Papers, folder 1–10. Personal interviews: Melvin Rader, November 4, 1974; Garland Ethel, October 15, 1975, Seattle. Albert F. Gunns, "Civil

Liberties and Crisis: The Status of Civil Liberties in the Pacific Northwest, 1917–1940," (Ph.D. dissertation, University of Washington, 1971), pp. 205–9. Albert A. Acena, "The Washington Commonwealth Federation: Reform Politics and the Popular Front," (Ph.D. dissertation, University of Washington, 1976), pp. 167–68.

17. *Regents Journal* 8 (June 9, 1933): 71; (October 24, 1936): 237–38; (January 23, 1937): 248; (March 27, 1937): 254–55; (April 1, 1939): 354. Gates, *First Century*, pp. 134–35. For Sieg's attitude on the student strikes see: University of Washington *Daily*, April 2, 3, 11, 1935, and April 23, 1936.

18. "Report of Committee A," *AAUP Bulletin* 27 (1941): 48.

19. Pro-America, founded in Seattle in 1932, was a national organization "devoted to the preservation of constitutional government." It voiced a common concern of the time that the New Deal would lead to a communistic U.S. Materials pertinent to the Laski controversy are found in President's Office Records, box 124.

20. Balmer to Sieg, March 6, 1939; Sieg to Balmer, April 20, 1939, President's Office Records, box 81. *Seattle Post-Intelligencer*, January 3, 1939, p. 4.

21. *Twenty-eighth Biennial Report from the Board of Regents to the Governor of Washington* (1945), pp. 9–31. *Twenty-ninth Biennial Report from the Board of Regents to the Governor of Washington* (1947), pp. 14–41. University of Washington *Bulletin*, January, 1947, p. 4; April 19, 1947, p. 3.

22. Calvin F. Schmid, *Social Trends in Seattle* (Seattle: University of Washington Press, 1944), p. 298 and *passim*. Oscar O. Winther, *The Great Northwest* (New York: Alfred A. Knopf, 1952), p. 430.

23. *Twenty-eighth Biennial Report of the Regents* (1945), pp. 39–41; *Regents Journal* 9: 647, 656.

24. *Public Education in Washington: A Report of a Survey of Public Education in the State of Washington*, George D. Strayer, director. Submitted to Governor Mon C. Wallgren, September 5, 1946, pp. 267–72.

25. Ibid., pp. 503–6.

26. Ibid., pp. 510–64.

27. Edwin R. Guthrie, "Evaluation of Faculty Service," *AAUP Bulletin* 31 (1945): 255–62; Vernon A. Mund, "The Economic Status of the Profession," *AAUP Bulletin* 33 (1947): 95–98. "Questionnaire," *AAUP Chapter Bulletin*, April, 1946; "Report of the Committee on Democratic Government, 1944," *AAUP Chapter Bulletin*, n.d., AAUP Records, box 1. *Strayer Survey*, pp. 560–61.

28. Minutes of the Meeting of the Budget Committee, April 9, 1947, Records of the Secretary of the Faculty, box 1. *AAUP Chapter Bulletin*, March, 1947, pp. 2, 3, UWAAUP Records, box 1. Allen to Robert G. Sproul, April 2, 1947, President's Office Records, box 115. Personal interviews: Laurel Lewis, March 2, 1976; Charles Martin, October 21, 1975; Lloyd Woodburne, March 9, 1976; Donald K. Anderson, January 28, 1976, all in Seattle.

29. *Old Truths and New Horizons*, p. 40.

30. Telford Taylor, *Grand Inquest: The Story of Congressional Investigations* (New York: Simon and Schuster, 1955), pp. 290–91 and *passim*.

31. Acena, "The Washington Commonwealth Federation," p. 438. Vern

Countryman, *Un-American Activities in the State of Washington* (Ithaca, N.Y.: Cornell University Press, 1951), pp. 10–11. Since the 1930s the House Un-American Activities Committee (HUAC) had become the chief forum of those who believed that New Deal economic and foreign policy gave too much advantage to Communists. An overall study is Walter Goodman, *The Committee: The Extraordinary Career of the House Committee on Un-American Activities* (New York: Farrar, Straus and Giroux, 1968).

32. *Seattle Post-Intelligencer*, December 13, 1946. According to former managing editor of the *Post-Intelligencer* Ed Stone, a major actor in the formation of the legislative investigation was reporter Fred Niendorff. Genuinely concerned about Communists on the campus, Niendorff wrote many articles on the committee's activities during its two-year existence. Tape-recorded interview between Stone and Richard Pelto, 1969, Pelto Collection.

33. Roger Sale, *Seattle Past to Present* (Seattle: University of Washington Press, 1976), pp. 144–49. Murray Morgan, *Skid Road: An Informal Portrait of Seattle* (New York: Viking Press, 1951), pp. 220–71. *Seattle Post-Intelligencer*, March 2, 1947, p. 1. Recall Drumheller's wish for a legislative investigation of the university in 1939.

34. University of Washington *Daily*, March 3, 1947. Gordon Newell, *Rogues, Buffoons and Statesmen* (Seattle: Hangman Press, Superior Publishing Company, 1975), p. 442.

35. *Seattle Post-Intelligencer*, March 2, 1947, p. 1.

36. *Journal of the House of the Thirtieth Legislature of the State of Washington* (1947), pp. 449, 572–73, 909. Countryman, *Un-American Activities in Washington State*, pp. 13–22. Countryman points out the similarities between the Washington legislation and that which established the Tenney Committee in California.

37. Acena, "The Washington Commonwealth Federation," p. 280, n. 3. In a 1966 letter to Acena, Farley did not disavow the statement, but wrote: "many statements that I never made were attributed to me." See also Morgan, *Skid Road*, p. 241, and Sale, *Seattle Past to Present*, p. 148. Also worthwhile is Fayette Krause, "Democratic Party Politics in the State of Washington during the New Deal: 1932–40" (Ph.D. dissertation, University of Washington, 1971).

38. Gates, *First Century*, p. 133; Eric F. Goldman, *Rendezvous with Destiny* (New York: Alfred A. Knopf, 1953), pp. 143–53; Thomas C. McClintock, "J. Allen Smith and the Progressive Movement: A Study in Intellectual History" (Ph.D. dissertation, University of Washington, 1959). Garland Ethel, personal interview, October 15, 1975, Seattle. An alternative view of the faculty is contained in Thomas Griffith, *The Waist High Culture* (New York: Harper and Brothers, 1959), pp. 22–33. Another account of Washington's radicalism is Norman H. Clark, *Washington: A Bicentennial History* (New York: W. W. Norton and Company, 1976), pp. 155–69.

39. Frank A. Warren III, *Liberals and Communism* (Bloomington: Indiana University Press, 1966). David Storey, "Sidney Hook and Arthur Schlesinger, Jr., Spokesmen for the Anti-Communist Left in American Political Thought Since 1940" (M.A. thesis, University of Washington, 1967).

40. Minutes of meeting between Allen and Executive Committee of the UWAAUP, March 12, 1947, President's Office Records, box 101; *UWAAUP Chapter Bulletin*, no. 5 (March, 1947), UWAAUP Records, box 1. Charles E. Martin, personal interview, October 21, 1975.

41. *UWAAUP Chapter Bulletin*, no. 5 (March, 1947); Allen to the Washington State Interim Committee for Investigation of Subversive Activities, March 25, 1947, President's Office Records, small box 11.

42. *Transcript of the Proceedings before the Faculty Committee on Tenure and Academic Freedom* 19: 1971–72. *Old Truths and New Horizons*, pp. 15–16.

Chapter II

1. Sketches of the committee members are derived from Vern Countryman, *Un-American Activities in the State of Washington* (Ithaca, N.Y.: Cornell University Press, 1951), pp. 17–18.

2. George F. Yantis to Allen, April 1, 1947, President's Office Records, box 12.

3. *Seattle Post-Intelligencer*, March 24, April 18, 1947.

4. *Seattle Post-Intelligencer*, April 12, 24, October 4, 1947. For Allen's early concern with AYD activities on campus, see Glen T. Nygreen to Allen, August 7, 1947, President's Office Records, box 13.

5. *Seattle Times*, October 26, 27, 29, November 7, 1947; *Seattle Post-Intelligencer*, October 26, 27, 28, 30, November 7, 8, 1947. The faculty member involved was a teaching assistant (English); he was dismissed, and his fellow prankster put on probation.

6. *Seattle Times*, November 2, 1947, p. 15. Cunningham was referring to Frances Farmer, whose fellow drama students helped her win a trip to New York via the U.S.S.R. by selling subscriptions to the *Voice of Action*, a Seattle labor paper which was the unofficial organ of the Communist party in Seattle in the 1930s. She used contacts established in New York theater to become one of the more popular movie actresses of the late 1930s and early 1940s. Her Bohemian lifestyle and espousal of causes, as well as her liaison with Clifford Odets (one of the "Hollywood 10"), attracted the attention of HUAC in 1947. Miss Farmer's autobiography, *Will There Really Be a Morning?* (New York: G. P. Putnam's Sons, 1972), seems to refute charges that she had ever been a Communist party member.

7. *First Report: Un-American Activities in Washington State, 1948, Report of Joint Fact-Finding Committee on Un-American Activities* (Olympia, 1948), pp. 1–91. For a detailed analysis of this first hearing, see Countryman, *Un-American Activities*, pp. 25–71.

8. *First Report*, pp. 101–12, 420–40, 370–76. Surprise testimony by Agnes Bridges, former wife of Harry Bridges, implicated the leader of the International Longshoremen's Union and adversary of Dave Beck, in Communist party activities. Her testimony corroborated testimony given earlier by Budenz. From 1937 to 1955 the U.S. government made almost continuous

attempts to deport Bridges on charges brought by reformed Communists like Budenz. Those attempts were unsuccessful.

9. Minutes of the Public Relations Committee, January 30, 1948, Records of the Secretary of the Faculty, box 1. Personal interview, Donald K. Anderson, January 28, 1976, Seattle.

10. *Minutes of the Faculty Senate of the University of Washington* 4(1946–48): 149, Office of the Secretary of the Faculty. *Spokane Spokesman-Review*, March 25, 1948; *Seattle Post-Intelligencer*, March 26, 27, 1948.

11. *Seattle Post-Intelligencer*, March 27, 1948; *Daily Olympian*, April 9, 1948; *Pasco Herald*, April 12, 1948; *Aberdeen World*, April 12, 1948, all in Regents Clipping File, box 46.

12. *Regents Journal* 9 (January 3, November 22, 1947): 845, 919. Beck to Allen, June 26, 1947, President's Office Records, box 127. Countryman, *Un-American Activities*, p. 194.

13. University of Washington *Record* 1 (April, 1949): 5; (May, 1949): 3. William S. Hopkins, telephone interview, January 26, 1976.

14. *Regents Journal* 10: 21, 24–25. *Seattle Post-Intelligencer*, April 23, 1948.

15. Fred Niendorff, "Red Quiz at University of Washington to Be Public," *Seattle Post-Intelligencer*, May 4, 1948.

16. Little to Drumheller, May 5, 1948, Balmer Papers, folder 13-5.

17. Personal interviews: Max Savelle, March 25, 1976; Giovanni Costigan, April 27, 1978, Seattle. Stirling to Allen, April 29, 1948, Faculty Committee on Tenure Hearings, President's Office Records, box 1 (hereafter cited as FCTH Records). Costigan, Savelle, and Stirling were not required to testify at the committee's public hearings, apparently because their activities were not deemed subversive enough. However, when Savelle was later cited by the Canwell Committee for supporting groups sympathetic to the Spanish Loyalists and to the abolition of the Dies Committee (HUAC), he protested to Allen. See *Second Report: Un-American Activities in Washington State, 1948*, pp. 346, 362; Savelle to Allen, April 29, 1949, FCTH Records, box 1.

18. Cain to Allen, May 7, 1948, FCTH Records, box 5.

19. Allen's notecards on May 12, 1948 faculty meeting, FCTH Records, box 2.

20. *Faculty Committee on Tenure Hearings Transcript* 8:693–95. Personal interviews: Donald K. Anderson, Max Savelle, J. Richard Huber.

21. Statement of Principles by the Executive Board of the University of Washington chapter of the AAUP, n.d., FCTH Records, box 4. The position of the AAUP was that faculty members should not be dismissed merely for being members of the Communist party. Since there is no date on the board's statement, it is not clear if this vote was taken before or after the national AAUP took its position. See "Report of Committee A for 1947," *AAUP Bulletin* 34(Spring, 1948): 122–33.

22. Allen Yarnell, *Democrats and Progressives: The 1948 Presidential Election as a Test of Post-War Liberalism* (Berkeley: University of California Press, 1974), pp. 87–107.

23. Lundberg to Allen, June 11, 1948, FCTH Records, box 2 (Lundberg's

emphases). The Pension Union lost its court fight when the state supreme court upheld the power of the legislature to appoint "interim" committees. See Countryman, *Un-American Activities*, pp. 68–70.

24. Harrison to Allen, June 22, 1948; Melden to Allen, June 22, 1948; Stirling to Allen, June 25, 1948; Benson to Allen, July 1, 1948, FCTH Records, box 2.

25. Lundberg to Harrison, June 23, 1948, FCTH Records, box 2.

26. University of Washington *Daily*, February 19, 1948, p. 1. R. G. Tyler was chairman of the Faculty Senate Committee on Public Relations. Brock Adams served as representative in Congress from 1965 until his appointment as secretary of the Department of Transportation in 1977.

27. University of Washington *Daily*, February 17, 1948.

28. *Regents Journal* 10: 20, 28; *Daily*, May 14, 20, 21, 1948; *Seattle Times*, May 17, 1948.

29. *Seattle Times*, May 21, 1948; Regents Papers, folder 5-24.

30. "Problems of Washingtonians," *Bulletin #1*, Washington Public Opinion Laboratory, 1948. Sam Stouffer, *Communism, Conformity and Civil Liberties* (Garden City, N.Y.: Doubleday and Co., 1955), pp. 55–58, 110–15.

31. *Regents Journal* 10 (June 12, 1948): 32.

32. *Seattle Post-Intelligencer* and *Seattle Times*, June 13, 1948.

33. *FCTH Transcript*, vol. 21. Max Savelle, personal interview.

34. University of Washington *Daily*, June 2, 1948.

35. Gundlach to Gene Hartley of CCNY, June 11, 1948, Gundlach Papers, folder 1-10.

36. Gundlach to Clifford O'Brien, June 28, 1948, Gundlach Papers, folder 1-10.

37. *Seattle Times*, June 30, 1948; *Seattle Post-Intelligencer*, June 30, July 2, 1948.

38. *Seattle Times*, July 8, 1948. Gundlach to Phillips, July 8, 1948, Gundlach Papers, folder 1-11.

39. Regents Papers, box 1; *Seattle Post-Intelligencer*, July 15, 16, 1948. Cf. Countryman, *Un-American Activities*, p. 74.

40. University of Washington *Daily*, June 21, 1948; *Longview* (Wash.) *Daily News*, July 17, 1948.

41. *Seattle Times*, July 18, 1948.

42. *Second Report*, pp. 42–43 and *passim*. The Appendix to this transcript of the hearings is a list of the "front organizations" and names of faculty members active in them. A thorough analysis of these proceedings can be read in Countryman, *Un-American Activities*, pp. 72–149.

43. *Seattle Post-Intelligencer*, July 21, 1948; cf. Mrs. Costigan's testimony, *Second Report*, pp. 120–24.

44. *Seattle Times*, July 21, 22, 25, 1948. Hilen was to become the university's senior counsel in the upcoming hearings before the Faculty Committee on Tenure. Like many Socialists, Thomas was vigorously anti-Communist at this time.

45. *Seattle Post-Intelligencer*, July 24, 1948.

46. Allen to Board of Regents, July 28, 1948, Regents Papers, folder 5-24.

47. Allen to Martin, September 1, 1948, Martin Papers, folder 77-12.

48. Memo, Charles E. Martin to deans, directors and executive officers, June 28, 1948; Martin to Allen, July 2, 15, 1948 Martin Papers, folder 77-12. Cf. Charles M. Gates, *First Century at the University of Washington, 1861–1961,* pp. 198–99. See also Peter C. Schaehrer, "McCarthyism and Academic Freedom—Three Case Studies," (Ed.D. dissertation, Teachers College, Columbia University, 1974), pp. 65–66. Schaehrer writes that this committee should have refused to consider any charges.

49. University of Washington Administrative Code, chapter 4, *Faculty Handbook* (1948), pp. 39–40. Martin to Allen, August 4, 1948; Martin to Benson, Faulkner, Harsch, and McMinn, August 24, 1948, Martin Papers, folder 77-12.

50. Cornu to Allen, August 16, 1948, FCTH Records, box 5. Martin to Allen, August 3, 4, 6, 19, and September 14, 1948, Martin Papers, folder 77-12.

51. Martin to H. K. Benson, August 24, 1948, Martin Papers, folder 77-12.

52. "Witch-Hunt in the Northwest," *New Republic* 119 (August 9, 1948): 11; Hopkins' reply: September 20, 1948, p. 28. Hopkins to Ralph Himstead, September 1, 1948, FCTH Records, box 4; in this letter to the AAUP's general secretary, Hopkins also assured him on Allen's handling of the affair.

53. *Regents Journal* 10 (August 13, 1948): 39. *Seattle Post-Intelligencer,* August 1, 1948.

54. Allen to Eisenhower, July 22, 1948, President's Office Records, small box 15; Allen to Eisenhower, August 9, 1948, FCTH Records, box 3. Allen did not mention the attack on Eisenhower delivered before the Canwell Committee by J. B. Matthews. See *Second Report,* pp. 44–45. Cf. Gates, *First Century,* pp. 199–200.

55. Allen to Frederick Middlebush, August 10, 1948; also to Malcolm Willey, August 11, and Justin Morrill, July 27, 1948, FCTH Records, box 3.

56. A. J. Carlson to Allen, July 7; Allen to Carlson, August 4, 1948, FCTH Records, box 5. Cohen believes that because Sophus Winther was the only witness to (incorrectly) name him a Communist party member, his name was dropped. Joseph Cohen, personal interview, March 24, 1978. For an account of Melvin Rader's struggle to clear himself, see his book *False Witness* (Seattle: University of Washington Press, 1969).

57. October 7, 1948, pp. 4–6. This portion of the letter seems aimed at a newspaper editor who had accused Allen of trying to subvert the Canwell Committee's work with another "trial" by the university. For a broad look at such hostility to the delay in firing professors, see the Regents Clipping File, box 48.

58. "Open Letter," pp. 5–7, 18.

59. Ibid., p. 10.

60. University of Washington *Daily,* October 5, 1948. Allen to Luce, October 26, 1948, FCTH Records, box 3. Cf. Gates, *First Century,* p. 202.

61. Eisenhower to Allen, November 3, 1948; Allen to Eisenhower, November 8, 1948, President's Office Records, small box 15.

Chapter III

1. Faculty Committee on Tenure Hearings Records, box 1; (hereafter cited as FCTH Records). For the full-length charges, see Appendix B. Garland Ethel, personal interview, October 15, 1975.

2. E. R. Wilcox to Gose, September 16, 1948, FCTH Records, box 1. University of Washington *Catalogue*, 1948–49.

3. FCTH Records, box 1. University of Washington *Daily*, October 14, 19, 21, 26, 29, November 17, 23, 1948; *Seattle Post-Intelligencer*, October 27, 1948.

4. *Faculty Committee on Tenure Hearings Transcript* (hereafter cited as *FCTH Transcript*) 1: 10–17. In both Canwell hearings, John Caughlan had often been called a Communist. Though university counsel pointed out Caughlan's activities as attorney for Communist party members several times during the hearings, it is impossible to know what effect this had on the committee. Huber remembers him as a capable attorney. J. R. Huber, personal interview, October 9, 1975.

5. *FCTH Transcript* 1: 119–22.

6. *FCTH Transcript*, vols. 4, 5, 6, 7.

7. *FCTH Transcript*, vols. 9, 10. Allen formed a high opinion of Gitlow and recommended him to Ferdinand Eberstadt of the Hoover Commission as someone to whom the National Security Council should listen. All correspondence in FCTH Records, box 3.

8. *FCTH Transcript* 8: 740–48. Stuart Browne [Sophus Winther], "A Professor Quits the Communist Party," *Harpers* 179 (July, 1939): 133–42. Garland Ethel expressed some sympathy with Winther's dilemma: testify or lose your job. Joseph Cohen, whom Winther falsely accused of Communist party membership, was less than sympathetic. Personal interviews: Ethel, October 15, 1978, and Cohen, March 24, 1978.

9. *FCTH Transcript*, vols. 11, 12. In November, 1977, Clayton van Lydegraf was arrested in Houston and charged with "conspiracy to violate the federal firearms act and possession of an unregistered explosive device." He was identified by the F.B.I. as head of the Prairie Fire organizing committee of the Weather Underground. A year later, van Lydegraf, sixty-two, was indicted by a Houston federal grand jury on charges of conspiring to bomb the offices of a California state senator. *Seattle Post-Intelligencer*, November 20, 1977, p. A-8, January 15, 1978, p. A-6, and November 8, 1978, p. B-4.

10. *FCTH Transcript*, vols. 12, 13, 14. According to J. Richard Huber, the quality of the defense testimony regarding the Communist party surpassed that of administration witnesses; personal interview, September 30, 1975. After Strong became chancellor at Berkeley, he was removed by the regents in the midst of the Free Speech crisis of 1965.

11. *FCTH Transcript*, vol. 15.

12. Ibid., vols. 15, 16, 17. Huber recalls the enthusiasm with which students testified for Phillips. Deep admiration for his teaching abides with Harrill Dabney, one of the students who testified for him; personal interview, August, 1975.

13. *FCTH Transcript*, vols. 16, 17. As an *ex officio* member of the committee, Allen frequently questioned witnesses. Since neither Huber nor Rex Robinson, members of the committee, can recall Allen's role in the hearings, an inference could be drawn that his presence did not unduly influence their thinking. It was a concern to defense counselors, however. For instance, on November 10, Allen said, "I hope that you gentlemen forget during the cross-examination that I happen to be President of the University." Caughlan replied, "I assure you that is going to be very difficult to do. . . ." Ralph Gundlach later assessed Allen's role as both prosecutor and jury in this way: "President Allen agreed that he helped make up the charges; he served as unfriendly witness against me, and on several occasions he critically cross-examined defense witnesses; he made clear his own feelings about the defendants and what the findings of the committee members should be; and he made several major procedural rulings. When the Tenure Committee was in doubt about its powers or procedures, it turned not to the Faculty but to the President." Gundlach to Charles M. Gates, November 14, 1962, Gundlach Papers, folder 1-2. Cf. Gates, *The First Century at the University of Washington, 1861–1961*, p. 199; and Peter C. Schaehrer, "McCarthyism and Academic Freedom," p. 90.

14. *FCTH Transcript*, vol. 31.

15. *Communism and Academic Freedom: The Record of the Tenure Cases at the University of Washington* (Seattle: University of Washington Press, 1949), pp. 29, 30, 36–40. This slim volume contains the charges, findings of the committee, and Allen's recommendations to the regents. It was later distributed to libraries, critics, and supporters of the decisions.

16. Ibid., pp. 30–41.

17. Ibid., pp. 52–54.

18. Ibid., pp. 48–49.

19. Ibid., pp. 85–86.

20. Ibid., pp. 87, 96.

21. Ibid., pp. 89–90.

22. Ibid., pp. 92–93.

23. *FCTH Transcript*, vol. 18. The attorney general's third list was introduced as evidence that Gundlach had participated in subversive groups: Exhibit #54, FCTH Records, box 8. The Consumer's Union was not on this list; the Seattle Labor School was listed as of November, 1947, but Gundlach had resigned from the school in March, 1947. See Gundlach to board of the Pacific Northwest Labor School, February 19, 1947, Gundlach Papers, box 1 (letter of resignation). Cf. Vern Countryman, *Un-American Activities in Washington State*, pp. 361–62.

24. "Statement to the Committee on Tenure," Gundlach Papers, folder 1-10.

25. Brief submitted by Gundlach, FCTH Records, box 1; *FCTH Transcript*, vol. 19. Countryman, *Un-American Activities*, p. 363; Countryman points out that "Gundlach could have reached his position on these issues by 'following' public opinion."

26. *FCTH Transcript*, vols. 24, 25. The adult education movement among unions was a common phenomenon of the 1940s. The idea of a national program of adult education died when it was denounced by management of General Motors as a Communist plot to subvert workers during congressional hearings on the subject. An account of University of Michigan involvement in the Worker's Education Movement is in: Peter E. Van DeWater, "Peace Maker: President Alexander G. Ruthven of Michigan and His Relationship to His Faculty, Students, and Regents" (Ph.D. dissertation, University of Michigan, 1970), pp. 173–86.

Gundlach and Franzke, like some other faculty members, were involved in both the Labor School and the AFT. Both came under fire from the AFL, which was engaged in jurisdictional disputes with the CIO. Since the leading AFL union in Seattle was Dave Beck's Teamsters, it is easy to see why Gundlach felt Beck was out to get him, as he later wrote to Ralph Fuchs (general secretary of the AAUP), February 13, 1956, Gundlach Papers, folder 2-3.

In October, 1948, the American Federation of Teachers revoked the charter of Local 401 following an investigation by national representatives which revealed "unprofessional activities" by its members. Franzke, who was then president of the local, resigned in protest. See Franzke to Allen, October 15, 1948, FCTH Records, box 4; *American Teacher* 33 (February, 1949): 9.

27. *FCTH Transcript*, vol. 25.

28. Ibid., vol. 18. DeLacy lost his bid for reelection in 1946, along with many other Democrats. He became an organizer for the Progressive party in Washington and in Ohio, and was later indicted for violations of the Smith Act. The 1947 oath said nothing explicit about Communists.

29. *FCTH Transcript*, vols. 18, 19.

30. Ibid., vol. 19.

31. Ibid., vols. 26, 27.

32. Ibid., vols. 27, 30. Gundlach Brief, Appendix C.

33. Ibid., vol. 8. James B. Conant, in *Education in a Divided World* (Cambridge: Harvard University Press, 1948), had upheld the necessity of tolerating diverse opinions in the face of ideological conflict; see pp. 178–80.

34. *FCTH Transcript*, vol. 8.

35. A. W. Martin to Allen, November 12, 1948, FCTH Records, box 4.

36. Himstead to Allen, Himstead to R. G. Tyler, telegrams, November 30, 1948, FCTH Records, box 4. *FCTH Transcript*, vol. 23, pp. 2589–92. Gundlach to Bonnie Bird [Gundlach], November 23, 1948, Gundlach Papers, folder 1-13. It should be noted that Allen left one sentence out of the published version of this letter. It contained Martin's estimate that the regents would probably want to "go further in this matter of discharge" than the AAUP would prefer.

37. *FCTH Transcript* 23: 2602–5; 25: 2862–63. Personal interviews: Roger Loucks and J. R. Huber, October, 1975; telephone conversation with Rex Robinson, December, 1975.

38. *FCTH Transcript* 32: 3776–77; Gose memo, n.d., FCTH Records, box 1. Cf. Countryman, *Un-American Activities*, pp. 361–70. Gundlach's attorney,

Clifford O'Brien, later argued that there should have been a new hearing for Gundlach with new charges; apparently the committee never considered such a course.

39. *Communism and Academic Freedom*, pp. 56–57, 67–70.

40. Ibid., p. 58.

41. Ibid., pp. 58–61, 69. In defending acknowledged Communists, Committee A also stressed the dangers faced by professors whose views were "left of center": "This is not a reference to crypto-Communists; this Association can have no sympathy with covert, deceitful methods. We are concerned with those sincere persons whose unconcealed views range from an emotional sympathy for the underdog, through various stages in social planning, to a reasoned belief in collectivism." *AAUP Bulletin* 34(Spring, 1948): 128.

42. *Communism and Academic Freedom*, pp. 70–72.

43. Ibid., pp. 64–72. Robinson and Huber, who had participated in research club discussion with Gundlach prior to the hearings, differed in their appraisals of Gundlach's scientific ability. Dr. Loucks indicated that Gundlach, like most scientists, had a few brilliant ideas. Personal interviews.

44. Ibid., pp. 65–66. This finding was forgotten when fifth amendment cases came up in the 1950s.

45. Ibid., pp. 99–104.

46. See the charges in Appendix B.

47. *FCTH Transcript*, vol. 22. Ethel, interview, October, 1975, and tape-recorded interview with R. H. Pelto, 1969, Pelto Collection.

48. *FCTH Transcript*, vols. 22, 23, 28. Understandably, Ethel felt betrayed by the president on the charge that he had failed to cooperate.

49. *Communism and Academic Freedom*, pp. 74, 76, 79–80.

50. *FCTH Transcript*, vols. 30, 31; tape-recorded interview, Jacobs with R. H. Pelto, 1969. Roberts tried to enlist anyone on the faculty who seemed sympathetic to the Popular Front against Fascism; in the case of Melvin Rader, for instance, he failed. Melvin Rader, personal interview, November, 1974.

51. Pelto interview with Jacobs, 1969.

52. *FCTH Transcript*, vol. 31. Boas was Jacobs' teacher at Columbia.

53. Ibid., vols. 21, 30.

54. *Communism and Academic Freedom*, pp. 74–75, 77–79.

55. *FCTH Transcript*, vols. 20, 21. Tape-recorded interview, Eby with R. H. Pelto, 1969, Pelto Collection. *Second Report: Un-American Activities in Washington State, 1948*, pp. 120–21, 162–63. Albert A. Acena, "The Washington Commonwealth Federation: Reform Politics and the Popular Front" (Ph.D. dissertation, University of Washington, 1976), pp. 143–48, 254, 438. Acena points out that membership of Communists in reform groups like the wcf made the Communist party consciously reformist; this symbiosis is not often noted by those concerned only with the pernicious nature of front groups.

56. *FCTH Transcript*, vol. 20; Eby, interview with Pelto.

57. Ibid.

58. *FCTH Transcript*, vol. 21.

59. Ibid., vol. 23. Since Allen had much to do with framing the charges, it is difficult to reason why Charge V was brought against Eby, Ethel, and Jacobs.

60. *Communism and Academic Freedom*, pp. 74, 76–79, 80.

61. Ibid., pp. 105–6.

62. Ibid., p. 107.

63. Ibid., p. 108. For another impression of Allen in the days before the decisions were made by the board, see T. V. Smith, *A Non-Existent Man, an Autobiography* (Austin: University of Texas Press, 1962), pp. 138–41. Smith admired Allen's open-minded attitude toward controversial persons and situations.

64. Allen to Board of Regents, January 19, 1949, FCTH Records, box 4. *Regents Journal* 10(February 19, 1949): 76. Butterworth, Phillips, and Gundlach were dismissed as of February 1, 1949.

Chapter IV

1. Neal Miller to Board of Regents, December 6, 1948, Regents Papers, folder 5–24. On the Suzzallo and Fisher matters, see above, chap. I. More letters from academics to Allen and the board are found in Faculty Committee on Tenure Hearings, box 2 (hereafter cited as FCTH Records). *Seattle Post-Intelligencer*, January 20, 1949.

2. *FCTH Transcript* 33: 3921–53.

3. Ibid., pp. 3955–62. While it is true that Canwell, Bienz, and Sydney Stevens were defeated in the election of 1948, it is not clear that their role on the Un-American Activities Committee had much to do with it. The elections of 1948 washed out many an errant Republican; Bienz had the misfortune to switch from the Democratic ticket at the wrong time. On the other hand, Arthur Langlie, a Republican, defeated incumbent Mon Wallgren in 1948. Much of his campaign was directed at Wallgren's "domination" by Dave Beck and "subversives" in the Democratic party; Langlie cited the findings of the Canwell Committee often. See George W. Scott, "Arthur B. Langlie: Republican Governor in a Democratic Age" (Ph.D. dissertation, University of Washington 1971), pp. 163–64.

4. *FCTH Transcript* 33: 3964–74. The university's senior counsel, Andrew Hilen, was ill during this last phase of the hearings.

5. *FCTH Transcript* 33: 3978–98. See also Terman to Allen, January 14, 1949, and Allen to Terman, January 20, 1949, FCTH Records, box 2.

6. *FCTH Transcript* 33: 4123. See also Peter C. Schaehrer, "McCarthyism and Academic Freedom—Three Case Studies" (Ed. D. dissertation, Teachers College, Columbia University, 1974), p. 171. Henry told Schaehrer in 1971 that, given the biases of the regents, he introduced the notion of "probation" as a way to give moderate regents like John King a way out. Eby credits Henry with saving his job while risking his own career; Henry moved behind the scenes cajoling the regents and blunting the impact of pressure groups such

as the American Legion. Eby, tape-recorded interview with R. H. Pelto, 1969, Pelto Collection.

7. *Seattle Post-Intelligencer*, January 23, 1949.

8. Ibid., January 23, 24, 1949.

9. Regents Clipping File on Subversive Activities, box 46.

10. Ibid.; FCTH Records, boxes 2 and 4.

11. *New York Times*, January 30, 1949, p. E-9. FCTH Records, box 5. Joel H. Hildebrand to Allen, January 27, 1949, FCTH Records, box 4.

12. University of Washington *Daily*, January 25, 26, 27, 28, February 1, 25, March 2, 1949.

13. *Seattle Post-Intelligencer*, January 27, 1949; University of Washington *Daily*, February 2, 1949; University of Washington *Record*, February, 1949. Kenneth Cole (Political Science) to Allen, January 29, 1949; George Lundberg (Sociology) to William Anderson, February 3, 1949, FCTH Records, box 2. T. Cook to W. Stull Holt, June 18, 1949, Holt Papers, folder 1-7. Cook later accepted a position at Johns Hopkins. Two copies of the Tenure Committee's transcript were available for inspection by interested parties.

14. *Seattle Times*, February 8, 1949, p. 17; *New York Times*, February 11, 1949.

15. Lundberg to William Anderson, February 3, 1949; E. O. Eastwood (Engineering) to Allen, March 8, 1949; Deans Gordon Marckworth (Forestry), Harold Wessman (Engineering), and Harry Burd (Business Administration) to Allen, April 5, 1949, FCTH Records, box 2. On the other hand, Herschel Roman (Biochemistry) expressed surprise that Allen could declare most faculty response was positive; most of the faculty he knew would have preferred Allen follow the faculty committee's recommendation. Roman to Allen, February 5, 1949, FCTH Records, box 2.

16. Transcript of debate between Harrison and Taylor, FCTH Records, box 4. University of Washington *Daily*, February 18, 1949. In a November, 1974, interview with the author, Taylor expressed disapproval of the regents decisions because they overrode the faculty committee's recommendations.

17. Ibid. Sidney Hook, *Heresy, Yes—Conspiracy, No* (New York: John Day Company, 1953), pp. 10–11. Rex Robinson, telephone interview, December, 1975.

18. *Minutes of the Faculty Senate of the University of Washington* 5 (1948–50): 69–76. W. Stull Holt, personal interview, October, 1974, Seattle.

19. See note 15 above. "An Open Letter to President Raymond B. Allen and the Board of Regents of the University of Washington," n.d., FCTH Records, box 1.

20. Personal interviews: Stull Holt, October, 1974; Abraham Keller, March 3, 1976; Laurel Lewis, March 2, 1976. Keller, who attempted to procure signatures from his colleagues, found all these factors in operation; Holt refused to sign the letter because it indicated approval of Ralph Gundlach's activities; Laurel Lewis found such statements too broad and vague.

21. "Should Communists Be Allowed to Teach in Our Colleges?" *Town Meeting* vol. 14 (March 1, 1949).

22. "Communism and Academic Freedom at the University of Washington," *American Scholar* 19 (Summer, 1949): 323–53.

23. Sidney Hook, "What Shall We Do About Communist Teachers?" *Saturday Evening Post*, September 10, 1949, and "Should Communists Be Permitted to Teach?" *New York Times Magazine*, February 27, 1949, pp. 7, 22–29. Meiklejohn, "Should Communists Be Permitted to Teach?" *New York Times Magazine*, March 27, 1949, pp. 10, 64–66. Transcript of telephone conversation between Hook and Allen, n.d., FCTH Records, box 1. Allen's reply to Meiklejohn appears in *New York Times Magazine*, May 8, 1949, pp. 33–35. Hook wrote extensively on this topic; see his "Academic Integrity and Academic Freedom: How to Deal with the Fellow-Traveling Professor," *Commentary* 8 (October, 1949): 329–39, where he attacks Meiklejohn and Lynd's position; an exchange of letters among them appears in *Commentary* 8 (December, 1949): 594–601.

24. I. L. Kandel, *School and Society* 69 (May 7, 1949): 331. Henry Steele Commager, "Red-Baiting in the Colleges," *New Republic*, July 25, 1949, pp. 10–13. A. M. Schlesinger, Jr., "The Right to Loathsome Ideas," *Saturday Review*, May 14, 1949, pp. 17–18, 47. Merritt E. Benson, "The Right to Demand Scholars," *Saturday Review*, September 10, 1949, pp. 34–35. Francis D. Wormuth, "On Bills of Attainder: A Non-Communist Manifesto," *Western Political Quarterly* 3 (March, 1950): 52.

25. *Spokane Spokesman-Review*, April 8, 1949. Walter Gellhorn, ed., *The States and Subversion* (Ithaca, N.Y.: Cornell University Press, 1952), pp. 102–3.

26. "Confidential Report on Communist Activities at the University of Washington," February 28, 1949, President's Office Records, box 126.

27. Memorandum, April 15, 1949, President's Office Records, box 126; George Taylor to Allen, April 12, 1949, FCTH Records, box 5; *Regents Journal* 10 (May 13, 1949):87. Condon had been recommended to head the National Bureau of Standards by then Secretary of Commerce Henry Wallace. That connection, plus his involvement with other scientists in the movement to put the Atomic Energy Commission in civilian hands, led J. Parnell Thomas of HUAC to demand review of his security clearance in 1948; Truman refused. See Walter Goodman, *The Committee: The Extraordinary Career of the House Committee on Un-American Activities* (New York: Farrar, Straus and Giroux, 1968), pp. 231–44.

28. *Seattle Times*, May 17, 1949; *Regents Journal* 10 (June 10, 1949): 103.

29. University of Washington *Record*, April, 1949, p. 16; *Thirty-first Biennial Report of the Regents* (1951), pp. 13–36. Donald K. Anderson to Benjamin Fine, October 13, 1949, President's Office Records, box 110. Anderson, Allen's assistant in charge of university relations and director of public relations, completed a questionnaire for Fine on research support.

30. *Time*, March 5, 1949; University of Washington *Daily*, July 28, 1949. Goodman, *The Committee*, p. 274. Robert W. Iversen, *The Communists and the Schools* (New York: Harcourt, Brace and Company, 1959), pp. 254–55. Textbooks under attack included Frank Magruder's venerable high school civics text, *American Government*, and Paul Samuelson's college text, *Economics*.

31. Carl Solberg, *Riding High: America in the Cold War* (New York: Mason and Lipscomb, 1973), pp. 111–25.

32. Allen to Jacobs, February 11, 1949, President's Office Records, box 15. Cf. Melvin Rader, *False Witness* (Seattle: University of Washington Press, 1969), pp. 118–20.

33. Rader, *False Witness*, pp. 154–55. *Regents Journal* 10 (October 29, 1949): 119. Guthman's Pulitzer Prize-winning articles on the Rader case appear in the *Seattle Times*, October 21, 22, 27, 1949. Rader, tape-recorded interview with R. H. Pelto, July, 1969, Pelto Collection. Cf. Vern Countryman, *Un-American Activities in the State of Washington* (Ithaca, N.Y.: Cornell University Press, 1951), pp. 286–331.

34. Cowley to Heilman, November 8, 1948; Heilman to Cowley, November 10, 1948, Heilman Papers, folder 11-9.

35. Heilman to Verne Ray, January 25, 1949, Heilman Papers, folder 11-9. *Regents Journal* 10 (May 13, 1949, and May 27, 1949): 87, 95. George Stuntz to Allen, May 25, 1949, President's Office Records, box 126.

36. An account of Cowley's testimony appears in Alistair Cooke, *A Generation on Trial* (New York: Alfred A. Knopf, 1952), pp. 194–96. The second trial began on November 17, 1949; Hiss was convicted of perjury and sentenced to five years in prison on January 21, 1950. Cowley to Heilman, November 21, 1949, Heilman Papers, folder 11-9.

37. Mrs. Donald Trueblood to Drumheller, December 7, 1949, President's Office Records, box 110; letters to President Allen concerning Cowley are in box 109. William D. Shannon to Allen, December 6, 1949; Arthur Paulsen to Allen, December 23, 1949, President's Office Records, small box 12. *Seattle Post-Intelligencer*, December 23, 1949. Many of these letters noted Cowley's resignation from the Office of Facts and Figures when, in 1942, Martin Dies "exposed" him as "one of the chief Communist intellectuals in the country." See Goodman, *The Committee*, pp. 127–28.

38. *Seattle Times*, December 28, 30, 1949. "Report to the Chairman of the State Americanism Commission of the American Legion," December 29, 1949, President's Office Records, box 101.

39. *Seattle Post-Intelligencer*, January 30, 1950. Heilman, personal interview, November, 1974, Seattle.

40. President's Office Records, box 121; *Seattle Post-Intelligencer*, January 5, 1950.

41. Senate Budget Committee Records, October, 1950, December, 1950, November, 1951, box 1.

42. Notes on meetings on university-legislature relations, President's Office Records, small box 18; Donald K. Anderson to Allen, May 26, 1951, small box 11. Minutes of the Public Relations Committee of the Faculty Senate, Faculty Senate Records, box 1. "Narrative Description," Board of Regents Buildings and Grounds Committee Records. Complaints about legislative favoritism toward the State College were recurring, but in this case seem justified: the 1951 legislature appropriated $10 million to the college, which

had 5,000 students, and $20 million to the university, which had 13,000 students. However, the cutbacks brought on the resignation of wsc President Wilson Compton.

43. *Regents Journal* 10(April 20, June 8, December 22, 1951): 194–96, 201, 239–40. See also, Scott, "Arthur B. Langlie," pp. 209–18.

44. *Journal of the House of the Thirty-first Legislature of the State of Washington* (1949), pp. 371–73, 1095–121. The special committee which investigated the Canwell Committee was headed by Arthur Paulsen, one of the chief critics of the way it handled the university inquiry. "Message of Arthur B. Langlie to the Thirty-second Legislature," January 10, 1951.

45. University of Washington *Daily*, March 1, 1951, p. 1. *Journal of the House of the Thirty-second Legislature* (1951).

46. *Daily*, February 6, p. 4; February 28, pp. 1, 4; March 1, p. 1; March 2, pp. 1, 4, 1951.

47. *Daily*, March 7, p. 1; March 8, pp. 1, 4, 1951. *Seattle Post-Intelligencer*, March 7, 1951, pp. 1, 3. Recall that Everest had been Langlie's assistant while on leave from the university in 1944 and 1949.

48. *Daily*, March 13, 1951; *Seattle Post-Intelligencer*, March 14, 1951, p. 6. Allen to Roderick, March 15, 1951; Irving Clark (ACLU) to Allen, March 27, 1951; Ken MacDonald (ACLU) to Allen, April 12; Solie Ringold (ADA) to Allen, May 15, 1951, President's Office Records, box 115.

49. Leonard Saari, personal interview, March 23, 1978, Seattle. Saari is currently Region 10 director for the secretary of commerce.

50. Report of the Independent Students' Committee, June 15, 1951; Saari to author, March 24, 1978, author's files. For another account of the Saari matter, see Robert MacIver, *Academic Freedom in Our Time* (New York: Columbia University Press, 1955), pp. 218–20.

51. *New York Times*, November 25, 1951, p. B-8. *Seattle Post-Intelligencer*, April 22, 1950, p. 1.

52. Charles E. Martin to Allen, October 20, 1947, President's Office Records, box 121. Allen to Chester Barnard, May 1, 1950, President's Office Records, box 120.

53. Wittfogel to Allen, August 17, 1951, President's Office Records, box 119. Many of the complaints about the Northwest IPR were lodged by a former member, Miller Freeman. His correspondence with Allen and the regents, in which he warned that the university was becoming entangled in an "unholy alliance" with the State Department, is found in President's Office Records, box 119. See also *Regents Journal* 10(August 24, September 21, 1951): 225–29. John N. Thomas, *The Institute of Pacific Relations* (Seattle: University of Washington Press, 1974), pp. 65–100.

In his bid for a senate seat in 1950, Canwell also raised charges against the faculty members who worked with the IPR; President's Office Records, small box 15. Personal interviews: Charles E. Martin, October 21, 1975; George Taylor, November, 1974.

54. *Seattle Post-Intelligencer*, May 21, 1951. *Regents Journal* 10(July 6,

1951):217. University of Washington *Record*, November, 1951, p. 1. Personal interviews: Donald K. Anderson, January 28, 1976, George Taylor; Charles E. Martin.

55. Allen to Guthrie, December 8, 1951, Allen Papers, folder 2-12. Personal interviews: Charles E. Martin; Laurel Lewis, March 2, 1976; Lloyd Woodburne, March 9, 1976; Donald K. Anderson. A good example of Allen's increasing frustration with a curtailed budget is his memo to the regents detailing reasons why extra money should be spent to hire a new dean of the Law School from outside the university: Regents Meeting Minutes, September 21, 1951, Presidents Office Records, box 127.

56. University of Washington *Daily*, December 12, 18, 1951. *Seattle Times*, December 23, p. 6; December 26, p. 6, 1951. *Time*, December 24, 1951, p. 40. UCLA *Daily Bruin*, November 14, 1952. Julian Barksdale, "Geology at the University of Washington," Publications in Geological Sciences, no. 4, p. 49. Barksdale states that Allen's selection by the California regents was a result of his conservative stand on Communists. According to *Who's Who in America*, Allen remained at UCLA until 1959. He served in several federal health positions from 1959 to 1972 in areas such as Indonesia, South America, and Bangladesh. From 1967 to 1970 he was also clinical professor of community medicine and international health at Georgetown University. He is now retired in Virginia.

57. Eby, tape-recorded interview with R. H. Pelto, 1969, Pelto Collection. Ethel, personal interview, October, 1975.

58. Ibid.

59. Jacobs, tape-recorded interview with R. H. Pelto, 1969.

60. Butterworth, tape-recorded interview with Pelto, 1969. Phillips, personal interview, December, 1975, San Francisco. *Daily*, October 28, 1969. Butterworth died in 1970. Phillips died in October, 1978. J. W. Robson to Allen, January 3, 1949, FCTH Records, box 2. David P. Gardner, *The California Oath Controversy* (Berkeley: University of California Press, 1967), pp. 12–19.

61. Gundlach Papers, box 2. "The Gundlach Case," *New Republic*, January 3, 1949, p. 31; this was a letter of concern initiated by Theodore Newcomb (Michigan), Harlow Shapley (Harvard), Ernest Hilgard (Stanford), Zechariah Chafee, Jr. (Harvard Law), Gordon Allport (Harvard), and others. "Report on the Dismissal of Dr. Ralph Gundlach," adopted by the APA, 1951; the committee that made the report found that Gundlach had not been dismissed due to lack of competence but because of his difficulties with the administration. See also Gundlach to Charles Newell, January 4, 1950, Gundlach Papers, folder 1-15. Gundlach to the author, May 12, 1978. For an example of Dr. Gundlach's recent publications, see Gundlach. "Birth Order Among Lesbians: New Light on an 'Only Child,'" *Psychological Reports* 40 (1977): 250. Gundlach lived in London until his death in August, 1978.

62. "Report of Committee A for 1948," *AAUP Bulletin* 35(Spring, 1949): 52–53, 65. Clipping, *Los Angeles Times*, May 8, 1949; Lutz to Martin, May 26, 1949, Martin Papers, folder 11-12.

63. *AAUP Bulletin* 36(Spring, 1950): 40–43. Telegram, Himstead to Warne, March 18, 1950, on which is a note from Warne to Gundlach; Warne to Bonnie Bird [Gundlach], March 28, 1950, Gundlach Papers, folder 2-3.

64. Gundlach to Ralph Fuchs (general secretary, AAUP), February 13, 1956, Gundlach Papers, folder 2-3. "Academic Freedom and Tenure in the Quest for National Security," *AAUP Bulletin* 42(Spring, 1956): 60–65. Though it would be interesting to see precisely what caused the AAUP to delay its investigation of the University of Washington cases for seven years, I have not been granted access to AAUP archives. The limited staff of the association and the location of pertinent files in various cities make such an investigation difficult; AAUP President William Van Alstyne to the author, April 26, 1976. Cf. Walter Metzger, *Academic Freedom in the Age of the University* (New York: Columbia University Press, 1955), p. 215, note 56.

Chapter V

1. Board of Regents statement, December 2, 1951, President's Office Records, box 125. *Seattle Times*, December 3, 1951; University of Washington *Daily*, December 4, 1951. Edwin Guthrie to Allen, January 24, 1946, Guthrie Papers, box 2; Schmitz to Balmer, September 28, 1948, Balmer Papers, folder 13-7; Allen to Guthrie, December 8, 1951, Allen Papers, folder 2-12. Much of the reasoning behind Schmitz's selection is contained in the addresses of Regents Donald Corbett and Thomas Balmer on the occasion of his inauguration: see pamphlet entitled "The Inauguration of Dr. Henry Schmitz, October 3, 1952."

2. Board of Regents statement, December 2, 1951. Faculty Senate resolution, December 6, 1951, President's Office Records, box 125. *Regents Journal* 10(December 22, 1951, and March 16, 1952): 239–40, 255. *Daily*, January 8, March 11, 1952; *Seattle Times*, March 16, 1952, p. 1. Lloyd Woodburne, personal interview, March 9, 1976.

3. *Seattle Post-Intelligencer*, March 17, 1952. George W. Scott, "Arthur B. Langlie: Republican Governor in a Democratic Age," (Ph.D. dissertation, University of Washington, 1971), p. 197–98.

4. Everest to deans and department heads on budget cutbacks, February, 1952, President's Office Records, box 113. *Thirty-second Biennial Report of the Regents to the Governor* (1953), pp. 4–6. Virgil Lee to Everest, March 5, 1952, President's Office Records, box 112. *Seattle Times*, January 8, p. 4; January 19, p. 8; January 23, 1952, p. 2. These articles by Ross Cunningham, a Langlie confidant, point out the seriousness of the legislature's problems vis à vis the university at a time of "international crisis akin to 1941."

5. Woodburne to Everest, June 11, 1952, President's Office Records, box 113.

6. *Regents Journal* 10 (June 8, 1951): 207.

7. George Lundberg to Schmitz, October 21, 1952, President's Office Records, box 102. Lundberg's "Prefatory Foreword," in Arthur Goddard, ed.,

Harry Elmer Barnes, Learned Crusader (Colorado Springs: Ralph Myles, 1968), is a summary of Lundberg's attempts to have Barnes lecture at the University of Washington.

8. Minutes of the University Executive Committee, March 4, 1952, President's Office Records, box 117. *Hearings Before the Committee on Un-American Activities, House of Representatives, Seventy-sixth Congress* (1938), vol. 1.

9. Lundberg to Frost, March 19, 1952, President's Office Records, box 102. Lundberg in *Learned Crusader*, pp. xxx–xxxi. Lundberg to Alfred Schweppe, April 3, 1952, Lundberg Papers, folder 11-18.

10. Howard L. Bevis to Everest, April 15, 1952, President's Office Records, box 117. Recall that Everest was a member of the Rainier Club.

11. Everett Nelson to Woodburne, June 23, 1952, President's Office Records, box 120.

12. For some idea of the volume of mail received by the university from patriotic groups and individuals, see President's Office Records, box 109.

13. *Regents Journal* 10(April 19, 1952): 265, 267, 280. Schmitz to deans and budget officers, August 28, 1952, President's Office Records, box 114. Schmitz, "Inaugural Address." While at Minnesota, Schmitz sent clippings and comments on the Weinberg and Oppenheimer matters to Regent Balmer; see Schmitz to Balmer, September 28, 1948, Balmer Papers, folders 13-7, 13-8, 13-12. For an account of the difficulties of Weinberg and Oppenheimer see Robert M. MacIver, *Academic Freedom in Our Time* (New York: Columbia University Press, 1955), p. 48.

14. President's Office Records, box 102, May 29, 1952. Cf. Hook, "The Technique of Mystification," *Partisan Review* 4 (December, 1937): 57–62. In 1937, Hook himself had only recently seen the light on Stalinist Russia, i.e., following the Dewey Commission Report on the Moscow Trials; this review is a good example of the polemical style Hook employed to refute his former leftist associates. An informative essay on Hook's odyssey from socialism to communism and back is Lewis Feuer, "From Ideology to Philosophy: Sidney Hook's writings on Marxism," in Paul Kurtz, ed., *Sidney Hook and the Contemporary World* (New York: John Day Company, 1968), pp. 36–49.

15. President's Office Records, box 102.

16. Anderson to Allen, June 9, 1952; memo, June 16, 1952, President's Office Records, box 102.

17. Woltman to Anderson, June 18, 1952, President's Office Records, box 102. John Cogley has described Fred Woltman as a prominent figure in blacklisting activities: *Report on Blacklisting* (New York: Fund for the Republic, 1956), 2: 90, 116. Recall that as a graduate student at the University of Pittsburgh, Woltman was fired by Sieg in 1929.

18. Everest to Burke, June 16, 1952, Robert B. Heilman Papers, folder 11-7.

19. Heilman to department members, June 15, 1952, Heilman Papers, folder 11-7. Heilman to Anderson, June 24, 1952, President's Office Records, box 102.

20. Burke to Everest, June 29, 1952, President's Office Records, box 102.

21. Ibid.

22. Ibid. Herbert Phillips, dismissed from the university as a Communist in 1949, had also been an editor of *Science and Society*, as Anderson noted in this compilation.

23. Burke to Everest, June 29, 1952.

24. Ibid.

25. Heilman to Schmitz, July 18, 1952, President's Office Records, box 102.

26. Ibid. Emphasis is Burke's.

27. Ibid. Heilman was, of course, referring to the fact that six of the university faculty subpoenaed by Canwell were English Department members; the Cowley episode was also fresh in memory.

28. Schmitz to Heilman, August 19, 1952; Burke to Schmitz, August 30, 1952; Heilman to Schmitz, August 26, 1952, President's Office Records, box 102. The oaths referred to by Heilman were the 1931 affirmation of the federal and state constitutions and the 1951 disclaimer of subversive activity.

29. Schmitz to Heilman, September 3, 1952, President's Office Records, box 102. Ames, for example, supported the Minutemen division of the American Protective League during the World War I lumber industry labor disputes involving the Industrial Workers of the World (IWW); see Albert F. Gunns, "Civil Liberties and Crisis: The Status of Civil Liberties in the Pacific Northwest, 1917–1940" (Ph.D. dissertation, University of Washington, 1971), pp. 21–24.

30. Kenneth Burke to Schmitz, September 2, 1952; Heilman to Schmitz, September 3, 1952; Schmitz to Heilman, September 5, 1952, President's Office Records, box 102. Actually, Schmitz already knew that Burke's appearance at Indiana had caused no problems, since Don Anderson had checked the matter with his counterpart there; see Ross Bartley to Anderson, July 21, 1952, President's Office Records, box 102.

31. Heilman to Schmitz, September 18, 1952, Heilman Papers, folder 11-7. Executive Committee members included Brents Stirling, J. B. Harrison, and E. E. Bostetter; their comments on early drafts of the letter are found in the same folder.

32. Heilman to Schmitz, September 18, 1952.

33. Ibid.

34. Schmitz to Heilman, President's Office Records, box 102. *Regents Journal* 10 (September 27, 1952): 352.

35. "The Inauguration of Dr. Henry Schmitz." Schmitz to Armstrong, September 16, 1952, President's Office Records, box 81.

36. Heilman to Schmitz, October 14, 1952, Heilman Papers, folder 11-7.

37. *Seattle Post-Intelligencer*, November 10, 14, 1952.

38. Paulsen to Schmitz, November 20, 1952, Heilman Papers, folder 11-7. University of Washington *Daily*, December 12, 1952.

39. Clise to Schmitz, November 17, 1952, President's Office Records, box 109. *Educational Guardian* 9 (December, 1952): 1, found in Heilman Papers, folder 11-7. Heilman to Schmitz, May 8, 1953; Schmitz to Heilman, May 18,

1953, President's Office Records, box 95. Besides publishing the *Guardian* and evaluating textbooks for un-American bias, Zoll's NCAE put out a series on "Red-ucators at Leading Women's Colleges." In compiling materials on Burke's political past, Donald Anderson had consulted Zoll's "Red-ucators at Bennington." Burke was one Bennington faculty member extensively covered in that broadside. For more on Zoll, see MacIver, *Academic Freedom in Our Time*, pp. 59–61.

40. Cowley to Heilman, November 24, 1952; Burke to Heilman, December 2, 1952, Heilman Papers, folder 11-7. Burke's emphasis. "An Old Liberal Looks to the New Year, 1953," may be regarded as Burke's poetic reflections on the autumn of 1952: Kenneth Burke, *Book of Moments, Poems 1915–54* (Los Altos: Hermes Publications, 1955), pp. 18–19. Twenty-three years later, in the autumn of 1975, Kenneth Burke was a Walker-Ames Lecturer in the University of Washington Department of English. For Malcolm Cowley's assessment of university security systems vis à vis writers, see Cowley, *The Literary Situation* (New York: Viking Press, 1954), pp. 219–36.

41. Schmitz to Heilman, September 30, 1952, President's Office Records, box 102.

42. "Inauguration of Dr. Henry Schmitz." Personal interviews: J. Richard Huber, November 9, 1975; Solomon Katz, November, 1974; Abraham Keller, March 3, 1976, Seattle.

43. *Regents Journal* 10 (April 19, 1952): 267; 11 (October 31, 1953; September 24, 1954; October 16, 1954): 191, 351, 362; 12 (May 19, 1956): 278–79. H. Stanley Bennett to Schmitz, May 13, 1953, President's Office Records, box 101. Arnold Stein, notes on meeting with President Schmitz, October 16, 1956, UWAAUP Records, box 3.

44. Washington State Legislature Budget Committee Report, President's Office Records, box 112; *Biennial Report of the Board of Regents* (1953), pp. 9–14.

45. Minutes of the Public Relations Committee of the Faculty Senate, President's Office Records, box 117. Max Savelle to Woodburne, December 2, 1952; Schmitz and Everest to members of the faculty, April 28, 1953, President's Office Records, box 112.

46. *Regents Journal* 11 (March 6, 1953): 50. Woodburne to Schmitz, December 4, 1953; Schmitz to Woodburne, December 14, 1953, President's Office Records, box 95.

47. Lundberg to Woodburne, May 26, 1953, President's Office Records, box 95. Personal interviews: J. R. Huber, November 9, 1975; Lloyd Woodburne, March 9, 1976, Seattle.

48. *Who's Who in the West* (Chicago: Marquis—Who's Who, 1954), pp. 213, 615. University of Washington *Daily*, June 23, 25, 1953. Scott, "Arthur B. Langlie," pp. 197, 238, 283, 491. Personal interviews: Huber, Keller, Woodburne.

49. *Seattle Times*, October 22, 1952, p. 2; *Seattle Post-Intelligencer*, October 23, 1952, p. 5.

50. *Seattle Times*, October 26, p. 8; October 27, 1952, p. 6. Scott, "Arthur B.

Langlie," pp. 238–44. Delores A. Van Wagenen, "Americans for Democratic Action in the Northwest," (M.A. thesis, University of Washington, 1963), pp. 115–19.

51. *Regents Journal* 11 (October 18, 1952; May 21, 1954): 7, 279. *Biennial Report of the Board of Regents* (1953–55), pp. 5–7. Woodburne to Schmitz, February 18, 1954; Everest to Woodburne, February 24, 1954, President's Office Records, box 94. Everest to the Board of Regents, "Hospital Development History," November, 1954, President's Office Records, box 95.

52. Lundberg to Schmitz, October 21, 1952, Heilman Papers, folder 11-7.

53. *Regents Journal* 10 (September 27, 1952): 352. Schmitz to Harsch, November 25, 1952, Harsch Papers, box 1. *Seattle Post-Intelligencer*, November 26, 1952; *Seattle Times*, December 30, 1952.

54. Everest to Combs, January 22, 1953, President's Office Records, box 109. *Hearings before the Subcommittee to Investigate the Administration of the Internal Security Act of the Senate Committee on the Judiciary, Subversive Influence in the Educational Process*, Eighty-third Congress, first session (1953), pp. 605–22.

55. Manley to Woodburne, March 24, 1953; Heilman to Schmitz, March 9, 1953; Schmitz to Heilman, March 23, 1953, President's Office Records, box 95.

56. Schmitz to Eva Anderson, March 23, 1953, President's Office Records, box 112.

57. *Hearings before the Committee on Un-American Activities, House of Representatives, Eighty-third Congress, Communist Methods of Infiltration (Education)*, vol. 3; *Congressional Record*, vol. 100 (March 31, 1954).

58. *Seattle Post-Intelligencer*, September 18, 1952, April 21, July 17, 18, 22, 24, 25, August 19, 1953. *Civil Liberties in Washington State* (newsletter of the Washington State chapter of the ACLU), vol. 1 (May, 1954). Through the ACLU, Phillips appealed his conviction and was cleared of the contempt charges in 1958: *Seattle Post-Intelligencer*, April 22, 1958, p. 3. For another account of these proceedings, see Gerald B. Nelson, *Seattle: The Life and Times of an American City* (New York: Alfred A. Knopf, 1977), pp. 61–66.

59. "Faculty Appointment Policy: Report of the Administrative Committee on Appointment Policy," University of Washington, 1953.

60. *Minutes of the Faculty Senate of the University of Washington* 7 (May 28, 1953): 52–54. *Regents Journal* 11 (June 12, 1953): 101. Schmitz to Harsch, March 2, 1954, Harsch Papers, box 1.

61. "The Rights and Responsibilities of Universities and Their Faculties: A Statement by the Association of American Universities," March 24, 1953. H. S. Bennett to Schmitz, May 13, 1953, President's Office Records, box 101. *Minutes of the Faculty Senate* 7 (May 27, 1954): 126. *Seattle Times*, May 28, 1954, p. 41.

62. Abraham Keller, personal interview, March 3, 1976.

63. Phillip M. Stern, *The Oppenheimer Case: Security on Trial* (New York: Harper and Row, 1969), pp. 60, 131. Harold P. Green, "The Oppenheimer Case: A Study in the Abuse of Law," *Bulletin of the Atomic Scientists* 33 (September, 1977): 57. Green, who resigned his position as an AEC attorney to

protest the Oppenheimer case, theorizes that Weinberg was acquitted because Truman ordered government prosecutors not to introduce Oppenheimer-related evidence. Green believes Truman had been advised that Oppenheimer would perjure himself.

64. Keller, personal interview. The development of the H-bomb is still shrouded in the secrecy of classified documents. Herbert F. York, one of its developers used certain declassified information to show that, regardless of propaganda, the U.S. achieved a truly "deliverable" H-bomb about three years before the U.S.S.R., which did not have an H-bomb until 1955. See York, *The Advisors: Oppenheimer, Teller, and the Superbomb* (San Francisco: W. H. Freeman and Company, 1976), pp. 10–11. Also Nuel Pharr Davis, *Lawrence and Oppenheimer* (New York: Simon and Schuster, 1968), pp. 334–35, 344. *Seattle Post-Intelligencer*, August 20, 1953, pp. 1, 2.

65. Keller, personal interview. See above, note 13.

66. *Hearings before the Committee on Un-American Activities, House of Representatives, Eighty-third Congress (1953–54), Investigation of Communist Activities in the Pacific Northwest*, 7: 6454–89. *Seattle Post-Intelligencer*, June 19, 1954. *Seattle Times*, June 18, 19, 1954. Keller, personal interview. Frank J. Donner, *The Un-Americans* (New York: Ballantine Books, 1961), pp. 70–71, 86, 118–19, 156.

67. Keller, personal interview.

68. Speakers' Requests File, President's Office Records, box 91. After receiving Heilman's approved request from Dean of Arts and Sciences Woodburne, Schmitz consulted Librarian H. C. Bauer and Fred Woltman of the *New York World Telegram*; both confirmed Humphries' Communist Front activities during the 1930s. Woltman to Schmitz, August 16, 1954; Schmitz to Woodburne, December 1, 1953, President's Office Records, box 91.

Chapter VI

1. See note 63, chapter V, above. John Major, *The Oppenheimer Hearing* (New York: Stein and Day, 1971); Thomas W. Wilson, Jr., *The Great Weapons Heresy* (Boston: Houghton Mifflin Company, 1970).

2. Major, *The Oppenheimer Hearing*, pp. 248–73. Nuel Pharr Davis, *Lawrence and Oppenheimer* (New York: Simon and Schuster, 1968), pp. 293–330. Herbert F. York, *The Advisors: Oppenheimer, Teller, and the Superbomb* (San Francisco: W. H. Freeman and Company, 1976), pp. 36–72.

3. *Seattle Post-Intelligencer*, August 20, 1953, pp. 1, 2. Harold P. Green, "The Oppenheimer Case: A Study in the Abuse of Law," *Bulletin of the Atomic Scientists* 33 (September, 1977): 12–16, 56–61. York, *The Advisors*, pp. 10–17.

4. *In the Matter of J. Robert Oppenheimer: Texts of Principal Documents and Letters of Personnel Security Board, General Manager and Commissioners. Washington, D.C. May 27, 1954, through June 29, 1954* (Washington, D.C.: U.S. Government Printing Office, 1954), pp. 13–21. Phillip M. Stern, *The Oppenheimer Case: Security on Trial* (New York: Harper and Row, 1969).

5. *Seattle Times*, June 5, 1954, p. 4. *Bulletin of the Atomic Scientists* 10 (May,

1954): 173–74. James Shepley and Clay Blair, Jr., "The Hydrogen Bomb: How the U.S. Almost Lost It," *U.S. News and World Report*, September 24, 1954, pp. 58–72, 88–107. Joseph and Stewart Alsop, "We Accuse!" *Harpers* 209 (October, 1954): 25–45. Diana Trilling, "The Oppenheimer Case," *Partisan Review* 21 (November–December, 1954): 604–35.

6. This account is derived from two sources, one public, the other unpublished. Schmitz's account is in "Report to the Faculty Senate," Senate Meeting Minutes, March 3, 1955. The "Draft Report of the Senate ad hoc Committee on Walker-Ames Appointment Practices and Policies" was the result of an investigation by a faculty committee chaired by H. Stanley Bennett (Anatomy) in the wake of the Oppenheimer controversy. The committee seems to have stopped work on the report in August, 1955, without submitting it to the senate. The draft is found in the papers of one of the committee members, Alfred Harsch, box 1 (hereafter cited as Draft Report). Manley later wrote Schmitz that since the AEC hearings had neither uncovered new evidence nor resulted in an indictment of Oppenheimer, he assumed that Schmitz would have no reason to change his mind on the desirability of the appointment. Manley to Schmitz, April 8, 1955, President's Office Records, box 95. On Manley's work with Oppenheimer at Los Alamos and after, see Davis, *Lawrence and Oppenheimer*, pp. 133–35, 264–67, and *passim*.

7. Edwin Uehling, personal interviews, November, 1974, and May 16, ˙1978. University of Washington *Daily*, February 16, 1955.

8. *Seattle Times*, February 16, 1955, p. 11.

9. *Daily*, February 17, 18, 1955.

10. *Seattle Post-Intelligencer*, February 19, 1955, p. 6. *Daily*, February 24, March 1, 1955. *Regents Journal* 12 (February 26, 1955): 26.

11. Ray Kenworthy (Physics) to Schmitz, February 18, 1955, President's Office Records, box 92. The caliber of the student leaders is evident from their later accomplishments. One of them, Robert Skotheim, is a historian and president of Whitman College (Washington). Another, Byron Coney, provided legal counsel for the faculty in the loyalty oath suit (1955–64, see chapter VII); he is a Seattle attorney. *Civil Liberties in Washington State* (newsletter of the Washington State chapter of the ACLU) 2 (March, 1955):1.

12. *Daily*, February 16, 17, 18, 1955. Heilman to executive officers, February 25, 1955, Heilman Papers, folder 11-7.

13. *Daily*, February 18, 1955, Oppenheimer's appointment as a Walker-Ames lecturer would have made him a nonvoting member of the University of Washington faculty for one week, the duration of his appointment.

14. Kenworthy to Schmitz, February 18, 1955, President's Office Records, box 92; Kenworthy to Schmitz, December 29, 1954, box 95. One such disagreement concerned the jurisdiction of the Cosmic Ray Laboratory; see correspondence between Dean Woodburne and Vice-President Everest, January and February, 1952, President's Office Records, box 118. Personal interviews: Uehling, November, 1974, May, 1978; and Ronald Geballe, March 19, 1978.

15. Allendoerfer to Schmitz, February 17, 1955, President's Office

Records, box 92. Hans Bethe, "Oppenheimer: 'Where He Was There Was Always Life and Excitement,'" *Science* 155 (1967): 1080.

16. "Pro Football Welcomed, But Oppenheimer Banned," *Argus*, February 19, 1955, p. 1. The *Portland Oregonian* and the *San Francisco Chronicle* as quoted in the *Daily*, February 24, 1955, p. 1.

17. *New Republic*, April 18, 1955, pp. 6, 7. Alex Gottfried also reported this conversation, which outraged several of the students who were themselves veterans of the Korean conflict. Gottfried, personal interview, March 22, 1976. See also, *Seattle Times*, February 18, 1955, p. 2.

18. *Journal of the House of the Thirty-fourth Legislature* (1955), pp. 533, 1416. *Seattle Post-Intelligencer*, March 22, 1955. The activities of the Velde Committee dominated the headlines of Seattle newspapers during its hearings on March 18, 19, 20.

19. Neddermeyer to Schmitz, February 28, 1955, Balmer Papers, box 13. *Daily*, February 17, 1955, p. 1. On Neddermeyer's atomic bomb work, see Davis, *Lawrence and Oppenheimer*, pp. 169–73, 216–22, 229–30.

20. Committee on Public Lectures and Concerts to Allendoerfer, February 28, 1955, President's Office Records box 92. *Minutes of the Faculty Senate of the University of Washington* 8 (March 3, 1955): 47–63.

21. *Minutes of the Faculty Senate*. The members of this special committee consisted of four faculty persons who had served on the Guthrie Committee: Stanley Bennett, Alfred Harsch, J. Richard Huber, and Sargent Powell.

22. *Daily*, March 9, 11, 1955.

23. President's Office Records, box 92. Laurel Lewis (Electrical Engineering), personal interview, March 2, 1976. Lewis, who supported the president, says Schmitz told him that he refused to commit the university to a position on Oppenheimer in an effort to maintain neutrality on the scientist's affairs.

24. *Daily*, March 8, 1955, p. 1. Scientists to Schmitz, March 14, 1955; Schmitz statement, March 22, 1955, President's Office Records, box 102. *Seattle Times*, March 16, 1955, p. 1.

25. Stull Holt to Perry Miller, March 7, 1955, Holt Papers, folder 11-3. Bennett to Everest, March 18, 1955, President's Office Records, box 102.

26. "Arrogant Cult," March 14, p. 12; "Phoney Issue," March 15, 1955, p. 12.

27. *Seattle Post-Intelligencer*, March 24, pp. 1, 5; March 25, 1955, pp. 1, 6. In a follow-up article, the *Seattle Times* reported (March 25, 1955, p. 36) that Oppenheimer had not understood the nature of Walker-Ames appointments and believed that he was invited for informal lectures only.

28. *Regents Journal* 12 (March 26, 1955): 44–45. Executive Committee of the Board of Trustees of the University of Washington Alumni Association, press release, March 28, 1955. President's Office Records, box 11. *Seattle Times*, March 26, 1955, p. 12; *Seattle Post-Intelligencer*, March 27, 1955, p. 18.

29. Holt to Schweppe, March 31, 1955; Schweppe to Holt, April 4, Holt Papers, folder 11-7. Recording, KJR radio debate, April 3, 1955, Holt Papers, folder 11-5. *Seattle Times*, March 31, 1955, p. 20. *Daily*, April 1, 1955. See President's Office Records, box 102, for additional faculty correspondence.

30. *Seattle Times*, March 26, p. 25, and April 6, 1955, p. 4. *Daily*, March 29, 1955, p. 1. For more rebuttals to Schweppe, see the *Daily*, March 30, 1955, p. 2: Frank Huennekens (Medicine) and P. E. Wilcox (Biochemistry) criticized the attorney's discourtesy and disrespect for faculty members who felt it their duty to protest Schmitz's decision. Ullman to Himstead, March 29, 1955, UWAAUP Chapter Records, box 3.

31. Schmitz to Dael Wolfle (administrative secretary, American Association for the Advancement of Science), March 26, 1955, President's Office Records, box 102. Schmitz wrote a similar letter to Detlov Bronk on March 26. There is no indication that the National Academy acted on the situation; the AAAS printed excerpts from the Schmitz letter in *Science* 121 (April 8, 1955): 491–92, but made no comment.

32. "Boycott Against the University of Washington," p. 20. John Manley, on leave in Europe, apprised the president of the international repercussions of his decision in a letter of April 10, 1955, President's Office Records, box 102.

33. Notes, anonymous, Holt Papers, folder 11-7. Everest Committee to Executive Committee of the Senate, April 1, 1955, Office of University Committees Records, box 8. Professor Birnbaum did not agree to the compromise statement.

34. Minutes of the Executive Committee of the Senate, April 4, 1955, President's Office Records, box 92. *Minutes of the Faculty Senate* 8 (April 7, 1955): 70–75. Note that eighty-six out of one hundred possible votes were cast.

35. *Seattle Times*, April 18, 1955, p. 10.

36. "Two Scientists," *Seattle Post-Intelligencer*, April 8, 1955, p. 20. Stevens was Public Relations Counsel for the West Coast Lumbermen's Association. Edward R. Murrow's famous interview with Oppenheimer was rejected for airing by the university's new television station in March; members of the ACLU obtained it for free showings in the University District through the Fund for the Republic. See *Civil Liberties in Washington State* 2 (April, 1955):1.

37. Draft Report, p. 73, Harsch Papers, box 1. Edwin Uehling, personal interview, May 16, 1978. *Journal of the House of the Thirty-fourth Legislature* (1955), pp. 840–48. *Seattle Post-Intelligencer*, February 22, 1955, pp. 1, 7. Those files that Canwell himself did not destroy were kept at the Seattle Office of the F.B.I. until December 17, 1971, when they were destroyed "in accordance with federal regulations." William Earl Whaley (supervisory special agent, F.B.I.) to the author, May 30, 1978.

38. Charles M. Gates, *First Century at the University of Washington* (Seattle: University of Washington Press, 1961), pp. 219–20. Hughes to Schweppe, April 2, 1955, President's Office Records, box 11. *Daily*, April 15, 1955, p. 2. *Regents Journal* 12 (June 10, 1955): 80.

39. *Daily*, April 19, 1955, p. 1. Draft Report, pp. 105–6. *Northwest Corner Newsletter* (Washington-Idaho Council of Churches), April 8, 1955, in Gordon Marckworth Papers, box 14.

40. "What Constitutes a University?" May 1, 1955, p. 11. See also Sieg to

Balmer, March 23, 1955, Balmer Papers, box 13. Personal interviews: Donald K. Anderson, January 28, 1976; Laurel Lewis, March 2, 1976.

41. Dean Harold Wessman to State Senator William Shannon, March 31, 1955, Holt Papers, folder 11-5. Woodburne to Manley, July 3, 1956, Woodburne Papers, box 1.

42. Wessman to Regent Charles Frankland, April 1, 1955, Holt Papers, folder 11-5. Cannon to D. H. MacKenzie, August 1, 1955, President's Office Records, box 95. Bryan to Everest, January 5, 1956, President's Office Records, box 103. Draft Report, pp. 62–71.

43. Harold Taylor, "The Dismissal of Fifth Amendment Professors," *The Annals of the American Academy of Political and Social Science* 300 (July, 1955): 81. Robert M. Hutchins, "The Meaning and Significance of Academic Freedom," *Annals of AAPSS* 300: 73. Schmitz to Robert Lampman, March 10, 1955, President's Office Records, box 102. Schmitz stated that his hiring of an unnamed physics faculty member proved that he and the regents would hire someone whose clearance had been revoked, provided he did not work with contract research. He also noted to Lampman that he had been sharply criticized by faculty in two colleges for his action. See also Kenworthy to Schmitz, December 29, 1954, President's Office Records, box 88.

44. Lundberg to Schmitz, January 21, 1955, Holt Papers, folder 11-3. Lundberg to John King, January 28, 1955, Lundberg Papers, folder 29-6. Lundberg to Schweppe, January 28, 1955, Lundberg Papers, folder 11-19. Lundberg, "Prefatory Foreword," in Arthur Goddard, ed., *Harry Elmer Barnes, Learned Crusader* (Colorado Springs: Ralph Myles, 1968), pp. xxxii–lii.

45. Holt to Schmitz, January 31, 1955; Lundberg to Holt, February 9, 1955, Holt Papers, folder 11-3. Lundberg, *Learned Crusader*, pp. 1–lii. Holt, personal interview, November, 1974.

46. Schmitz to Holt, February 4, 1955; Holt to Schmitz, February 17, 1955, Holt Papers, folder 11-3.

47. Woodburne to Schmitz, June 17, 1955, President's Office Records, box 95. Manley to Schmitz, January 19, 1956; memo: "Message to Oppenheimer," January 28, 1956, President's Office Records, box 102. *Regents Journal*, vol. 12 (January 20, 1956). *Daily*, January 24, 25, 1956. *Seattle Times*, September 21, 1956, p. 2. Edwin Uehling, personal interviews, November, 1974, May, 1978.

48. President's Office Records, box 109. *Daily*, January 18, 1956.

49. *AAUP Bulletin* 42 (Spring, 1956): 49–64. Correspondence between Schmitz and the AAUP's general secretary, Ralph Fuchs, on early drafts of the Special Committee's Report is in President's Office Records, box 82. The case of the philosophical anarchist was that of George Woodcock, whom Heilman vainly sought to appoint despite immigration restrictions. When protests to the State Department failed, Woodcock took a position at the University of British Columbia. Heilman to Schmitz, April 5, 1956, President's Office Records, box 95.

50. Lutz to Martin, April 8, 1956; Martin to Schmitz, n.d., President's Office Records, box 88. Cf. Robert W. Iversen, *The Communists and the Schools* (New York: Harcourt, Brace and Company, 1959), pp. 334–54.

51. Notes on the meeting of April 12, 1956, UWAAUP Chapter Records, box 3. Moley, "The Pink Flag Flies," *Newsweek*, April 23, 1956, p. 104.

52. "The AAUP and Academic Integrity," *The New Leader*, 39 (May 21, 1956): 19–21. Hook and Fuchs, "A Joint Statement on a Matter of Importance," *AAUP Bulletin* 42 (Winter, 1956): 692–95.

53. *AAUP Bulletin* 39 (1953): 239; 41 (1955): 152; 44 (1958): 357. Interviews: Abraham Keller, March 3, 1976; Alex Gottfried, March 23, 1976.

54. Schmitz to Heilman, April 16, 1956, President's Office Records, box 95. *Regents Journal* 12 (April 14, May 19, July 14, 1956): 260–62, 278–79, 306–7. *Daily*, March 6, 8, 29, April 17, 1956.

55. "Wanted: Prestige," *Time*, February 24, 1958, p. 81. Anderson letter, *Time*, March 24, 1958, p. 8. Board of Deans to regents, February 25, 1958, Woodburne Papers, box 1. *Regents Journal*, November 21, 1958. Arnold Stein to Charles M. Harris (president of the board), December 6, 1958, UWAAUP Records, box 3.

56. "The Promise of a University: An Appreciation of J. Allen Smith," *Pacific Northwest Quarterly* 46 (July, 1955): 71. Harrison's note 14 reads: "It may not be amiss here to repeat the laconic comment of a colleague that this designation comes 'at the wrong end of the thousand years.'"

Chapter VII

1. Harold M. Hyman, *To Try Men's Souls: Loyalty Tests in American History* (Berkeley: University of California Press, 1959), pp. 338–39 and *passim*. *Senate Journal of the Twenty-second Legislature of the State of Washington* (1931), pp. 437, 550, 587. Section 2, Chapter 103, Laws of 1931. Section 2, Chapter 287, Laws of 1947. *House Journal of the Thirty-second Legislature of the State of Washington* (1951), pp. 23, 30.

2. Chapter 254, Laws of 1951. Chapter 142, Laws of 1953. *Journal of the Senate of the Thirty-third Legislature of the State of Washington* (1953), pp. 25, 38, 54, 59. Message of Arthur B. Langlie to the Thirty-fourth Legislature, January 12, 1955, p. 3. *Journal of the House of the Thirty-fourth Legislature*, pp. 533, 632–33. Chapter 377, Laws of 1955. *Seattle Post-Intelligencer*, August 30, 1955, p. 4.

3. Schmitz to the faculty, May 25, 1955; Everest to the faculty, June 30, 1955, President's Office Records, box 106. Temporary Steering Committee to colleagues, June 27, 1955, Howard L. Nostrand private files. Personal interviews: Melvin Rader, November 4, 1974; Alex Gottfried, March 23, 1976; Max Savelle, March 26, 1976; Howard L. Nostrand, June 6, 1978.

4. *Civil Liberties in Washington State* (newsletter of the Washington State chapter of the ACLU), vol. 3 (September, 1955). *Seattle Post-Intelligencer*, August 30, 1955, p. 4. University of Washington *Daily*, October 14, 1955, p. 1.

5. *Daily*, October 19, 1955, p. 2; November 9, 1955, p. 1; November 10, 1955, p. 1. *Minutes of the Faculty Senate of the University of Washington* 8 (1954–56): 33.

6. Howard L. Nostrand, personal interview, June 5, 1978. Hans Neurath,

notes on conversation with President Schmitz, September 26, 1955, UWAAUP Records, box 3. Everest to Dean L. J. Elias, October 26, 1955, Nostrand private files Arval Morris, personal interview, April 7, 1978.

7. Nostrand to Arthur Barnett et al., October 17 and 27, 1955; Nostrand, "One point for a composite formulation," October, 1955, Nostrand private files.

8. Matchett to Nostrand, September, 1955; Keller to Nostrand, October, 1955, Nostrand private files.

9. *Daily*, April 30, 1957, p. 1. Savelle, "In This Matter of the Oath," *Columns* 41 (May–June, 1957): 1. Nostrand vs. Balmer, 53 Wn. 2d 460; 335 P. 2d 10 (1959). *Civil Liberties in Washington State*, vol. 5 (May–June, 1957) and vol. 7 (January–February, 1959).

10. *Daily*, October 27, 1959, p. 1. Nostrand v. Little, 362 U.S. 474 (1960). Nostrand v. Little, 58 Wn. 2d 111; 361 P. 2d 551 (1961). Nostrand v. Little, 368 U.S. 436 (1962).

11. Daniel Bell, ed., *The Radical Right* (Garden City, N.Y.: Anchor Books, 1964), pp. 1–8. Alan F. Westin, "Anti-Communism and the Corporations," *Commentary* 36 (December, 1963): 479–87. William K. Wyant, Jr., "Speaking of Extremists, Who's Playing Right Field?" *New Republic*, September 19, 1964, pp. 12–16.

12. Alex Gottfried and Sue Davidson, "New Right in Action," *The Nation*, July 29, 1961, pp. 48–51. Melvin Rader, "Teaching about Communism," *Teachers College Record* 64 (April, 1963): 577–83.

13. Charles E. Odegaard, "Inaugural Address," in *Man and Learning in Modern Society* (Seattle: University of Washington Press, 1959), p. 184. Donald K. Anderson, "The Odegaard Years," *The University of Washington Report*, vol. 4 (Summer, 1973).

14. *Regents Journal*, January 15, 1960; *University of Washington Faculty Handbook*, 2:2–3. Heilman to Odegaard, May 11, 1962, President's Office Records, box 22. Anderson, "The Odegaard Years." Personal interviews: Laurel Lewis, March 2, 1976; Howard L. Nostrand, June 5, 1978.

15. UWAAUP Records, box 2. John F. Kennedy, "The Loyalty Oath—An Obstacle to Better Education," *AAUP Bulletin*, vol. 44 (Spring, 1959).

16. UWAAUP Records, box 2. *Daily*, November 19, 20, 1959; October 18, 1962. *AAUP Bulletin* 48 (Summer, 1962): 180. For an account of the conservative "Students' National Committee for the Loyalty Oath," see M. Stanton Evans, *Revolt on the Campus* (Chicago: Henry Regnery Company, 1961), chapter 4.

17. Charles C. Alexander, *Holding the Line: The Eisenhower Era, 1952–1961* (Bloomington: Indiana University Press, 1975), pp. 289–90. Carl Solberg, *Riding High: America in the Cold War* (New York: Mason and Lipscomb, 1973), pp. 419, 431. Westin, "Anti-Communism and the Corporations." Gottfried and Davidson, "New Right in Action."

18. Giovanni Costigan, personal interview, April 27, 1978. *Daily*, January 24, 25, February 2, 10, 14, 16, 1962. "Costigan file," President's Office

Records, box 47. Gottfried and Davidson, "New Right in Action." For another account of the "Communism on the Map" controversy, see Fred J. Cook, *The Warfare State* (New York: Macmillan Company, 1962). pp. 298–303.

19. Press release, February 1, 1962, President's Office Records, box 34. *Daily*, February 9, 13, 1962.

20. Recall that the Loyalty Oath suit had resulted in the state supreme court's disallowance of the list as an index of subversion.

21. Report to the senate, April 12, 1962. The regents approved Odegaard's statement on off-campus speakers at their April 27 meeting. Ironically, Joseph Drumheller and John L. King were again serving as members of the board as they had been in 1946, at the beginning of the Cold War era.

22. President's Office Records, box 34. This faculty statement endorsed the position taken by the University of Oregon faculty in March, 1962, and was in conformity with the position of the AAUP. See *AAUP Bulletin* 43 (Summer, 1957): 363.

23. Heilman to Odegaard, May 11, 1962, President's Office Records, box 22.

24. Odegaard to the faculty, May 29, 1962, President's Office Records, box 33. *Journal of the House of the Thirty-eighth Legislature* (1963), Extraordinary Session, pp. 127–28. *Seattle Post-Intelligencer*, March 29, 1963.

25. Regents Little and Harold Shefelman to Odegaard, May, 1963; Little to Odegaard, August 19, 1963, President's Office Records, box 33. This file also contains the results of a National Association of State Universities survey which showed that only the universities of Wisconsin, Minnesota, Oregon, and Cornell had open policies allowing anyone to speak. The report concluded that 1962 was "the worst year in a decade" for political freedom on campuses surveyed.

26. "Report of the Ad Hoc Committee of the Senate on Speaker Policy," November 8, 1963, Secretary of the Faculty Records, box 9.

27. *Minutes of the Faculty Senate* 14 (1963–64): 132–33. Transcript of Odegaard's remarks to senate meeting of January 6; Odegaard to the Board of Regents, January 17, 1964, President's Office Records, box 33. *Regents Minutes*, January 24, 1964. Charles E. Odegaard, personal interview, June 21, 1976.

28. Mrs. Joseph E. Hurley to Board of Regents, January 31, 1964, President's Office Records, box 34. *Argus*, February 7, 1964, p. 1. *Seattle Times*, February 7, 1964, p. 1. Robert Waldo to Odegaard, February 28 and April 24, 1964. As director of university relations, Waldo kept a running count of letters, petitions, etc., President's Office Records, box 33. *Regents Minutes*, March 24, 1964.

29. Geballe et al. to faculty, February 6, 1962; UWAAUP Executive Committee to AAUP members, February 13, 1962, Nostrand private files. Executive Committee of UWAAUP to faculty, April 20, 1962, President's Office Records, box 22. Personal interviews: Arval Morris, April 7, 1978; Howard L. Nostrand, June 5, 1978.

30. *Regents Journal*, May 28, 1962. Memo, President's Office to university staff, May 28, 1962. Maki to faculty and staff, May 29, 1962, President's Office Records, box 22. *Seattle Times*, May 26, pp. 1, 6, and May 27, p. 72.

31. UWAAUP questionnaire, May–June, 1962, Arval Morris private files. For faculty criticism of the ACLU, see *Daily*, April 4, 1962, p. 2. An overview of the broad attack on the Washington State ACLU in the early 1960s is in *Argus*, February 15, 1963, p. 1.

32. *Transcript of Record, Baggett v. Bullitt, Supreme Court of the United States, October Term 1963, No. 220*, pp. 9–17. The sixty-four plaintiffs included four undergraduates whose status as complainants was dismissed by the federal court in July, 1962, because they were judged to have no "direct legal interest" in the case; *Seattle Times*, July 14, 1962, p. 1.

33. *Transcript of Record, Baggett v. Bullitt*, pp. 26–34. *Seattle Times*, June 26, 1962, p. 25.

34. Griffiths to E. H. Kantorowicz, June 28, 1962, President's Office Records, box 22. Gordon Griffiths, personal interview, October, 1974. Regent Neylan was also counsel to the Hearst Press. For an account of the California case see David P. Gardner, *The California Oath Controversy* (Berkeley: University of California Press, 1967). Correspondence pro and con the oath suit is in President's Office Records, box 22. See also Arval Morris, "The University of Washington Loyalty Oath Case," *AAUP Bulletin* 50 (September, 1964): 221–32.

35. Arval A. Morris and Kenneth A. MacDonald, *Brief of the Appellants: Baggett v. Bullitt, In the Supreme Court of the United States, October Term 1963, No. 220.*

36. Ibid., pp. 138–50 and *passim*.

37. Ibid., pp. 98–100, 159–61.

38. John J. O'Connell et al., *Brief of Appellees: Baggett v. Bullitt, In the Supreme Court of the United States, October Term 1963, No. 220.*

39. Baggett v. Bullitt, 215 F. Supp. 439 (1963). *Seattle Times*, February 12, 1963, p. 3.

40. Baggett v. Bullitt, 12 L. 3d. 2d 377, 387 (1964). *Seattle Times*, June 1, 1964, p. 1.

41. Morris to Odegaard, June 2, 1964, President's Office Records, box 22.

Epilogue

1. Gundlach to Charles M. Gates, November 14, 1962, Gundlach Papers, folder 1-12.

2. Personal interviews: Garland O. Ethel, October 15, 1975; Abraham Keller, March 3, 1976; Howard Nostrand, June 5, 1978. Recall also the affidavit of W. Stull Holt in *Baggett v. Bullitt* concerning informers on campus, above chapter VII. Since the University of Washington was one of those institutions involved, note the comments of faculty surveyed in Paul F. Lazarsfeld and Wagner Thielens, Jr., *The Academic Mind: Social Scientists in a Time of Crisis* (Glencoe, Ill.: Free Press of Glencoe, 1958), pp. 225–27.

3. Draft Report of the Senate Ad Hoc Committee on Walker-Ames Appointment Practices and Policies, August, 1955, pp. 63–71, Harsch Papers, box 1. Charles E. Odegaard, personal interview, June 21, 1976.

4. Allen to Ralph Fuchs, February 15, 1956, President's Office Records, box 82.

5. Winston Ivan King, "The Public Image of the University of Washington in Selected Small Communities—with Special Attention to Factors of System Reciprocity and Autonomy," (M.A. thesis, University of Washington, 1964), pp. 82–84.

6. On Rostow and Rusk, see *National Review* 21 (May 6, 1969): 455. For other such incidents involving "traditional-conservative" professors, see Anthony T. Bouscaren, "Bias and Discrimination in Higher Education," in Charles A. Moser, ed., *Continuity in Crisis* (Washington, D.C.: University Professors for Academic Order, 1974), pp. 39–43.

Selected Bibliography

Manuscript Collections in the University of Washington Library

The University of Washington President's Office Records, of primary importance to this study, are arranged in three accessions. The largest accession has been reinventoried since my research; therefore box numbers cited in the notes are no longer current, although they can still be used by referring to the original inventory, which is available in the library. A second smaller accession of President's Office Records contains miscellaneous items and was largely unprocessed; it is referred to in the notes as President's Office Records, small box __. The third group of President's Office Records contains correspondence relative to the Canwell investigation and the proceedings of the Faculty Committee on Tenure. This collection is referred to in the notes as Faculty Committee on Tenure Hearing Records (FCTH Records).

The transcript of the 1948 hearings by the Faculty Senate Committee on Tenure and Academic Freedom (referred to in the notes as *FCTH Transcript*) is arranged in thirty-four volumes in document cases.

Other important documents located in the archives are: Minutes of the Faculty from before 1940, University of Washington chapter of the American Association of University Professors (AAUP), Instructors Association Records, Records of the Secretary of the Faculty and Office of University Committees, Regents' Records.

Collections of personal papers researched included those of Thomas Balmer, Garland O. Ethel, Charles M. Gates, Ronald Geballe, Ralph Gundlach, Edwin Guthrie, Alfred E. Harsch, Robert B. Heilman, W. Stull Holt, George Lundberg, Charles E. Martin, Henry Schmitz, Frank G. Williston, Lloyd Woodburne. The Richard H. Pelto Tape-recording Collection, recorded in 1969, contains valuable comments by principals in the events of 1948–49.

Official Records in Administrative Offices

The minutes of University of Washington Board of Regents meetings are bound in volumes known as the *Regents Journal* (after 1963, *Regents Minutes*), and are located in the Office of the Secretary to the Board of Regents. Official *Faculty Senate Meeting Minutes* are bound in volumes located in the Office of the Secretary of the Faculty.

Publications of the University of Washington

Periodicals issued by the university administration provide valuable source materials. These include: *Biennial Reports of the Board of Regents to the Governor of Washington*, the *University of Washington Bulletin* (includes *Catalogue* issues), the *University of Washington Record*. The Alumni Association's *Alumnus* and student publications such as the *Daily*, *Tyee* (yearbook), and *Columns* were also consulted.

Communism and Academic Freedom: The Record of the Tenure Cases at the University of Washington was issued by the University of Washington Press in 1949. Recognizing the importance of their decisions in 1949, the regents published this volume for distribution to critics and supporters of their action against Communist party faculty members. It contains the findings of the Faculty Committee on Tenure, Allen's recommendations to the board, and the charges on which they were founded.

The following commemorative volumes were also consulted: *Old Truths and New Horizons: Addresses Delivered at the Inauguration of Dr. Raymond B. Allen as President of the University of Washington*, May 22–24, 1947, (Seattle: University of Washington Press, 1949); *Man and Learning in Modern Society. Papers and Addresses Delivered at the Inauguration of Charles E. Odegaard as President of the University of Washington, November 6 and 7, 1958* (Seattle: University of Washington Press, 1959); "The Inauguration of Dr. Henry Schmitz as President of the University of Washington," Seattle, Washington, October 3, 1952.

Government Documents

Also consulted were the *Senate and House Journals of the Legislature of the State of Washington* for actions that affected the university. Transcripts of the Canwell Committee hearings are contained in *First and Second Reports: Un-American Activities in Washington State, 1948*. Various volumes of *Hearings before the Committee on Un-American Activities of the U.S. House of Representatives* contain the grist for allegations of "subversive activities" by persons mentioned above. Particularly interesting are those for the "Investigation of Communist Activities in Seattle," Eighty-third Congress (1953–54), vol. 7, and Eighty-fourth Congress (1955), vol. 7.

Public Education in Washington: A Report of a Survey of Public Education in the State of Washington, prepared by George D. Strayer, director, was submitted to

Governor Mon C. Wallgren on September 5, 1946. The Strayer Survey provided impetus for faculty reforms and legislative support in the postwar era.

Contemporary and Historical Accounts Concerning the University of Washington and State Politics

Books, dissertations, theses

Acena, Albert A. "The Washington Commonwealth Federation: Reform Politics and the Popular Front." Ph.D. dissertation, University of Washington, 1975.

Barksdale, Julian D. *Geology at the University of Washington, 1895–1973.* Publications in Geological Sciences, no. 4, University of Washington, Seattle. A useful study of the evolution of a department offering observations on university administrators.

Barth, Alan. *The Loyalty of Free Men.* New York: The Viking Press, 1951. Offers an analysis of the university's dismissal of Communist professors, pp. 218–22.

Caute, David. *The Great Fear: The Anti-Communist Purge under Truman and Eisenhower.* New York: Simon and Schuster, 1978. Offers some details on dismissed University of Washington professors.

Clark, Norman H. *Washington: A Bicentennial History.* New York: W. W. Norton and Company, 1976.

Cook, Fred J. *The Warfare State.* New York: The Macmillan Company, 1962. Pages on Giovanni Costigan's efforts to expose the film "Communism on the Map" as right-wing propaganda.

Countryman, Vern. *Un-American Activities in the State of Washington.* Ithaca, N.Y.: Cornell University Press, 1951. With Rockefeller Foundation funds, Countryman spent the summer of 1949 studying the events of 1947–49; his work is notable for its thorough attention to legal details involved in the Canwell investigations.

Eaton, William Edward. *The American Federation of Teachers, 1916–1961.* Carbondale: Southern Illinois University Press, 1975. Interesting observations on University of Washington's Local 401.

Gates, Charles M. *The First Century at the University of Washington, 1861–1961.* Seattle: University of Washington Press, 1961.

Griffith, Thomas. *The Waist-High Culture.* New York: Harper and Brothers, 1959. Contains some unsympathetic comments about University of Washington professors during the author's journalism studies in the 1930s.

Gunns, Albert Francis. "Civil Liberties and Crisis: The Status of Civil Liberties in the Pacific Northwest, 1917–1940." Ph.D. dissertation, University of Washington, 1971.

King, Winston Ivan. "The Public Image of the University of Washington in Selected Small Communities—With Special Attention to Factors of System Reciprocity and Autonomy." M.A. thesis, University of Washington, 1964.

Krause, Fayette. "Democratic Party Politics in the State of Washington During the New Deal: 1932–40." Ph.D. dissertation, 1971.

McClintock, Thomas C. "J. Allen Smith and the Progressive Movement: A Study in Intellectual History." Ph.D. dissertation, University of Washington, 1959.

MacIver, Robert M. *Academic Freedom in Our Time*. New York: Columbia University Press, 1955. A companion volume to Richard Hofstadter and Walter P. Metzger's *Development of Academic Freedom in the United States*, this is a full analysis of the problems of the early 1950s, including those at the university.

McKibben, Gordon Charles. "Nonpartisan Politics: A Case Study of Seattle." M.A. thesis, University of Washington, 1954.

McWilliams, Carey. *Witch Hunt: The Revival of Heresy*. Boston: Little, Brown and Company, 1950. Book 2 of this study, entitled "Witchcraft in Washington State," deals with the Canwell investigations.

Menefee, Selden, *Assignment: USA*. New York: Reynal and Hitchcock, 1943. An impressionistic account of the nation at war, with parts devoted to Seattle. The author was a former university instructor active in left politics and Local 401, AFT.

Morgan, Murray. *Skid Road: An Informal Portrait of Seattle*. New York: Viking Press, 1951.

Nelson, Gerald B. *Seattle: The Life and Times of an American City*. New York: Alfred A. Knopf, 1977.

Newell, Gordon. *Rogues, Buffoons and Statesmen*. Seattle: Hangman Press, Superior Publishing Company, 1975.

O'Connor, Harvey. *Revolution in Seattle, A Memoir*. New York: Monthly Review Press, 1964.

Rader, Melvin. *False Witness*. Seattle: University of Washington Press, 1969. A personal account of a philosophy professor's attempts to clear his name after false accusations by a Canwell Committee witness, a struggle that continued into the 1960s.

Sale, Roger. *Seattle Past to Present*. Seattle: University of Washington Press, 1976.

Schaehrer, Peter C. "McCarthyism and Academic Freedom—Three Case Studies." Ed. D. dissertation, Teachers College, Columbia University, 1974. One of the cases examined is that of the University of Washington, 1948–49.

Schmid, Calvin F. *Social Trends in Seattle*. Seattle: University of Washington Press, 1944. Schmid's work is especially valuable for its picture of the Pacific Northwest during the war. A university sociologist, Schmid also collected data on demographic factors specific to the university. With others he prepared *Studies in Enrollment Trends and Patterns, Part I—Regular Academic Year: 1930 to 1964*. University of Washington, Seattle, 1966.

Stewart, Edgar I. *Washington, Northwest Frontier*. 4 vols. New York: The Lewis Historical Company, 1957.

Tone, Eugene Patrick. "A Study of Academic Tenure at the University of Washington." Ed.D. dissertation, Washington State University, 1969. Tone concludes that the university violated its administrative code by dismissing Professors Herbert Phillips and Joseph Butterworth.

Van Wagenen, Delores. "Americans for Democratic Action in the Northwest." M.A. thesis, University of Washington, 1963.

Articles

"Academic Freedom and Tenure in the Quest for National Security." *AAUP Bulletin* 42 (Spring, 1956): 49–107. The report of a special committee of the American Association of University Professors which investigated the university's actions of 1948–55.

Allen, Raymond B. "Communists Should Not Teach in American Colleges." *Educational Forum* 13 (May, 1949): 433–40.

American Scholar Forum. "Communism and Academic Freedom at the University of Washington." *American Scholar* 18 (Summer, 1949): 323–53.

Benson, Merritt E. "The Right to Demand Scholars." *Saturday Review*, September 10, 1949, pp. 34–35. A member of the tenure committee defends the actions of President Raymond B. Allen and the university regents.

Browne, Stuart [Sophus K. Winther]. "A Professor Quits the Communist Party." *Harpers* 179 (July, 1937): 133–42. A University of Washington English professor's reaction to the events of the 1930s.

Commager, Henry Steele. "Red-Baiting in the Colleges." *New Republic*, July 25, 1949, pp. 10–13. A forceful attack on the university's 1949 decisions.

Cowley, W. H. "Academic Government." *Educational Forum* 15 (January, 1951): 217–29. Criticism of the regents' failure to allow faculty participation in decision-making.

Hutchins, Robert M. "The Meaning and Significance of Academic Freedom." *The Annals of the American Academy of Political and Social Science* 300 (July, 1955): 72–78.

Gottfried, Alex, and Davidson, Sue. "New Right in Action." *Nation*, July 29, 1961, pp. 48–51. A university political scientist looks at the Pacific Northwest in the early 1960s.

Guthrie, Edwin R. "Evaluation of Faculty Service." *AAUP Bulletin* 31 (Summer, 1945): 255–62. Dean of faculties and of the Graduate School, Guthrie attracted favorable attention to the university, since other institutions struggled with similar problems. See also the Mund article below.

Harrison, Joseph B. "The Promise of a University: An Appreciation of J. Allen Smith." *Pacific Northwest Quarterly* 46 (July, 1955): 65–71.

Hook, Sidney. "Academic Integrity and Academic Freedom." *Commentary* 8 (October, 1949): 329–39. For rejoinders to this article by one of President Allen's most prolific defenders, see the December issue, pp. 594–601.

———. "The Fellow Traveler: A Study in Psychology." *New York Times Magazine*, April 17, 1949, pp. 9, 20–24.

———. "Should Communists Be Permitted to Teach?" *New York Times Magazine*, February 17, 1949, pp. 7, 22–29.

Keller, Abraham C. "State University Professors Meet the State." *AAUP Bulle-*

tin 36 (Spring, 1950): 67–74. The University of Washington's Community Forum Program.

Lampman, Robert J. "Red Probes and Academic Freedom." *The Progressive* 13 (March, 1949): 20–22. A university economics professor looks at the events of 1948–49.

Lundberg, George. "Prefatory Foreword." in Goddard, Arthur, ed. *Harry Elmer Barnes, Learned Crusader: The New History in Action.* Colorado Springs: Ralph Myles, 1968. An account of Lundberg's attempts to have Barnes speak at the university.

McCarthy, Mary. "Circus Politics in Washington State." *Nation*, October 17, 1936, pp. 442–44.

Meiklejohn, Alexander. "Should Communists Be Allowed to Teach?" *New York Times Magazine*, March 27, 1949, pp. 10, 64–66. For President Allen's rejoinder to this attack, see the issue of May 8, 1949, pp. 33, 35.

Miller, Joe. "Dave Beck Comes Out of the West." *Reporter* 9 (December 8, 1953): 20–23.

Morris, Arval A. "The University of Washington Loyalty Oath Case." *AAUP Bulletin* 50 (September, 1964): 221–32.

Mund, Vernon A. "The Economic Status of the Profession: The University of Washington." *AAUP Bulletin* 33 (Spring, 1947): 95–98.

Patterson, James T. "The New Deal in the West." *Pacific Historical Review* 38 (1969): 317–27.

Rader, Melvin. "Teaching About Communism." *Teachers College Record* 64 (April 19, 1963): 577–83. On efforts by rightist pressure groups to compel schools to teach "anti-Communist" courses through the 1963 Washington State legislature.

Savelle, Max. "Democratic Government of the State University: A Proposal." *AAUP Bulletin* 43(1957): 323–28.

———. "The Teacher and Intellectual Freedom in the United States." *The Pacific Spectator* 10 (Winter, 1956): 15–26.

Scates, Shelby. "The Odegaard Regime." *Argus*, February 6 and 12, 1965.

Schlesinger, Arthur M., Jr. "The Right to Loathsome Ideas." *Saturday Review*, May 14, 1949, pp. 17–18, 47.

Scott, George W. "The New Order of Cincinnatus: Municipal Politics in Seattle During the 1930's." *Pacific Northwest Quarterly* 65 (October, 1973): 137–46.

Seattle Magazine, vol. 4 (February, 1967). Most of this issue is devoted to an analysis of the University of Washington faculty, administration, and students.

Sieg, Lee Paul. "What Constitutes a University." *Seattle Times Sunday Magazine*, May 11, 1955, p. 11. A former university president analyzes faculty-administration relationships in light of the Oppenheimer controversy.

Smith, T. V. "Democratic Compromise and the Higher Learning at Seattle." *School and Society* 69 (February 26, 1949): 137–41.

Taylor, Harold. "The Dismissal of Fifth Amendment Professors." *The Annals of the American Academy of Political and Social Sciences* 300 (July, 1955): 79–86.

Westin, Alan F. "Anti-Communism and the Corporations." *Commentary* 36 (December, 1963): 479–87.

Wormuth, Francis D. "On Bills of Attainder: A Non-Communist Manifesto." *Western Political Quarterly* 3 (March, 1950): 52–65.

Sources of General Background

Books

Alexander, Charles C. *Holding the Line: The Eisenhower Era, 1952–1961.* Bloomington: Indiana University Press, 1975.

Arnold, William. *Shadowland*. New York: McGraw-Hill, 1978.

Belfrage, Cedric. *The American Inquisition, 1945–1960.* Indianapolis, Ind.: Bobbs-Merrill, 1973.

Bell, Daniel, ed. *The Radical Right*. Garden City, N.Y.: Doubleday and Co., 1964.

Brown, Ralph S., Jr. *Loyalty and Security: Employment Tests in the United States.* New Haven: Yale University Press, 1958.

Carr, Robert K. *The House Committee on Un-American Activities: 1945–1950.* Ithaca, N.Y.: Cornell University Press, 1952.

Chambers, Merritt M. *The Colleges and the Courts since 1950.* Danville, Ill.: Interstate Publishers and Printers, 1964.

Conant, James Bryant. *Education in a Divided World.* Cambridge, Mass.: Harvard University Press, 1948.

Cooke, Alistair. *A Generation on Trial: U.S.A. v. Alger Hiss.* New York: Alfred A. Knopf, 1952.

Cowley, Malcolm. *The Literary Situation.* New York: Viking Press, 1954.

Davis, Nuel Pharr. *Lawrence and Oppenheimer.* New York: Simon and Schuster, 1968.

Cremin, Lawrence A. *The Transformation of the School.* New York: Alfred A. Knopf, 1961. The reaction against progressive education played a role in the domestic Cold War; see pp. 328–53.

Dilling, Elizabeth. *The Red Network: A "Who's Who" and Handbook of Radicalism for Patriots.* Kenilworth, Ill.: by the author, 1934. Sourcebook for rightist groups into the 1960s.

Donner, Frank J. *The Un-Americans.* New York: Ballantine Books, 1961.

Evans, M. Stanton. *Revolt on the Campus.* Chicago: Henry Regnery Company, 1961. The conservative intellectual student movement.

Farmer, Frances. *Will There Really Be a Morning?* New York: G. P. Putnam's Sons, 1972. Ms. Farmer's autobiography offers some glimpses of the University of Washington during the 1930s.

Freeland, Richard M. *The Truman Doctrine and the Origins of McCarthyism.* New York: Alfred A. Knopf, 1972.

Gardner, David P. *The California Oath Controversy.* Berkeley: University of California Press, 1967. Events in Washington influenced those in California.

Goldman, Eric F. *The Crucial Decade—And After: America, 1945–1960.* New York: Random House, 1960.

————. *Rendezvous with Destiny: A History of Modern American Reform.* New York: Alfred A. Knopf. 1953.

Goodman, Walter. *The Committee: The Extraordinary Career of the House Committee on Un-American Activities.* New York: Farrar, Straus and Giroux, 1968.

Griffith, Robert, and Theoharis, Athan, eds. *The Specter: Original Essays on the Cold War and the Origins of McCarthyism.* New York: Franklin Watts, 1974.

Hicks, Granville. *Where We Came Out.* New York: Viking Press, 1954. A famous ex-Communist examines the events of the postwar years in light of the 1930s.

Hofstadter, Richard. *Anti-Intellectualism in American Life.* New York: Random House, 1962.

————, and Metzger, Walter P. *The Development of Academic Freedom in the United States.* New York: Columbia University Press, 1955.

Hook, Sidney. *Heresy, Yes—Conspiracy, No.* New York: John Day Co., 1953.

Hyman, Harold M. *To Try Men's Souls: Loyalty Tests in American History.* Berkeley: University of California Press, 1959.

In the Matter of J. Robert Oppenheimer: Texts of Principal Documents and Letters of the Personnel Security Board, General Manager, Commissioners, Washington, D.C. May 27, 1954 through June 29, 1954. Washington, D.C.: U.S. Government Printing Office, 1954.

In the Matter of J. Robert Oppenheimer: Transcript of Hearing before the Personnel Security Board, Washington, D.C. April 12, 1954 through May 6, 1954. Washington, D.C.: U.S. Government Printing Office, 1954.

Iversen, Robert W. *The Communists and the Schools.* New York: Harcourt, Brace and Company, 1959.

Jencks, Christopher, and Riesman, David. *The Academic Revolution.* Garden City, N.Y.: Doubleday and Co., 1968.

Joughin, Louis, ed. *Academic Freedom and Tenure.* Madison: University of Wisconsin Press, 1967.

Kirk, Russell. *Academic Freedom—An Essay in Definition.* Chicago: Henry Regnery Company, 1955. The conservative intellectual viewpoint.

Kurtz, Paul, ed. *Sidney Hook and the Contemporary World.* New York: John Day Company, 1968.

Lazarsfeld, Paul F., and Thielens, Wagner, Jr. *The Academic Mind: Social Scientists in a Time of Crisis.* Glencoe, Ill.: Free Press of Glencoe, 1958.

Lyons, Eugene. *The Red Decade: The Stalinist Penetration of America.* New York: Bobbs-Merrill Company, 1941.

Major, John. *The Oppenheimer Hearing.* New York: Stein and Day, 1971.

Michelmore, Peter. *The Swift Years: The Robert Oppenheimer Story.* New York: Dodd, Mead and Company, 1969.

Miller, Douglas T., and Nowak, Marion. *The Fifties: The Way We Really Were.* Garden City, N.Y.: Doubleday and Company, 1977.

Moser, Charles A., ed. *Continuity in Crisis: The University at Bay.* Washington, D.C.: University Professors for Academic Order, 1974.

Nash, George H. *The Conservative Intellectual Movement in America since 1945.* New York: Basic Books, 1976.

Ogden, August R. *The Dies Committee*. Washington, D.C.: Catholic University of America Press, 1943.

O'Neill, William L. *Coming Apart: An Informal History of America in the 1960's*. Chicago: Quadrangle Books, 1971.

Overstreet, Harry and Bonaro. *The Strange Tactics of Extremism*. New York: W. W. Norton and Company, 1964.

Rogin, Michael Paul. *The Intellectuals and McCarthy: The Radical Specter*. Cambridge, Mass.: M.I.T. Press, 1967.

Saposs, David J. *Communism in American Politics*. Washington, D.C.: Public Affairs Press, 1960.

Schlesinger, Arthur M., Jr. *The Vital Center*. Boston: Houghton Mifflin Company, 1949.

Solberg, Carl. *Riding High: America in the Cold War*. New York: Mason and Lipscomb, 1973.

Stern, Philip M. *The Oppenheimer Case: Security on Trial*. New York: Harper and Row, 1969.

Stouffer, Sam. *Communists, Conformity, and Civil Liberties*. Garden City, N.Y.: Doubleday and Co., 1955.

Taylor, Telford. *The Grand Inquest: The Story of Congressional Investigations*. New York: Simon and Schuster, 1955.

Thomas, John N. *The Institute of Pacific Relations: Asian Scholars and American Politics*. Seattle: University of Washington Press, 1974.

Warren, Frank A., III. *Liberals and Communism*. Bloomington: Indiana University Press, 1966.

Wechsler, James. *Revolt on the Campus*. 1935; Americana Library reprint edition, Seattle: University of Washington Press, 1973. College students in the 1930s.

Wilson, Thomas W., Jr. *The Great Weapons Heresy*. Boston: Houghton Mifflin Company, 1970.

Yarnell, Allen. *Democrats and Progressives: The 1948 Presidential Election as a Test of Post-War Liberalism*. Berkeley: University of California Press, 1974.

York, Herbert F. *The Advisors: Oppenheimer, Teller, and the Superbomb*. San Francisco: W. H. Freeman and Company, 1976.

Articles

Alsop, Joseph, and Alsop, Stewart. "We Accuse!" *Harpers* 209 (October, 1954): 25–45.

Bolinger, Dwight L. "Who Is Intellectually Free?" *Journal of Higher Education* 25 (December, 1954): 464–67. Bolinger's point is that Communists are not unique; most human minds are biased to one degree or another.

"The Climate of Opinion and the State of Academic Freedom." *American Sociological Review* 21 (June, 1956): 353–57.

Curti, Merle. "Intellectuals and Other People." *American Historical Review* 40 (January, 1955): 259–82.

Frankel, Charles. "The Government of Scholarship." *AAUP Bulletin* 41 (Winter, 1955): 696–712.

Gideonese, Harry D. "Academic Freedom: A Decade of Challenge and Clarification." *The Annals of the American Academy of Political and Social Science* 301 (September, 1955): 75–85. Argues that Communist party membership is prima facie evidence of unfitness to teach.

Hyman, Herbert S., and Sheatsley, Paul B. "Trends in Public Opinion on Civil Liberties." *Journal of Social Issues* 9 (1953): 6–16.

Johnson, Oakley C. "Campus Battles for Freedom in the Thirties." *Centennial Review* 14 (1970): 341–66.

Jones, Howard Mumford. "How Much Academic Freedom?" *Atlantic Monthly* 191 (June, 1953): 36–40. ". . . leave reason free to combat error."

Metzger, Walter P. "Some Perspectives on the History of Academic Freedom." *Antioch Review* 13 (September, 1953): 275–87.

Murphy, Charles. "McCarthyism and Businessmen." *Fortune* 49 (April, 1954): 156–58, 180–94.

Perry, Ralph Barton. "Academic Freedom." *The Harvard Education Review* 23 (Spring, 1953): 71–76.

Sanford, Nevitt. "Individual and Social Change in a Community under Pressure: The Oath Controversy." *Journal of Social Issues* 9 (1953): 25–42.

Schlesinger, Arthur M., Jr. "The Oppenheimer Case." *Atlantic Monthly* 194 (October, 1954): 29–36.

Seigel, Kalman. "College Freedoms Being Stifled by Students' Fear of Red Label." *New York Times*, May 10, 1951, pp. 1, 28.

Shepley, James, and Blair, Clay, Jr. "The Hydrogen Bomb: How the U.S. Almost Lost It." *U.S. News and World Report*, September 24, 1954, pp. 58–72, 88–107.

Shryock, Richard. "The Academic Profession in the United States." *AAUP Bulletin* 38 (Spring, 1952): 32–70.

Stember, Herbert. "Student Opinion on Issues of Academic Freedom." *Journal of Social Issues* 9 (1953): 43–47.

Stoke, Harold W. "Academic Freedom." *Journal of Higher Education* 20 (October, 1949): 346–56. Stoke, who became dean of the Graduate School under President Allen, argued that "the prospect of damage from Communist toleration is greater than from Communist suppression."

Trilling, Diana. "The Oppenheimer Case." *Partisan Review* 21 (November–December, 1954): 604–35. A virulent anti-Stalinist deplores the "tragic ineptitude" of projecting upon Dr. Oppenheimer the "punishment we perhaps owe to ourselves for having once been so careless with our nation's security."

Van den Haag, Ernest. "McCarthyism and the Professors." *Commentary* 27 (February, 1959): 179–82. A review of Lazarsfeld and Thielens' *Academic Mind*, in which the reviewer found the social scientists described "public heroes and private cowards."

Woodcock, John. "An Interview with Kenneth Burke." *Sewanee Review* 85 (Fall, 1977): 704–18.

Wyant, William K. "Speaking of Extremists, Who's Playing Right Field?" *New Republic*, September 19, 1964, pp. 12–16.

Index